W9-AYK-198

PRAISE FOR JOE FOLLANSBEE'S BOOKS
The Fyddeye Guide to America's Maritime History

Any serious student of the maritime heritage of America will find this an invaluable addition to their library — and the more general reader will find it becomes well-thumbed as a comprehensive guide.

—Julian Stockwin, author of Stockwin's Maritime Miscellany and the Thomas Kidd novel series

In general, I am very impressed by the scope, organization and level of detail. Highly recommended.

—Rick Spilman, The Old Salt Blog

Between its glossy covers, this impressive work contains everything a person could want in the way of information about our country's historic maritime treasures, as well as some interesting articles. Whether you are doing research of a scholarly nature, or simply planning a vacation, the well-organized format (indexed by city) makes it easy to find not only heritage vessels and sites, but also organizations, educational resources, and more.

—Candace Brown, Good Life Northwest

Anyone with an interest in tall ships, lighthouses, historic ships, maritime museums, or any of a number of other maritime topics/locations/organizations will find Joe Follansbee's *The Fyddeye Guide to America's Maritime History* a much needed and valuable reference.

—Hal Barstow, Los Angeles Maritime Institute

The Fyddeye Guide is a great reference for when you're planning a vacation or you find yourself in a city and want to know what maritime attractions are located in the area.

—Cindy Vallar, Pirates and Privateers

Bet: Stowaway Daughter

The portrayal of Bet and her love for her father...pulled me along until the exciting last pages.

—Barbara Sjoholm, author of *The Pirate Queen: In Search of Grace O'Malley and Other Legendary Women of the Sea*

I love this novel! I don't know if having daughters has influenced the author but Joe Follansbee has conceived a smart, gutsy, yet very believable female protagonist whom I cheered for from page one.

—Linda Collison, author of *Star-Crossed* and The Patricia MacPherson Nautical Adventure Series

The strength of the book is a result of painstaking research by the author and clearly reflects his grasp of maritime history in and around Puget Sound and Alaska.

—Steven Wells, author of *Ginger's Story: A Golden Retriever Reflects Upon Her Life With Humans*

Joe Follansbee has created a memorable new character in Bet Lindstrom.

—Tamara Bunnell, history teacher, The Northwest School

THE FYDDEYE
GUIDE TO AMERICA'S LIGHTHOUSES

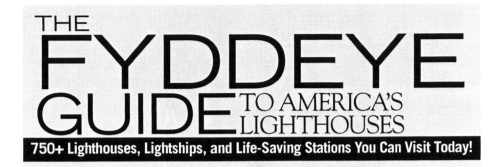

750+ Lighthouses, Lightships, and Life-Saving Stations You Can Visit Today!

edited by JOE FOLLANSBEE

with a foreword by New England lighthouse photographer Jeremy D'Entremont

Copyright © 2012 Fyddeye Media
All rights reserved.

ISBN: 0984905405
ISBN-13: 9780984905409
Library of Congress Control Number: 2011944952

Fyddeye, Seattle, WA

Cover photo of the West Quoddy Head Lighthouse © 2012 Jeremy D'Entremont http://lighthouse.cc/

CONTENTS

CONTENTS

DEDICATION

For Emily and Abbey

ABOUT THE AUTHOR

Joe Follansbee is the author of seven books, including *Shipbuilders, Sea Captains and Fishermen: The Story of the Schooner Wawona*, *The Fyddeye Guide to America's Maritime History*, and *The Fyddeye Guide to America's Lighthouses*. He runs a companion website to the *Fyddeye Guides* at www.fyddeye.com. He also works as the communications director for the tall ships *Lady Washington* and *Hawaiian Chieftain*. He has written a novel for young adults, *Bet: Stowaway Daughter*, based on his research into Pacific Northwest maritime history. He lives in Seattle with his wife, two daughters, four chickens, and a rat.

INTRODUCTION

Welcome to the *Fyddeye Guide to America's Lighthouses*, the resource that makes your heritage travel planning easier by showing you hundreds of fascinating lighthouses you can visit today on the east coast, Great Lakes, Gulf Coast, and the west coast, including *Alaska and Hawaii*. Few pieces of Americana have as much *Wow!* factor as the lighthouse, and they're one of the most easily recognizable landmarks in any port city or town, saltwater or freshwater. But oddly enough, most Americans have only visited one or two lighthouses on family trips or travels after retirement, often because these fascinating artifacts are hard to find or hidden from view. And even the residents of larger cities are barely aware of the lighthouses that serve local mariners and those coming from ports worldwide. *The Fyddeye Guide to America's Lighthouses* makes the lighthouse as easy to discover as any local attraction.

The lighthouse *Guide* is the second in the *Fyddeye Guide* series, which includes the *Fyddeye Guide to America's Maritime History*, a travel and research directory to more than 2,000 maritime museums, tall ships, historic ships, and of course, lighthouses. The lighthouse *Guide* focuses on the 750 or so maritime sentinels that dot the shores of the U.S. The book is divided into chapters reflecting this distribution on America's four coasts, with additional chapters on preserved lightships and life-saving stations, which were often associated with a lighthouse. At the beginning of each chapter, you'll find a Quick Response, or "QR" code, which looks something like a bar code. You can use the QR or bar code reader app on your iPhone, Android phone, or other mobile device to read the code, which will take you to a page on the Fyddeye website with the latest lighthouse information.

The *Fyddeye Guide to America's Lighthouses* contains information similar to that found on its companion Fyddeye website at www.fyddeye.com. The printed *Guide* includes information not found on the website, such some recommended lighthouses if your time is limited. The *Guide* also offers three itineraries with maps for lighthouses in New England and the Mid-Atlantic states, Michigan, and California. However, all books, especially travel guides and directories, are snapshots in time; they quickly go out of date. Email addresses change frequently, for example. If a listing in the *Fyddeye Guide* piques your interest, consider checking the online listing for the same lighthouse to see if the contact information, for example, is updated. You can also sign up for the *Fyddeye Guide* newsletter for the latest information about the guides. And each lighthouse listing on the website has a feature not practical for a printed book: a Google Map to each lighthouse location.

Lighthouses come in all shapes and sizes, and the ownership ranges from the U.S. Coast Guard to private citizens. That means you should follow a few simples rules before a visit. First, check the "Operated by" portion of the lighthouse listing. The vast majority of lighthouses are operated by a public entity, such as the Coast Guard, or a historical society or similar non-profit organization, which allows visitors and gives tours. Most lighthouses, particularly those operated by the federal government, offer at least access to the grounds, if not the tower. A few lighthouses are on government installations and may be off limits for security reasons. Some lighthouses are in very remote locations and may require an adventurous spirit to visit. Virtually all lighthouses operated by a "private owner" are private property, and in some cases, people live there. Don't go on the property without permission from the owner. When in doubt, call the listed phone number or send an email. Or visit the lighthouse website to get the latest information on tours.

A word on lighthouses owned and operated by historical societies or small museums. Ninety percent or more of these organizations are supported by a small, but dedicated cadre of volunteers and donors who are the unsung heroes of maritime heritage preservation and interpretation. A government or foundation may award a grant now and then, but the hard work, including fundraising, is accomplished by local citizens proud of their community's history and landmarks. Respect their work, and put a few dollars in the donation jar when you visit. Better yet, become a member of your own local history society or community museum. You'll be amazed at what you'll discover about your home town and its history.

In the meantime, think about exploring your local maritime heritage, especially lighthouses. *The Fyddeye Guide to America's Lighthouses* will be your constant companion.

How to read a typical *Guide* listing called an "attraction":

CAPE ANN LIGHTHOUSE

✟ Established in 1771, two lighthouse were built together on Thacher Island, also known as Cape Ann. Two new towers were constructed of granite in 1961. The light on the northeast tower was shut down in 1932. The lighthouse is now owned by the City of Rockport. *Address:* Cape Ann Light *City:* Rockport *State:* MA *Zip:* 01966 *Phone:* 617-599-2590 *Web:* www.thacherisland.org *Email:* info@thacherisland.org *Visitors welcome?* Yes *Hours:* Contact attraction directly *Admission:* Contact attraction directly *Operated by:* Thacher Island Association *NR?* Yes *NHL?* Yes *Year established/built:* 1771 *Latitude:* 42.6368 *Longitude:* -70.5749 Accommodations for overnight and/or long-term stays available.

✢ This lighthouse welcomes visitors for overnight stays. It may also have a volunteer keeper program, which allows visitors to stay for as long as a month with specific duties, such as maintaining the lighthouse grounds and giving tours.

Address/City/State/Zip: Street address or approximate location, sometimes nearest city, as in the case of some remote lighthouses.

Phone: Information phone

Toll-free: Toll-free phone

Web: Website

Email: Email address

Visitors welcome? Available for tours or visits? (Yes/No)

Hours: Operating hours, if available for visits

Admission: Admission fee, if available for visits

Operated by: Organization operating the attraction

NR? Is the attraction listed on the National Register of Historic Places?

NHL? Is the attraction listed as a National Historic Landmark?

Year established/built: Year constructed or established, if more than one structure

Latitude/Longitude: Approximate latitude and longitude of the attraction

Accommodations for overnight and/or long-term stays available. See the note for ✢.

Notes: The National Register of Historic Places is official list of cultural resources worthy of preservation in the United States. A National Historic Landmark is a similar list, but more prestigious and exclusive with tighter criteria. The latitude and longitude items are based on information, such as addresses, provided by the attraction owner or listed in publicly accessible map resources. *Guide* readers should double-check these before using them in GPS-enabled devices.

FOREWORD

I have vivid memories of some of my earliest visits to lighthouses around three decades ago, when lighthouse fever was first burning in my veins. It was an immeasurable thrill to drive some winding, picturesque coastal road until a particular lighthouse came into view for the first time. In the intervening years, I've researched the history of many lighthouses and I've led tours to quite a few. The lighthouses of New England are like old friends to me now, but I still feel that rush of excitement when I travel outside of my region and see lighthouses that are new to me. The lighthouse bug isn't something you get over; it's a chronic disease. And it's contagious.

At a keynote speech at an event celebrating the 200th anniversary of a federal lighthouse service in 1989, the late historian F. Ross Holland summed up the appeal of lighthouses about as succinctly as anyone ever has. "Americans love lighthouses," he said, adding:

> Artists and photographers find them picturesque. The dreamer finds them romantic. The boaters find them comforting. The navigator finds them helpful. The shore walker finds them peaceful. The historic preservationist feels they make a statement about a period of time. The historian is fascinated with the human and technological story they embody. And the idealist is drawn to them because they symbolize man's humanity to man. Americans truly like and respect their historic structures, but it seems to me there's a special place in their hearts they reserve for lighthouses.

I can't improve on Mr. Holland's statement, but I'd like to offer a suggestion. When you visit a lighthouse, any lighthouse, try and listen to what it has to say. You're not likely to hear actual voices, although some paranormal investigators might suggest otherwise. But if you open yourself up and allow the essence of these structures and locations wash over you, you might be surprised.

Lighthouses are more than physical structures made of brick, stone, wood, or iron. The spirit of the lighthouse keepers and families who devoted their lives to the service of safe navigation is still present. When you climb the stairs in a lighthouse, think of who climbed those stairs before you. When you savor a spectacular view from a lighthouse lantern, think of the beauty and tragedy witnessed by those who lived there a century or more ago.

Every lighthouse embodies the sum total of its human history. The lights are all automated now, but the spirit of the keepers is very much alive in the preservation organizations that now care for many of the lighthouses. If you derive any pleasure from your lighthouse visits, please keep in mind the fact that many small organizations are struggling daily to preserve this wonderful history and to make it available to the public. Please consider donating and perhaps volunteering some of your time to this worthy cause.

During my early lighthouse hunting, I was often accompanied by a guidebook by Kenneth Kochel. His guide to Atlantic coast lights was ahead of its time and can be considered the granddaddy of the many lighthouse guidebooks available today. Little did I know that I would eventually write some guidebooks of my own. I've specialized in the northeast, and a handful of other writers have published guides for specific regions of the United States.

The Fyddeye Guide to America's Lighthouses is unusual in that it covers the entire U.S., with lightships and life-saving stations included as well. It includes the basic information you'll want when planning a lighthouse visit, along with contact information to lead you to whatever additional information you require. I'm pleased that it also includes a primer on lighthouse history and technology.

All in all, this is a welcome addition to the bookshelf of any lighthouse buff, from the casual to the obsessed. May it serve you well on your lighthouse adventures.

Jeremy D'Entremont
Portsmouth, New Hampshire
Fall 2011

CHAPTER 1

East Coast Lighthouses

St. Simons Island Lighthouse, St. Simons, Georgia

Lighthouses you can visit today in the states of Connecticut, Delaware, Florida (Atlantic Coast), Georgia, Maine, Maryland, Massachusetts, New Hampshire, New Jersey, New York (Atlantic Coast), North Carolina, Pennsylvania, Rhode Island, South Carolina, Vermont, Virginia, as well as Puerto Rico and the U.S. Virgin Islands.

Use your smart phone's QR or bar code reader to visit this Fyrdeye web page.

FYDDEYE RECOMMENDS:

Assateague Lighthouse, Virginia	Montauk Point Lighthouse, Montauk, New York
Bald Head Island (Old Baldy) Lighthouse, Bald Head Island, North Carolina	Navesink Lighthouse, Highlands, New Jersey
Barnegat Lighthouse, Barnegat Light, New Jersey	Ponce de Leon Inlet Lighthouse, Ponce Inlet, Florida
Beavertail Lighthouse, Jamestown, Rhode Island	Portland Head Lighthouse, Cape Elizabeth, Maine
Cape Ann Lighthouse, Rockport, Massachusetts	Portsmouth Harbor Lighthouse, New Castle, New Hampshire
Cape Hatteras Lighthouse, Buxton, North Carolina	Saugerties Lighthouse, Saugerties, New York
Castillo San Felipe Del Morro Lighthouse	St. Simons Island Lighthouse, St. Simons Island, Georgia
Monhegan Island Lighthouse, Monhegan, Maine	Stonington Harbor Lighthouse, Stonington, Connecticut

A Fyddeye primer on the past, present, and future of lighthouses

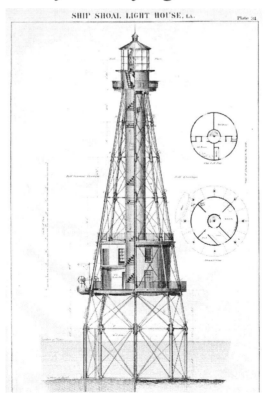

Ship Shoal Lighthouse, a typical lighthouse in the shallow waters of the Gulf Coast

The tall, stately tower of the lighthouse stands as one of the most iconic symbols of maritime culture, and it's entered the popular culture as a symbol of security and steadfastness in the face of adversity. Of course, the lighthouse has always had a practical purpose as a beacon guiding mariners to safe harbor or around hidden dangers. Here's a short primer on the lighthouse, its past, present, and possible future.

Human beings have signaled coastal dangers with lights since time immemorial, starting with bonfires on headlands or hilltops. The first signal fires built on short wood or stone platforms could also have warned mariners away from dangerous rocks or shoals. The first structure designed as a lighthouse marking the entrance to a port was the Lighthouse of Alexandria near the mouth of the Nile River in Egypt. Though some of the details are in dispute, the stone tower rose as much as 450 feet above the water, and the fire in its lantern, reflected by a mirror—possibly polished bronze or copper—could be seen 35 miles away. Built in the 3rd century B.C., the lighthouse was operational for nearly 1,300 years, until it was destroyed by a series of earthquakes. In 1994, divers discovered the remains of the lighthouse underwater near modern Alexandria.

The Greeks and Romans built a number of stone lighthouses around the Mediterranean Sea, including Pontus, the port of Rome, and one at Boulogne, France, across the Dover Strait from Britain, which was constructed by the notorious Roman emperor Caligula. In the Middle Ages, Italian city-states dependent on sea trade, such as Genoa, built lighthouses, and European kings built structures in France, Germany, Ireland, Sweden, and other states with long and rugged coastlines. Although structures designed specifically as lighthouses seem to be primarily a European and Near East phenomenon, Arab and Asian powers with merchant fleets sometimes put signal fires at the top of a mosque's minaret.

The history of the modern lighthouse began in the 17th century, particularly as Great Britain rose as a sea power. Increasingly dependent on shipping for trade, the British government needed ways to reduce the risks to men and ships bringing goods from all over the world. Trinity House, Great Britain's government agency in charge of lighthouses, built its first lighthouse in 1609. But the first true modern lighthouse—with the classic tapering tower rising to a bright beacon—was the Eddystone Lighthouse, lit in 1698. Located off the coast of Cornwall, it started as a wooden tower anchored by 12 iron stanchions embedded in hard rock. It was swept away in a storm in 1703, and the government replaced it with another wood tower, which was destroyed by fire in 1755. The third tower, this time made of stone, lasted until 1877, at about the time when the tower in use today was constructed. The new fourth tower stands right next to the stub of the third tower.

The first lighthouse tower in the Americas was probably built by the Spanish at St. Augustine (now in Florida) in the 16th century. But some argue that the first true lighthouse in the New World—Boston Light—appeared on Little Brewster Island off the entrance to Boston Harbor in 1716. The next light in New England, at Brant Point, Massachusetts, was constructed in 1746 to mark the entrance to Nantucket Harbor. Britain's colonies, like the mother country, were almost totally dependent on sea trade, and lighthouses became critical safety measures. A dozen lighthouses were in operation by the Revolutionary War, and they become battlegrounds; the British destroyed Boston

Light in 1776. After the war, the new government of the United States started building more lighthouses. President George Washington's earliest acts included the construction of lighthouses at Montauk Point, New York and Seguin Island, Maine.

Over the years in the United States, responsibility for lighthouses passed through several government departments and agencies, starting with the Bureau of Lighthouses, formed in 1789. The government formed the Lighthouse Board in 1852, which gave way to the Lighthouse Service in 1910. Congress finally handed responsibility for lighthouses and other navigational aids to the Coast Guard in 1939, where it remains. The last lighthouse built by the federal government went up in 1962 at the entrance to Charleston Harbor in South Carolina.

WHAT MAKES A LIGHTHOUSE?

What is a lighthouse? Some people include virtually every navigation light or marker on a saltwater or freshwater coast, or a navigable river, as a "lighthouse." But most people understand a lighthouse to include at least a bright, slowly flashing beacon on some sort of structure taller than a man's height. The *Fyddeye Guide to America's Lighthouses* narrows the definition further, focusing on structures with that "lighthouse look" that you can visit, or at least get close to by land or water, with a few exceptions.

Lighthouses—more properly called light stations—come in all shapes and sizes. There's the classic masonry or concrete tower that rises from a short pedestal to a height of a hundred or more feet, but that's the minority of lighthouse structures. Some are barely more than a skeleton of iron or steel, such as the lighthouse at the entrance to the harbor at Duluth, Minn., although the skeletal tower may have replaced a classic tower form that once stood on the site. Some lighthouses are sturdy residential-style structures with a lighthouse lantern on top, such as West Point Lighthouse in Seattle. Some lighthouses sit within a hundred yards or less of the surf line; others are perched on a cliff several hundred feet above the sea, such as Makapuu Lighthouse in Hawaii. A number of lighthouses, particularly in the Gulf Coast states and Florida, sit on stilts or pilings driven into the sea bed offshore, such as Carysfort Reef Light off Key Largo, Florida. Others, especially on the mid-Atlantic coast and New England, are built on caissons, watertight compartments that sit on the sea bed at harbor entrances or underwater hazards. These structures, such as the lighthouse off Orient Point, New York, have a squat appearance that reminded mariners of a coffee pot. Others like to call them "spark plug" lighthouses. A few lighthouses come in pairs, sometimes several miles apart. Called "range lights," mariners lined their vessel up with the two lights in order to find a channel in a river or estuary.

During the heyday of lighthouses from the late 18th century through the mid-20th century, most lighthouses were almost completely self-sustaining and independent. Many were in extremely remote locations, dozens or hundreds of miles from settlements, such as Destruction Island off the northwestern tip of Washington state. Some could only receive visitors a few times a year. Offshore lighthouses were usually single units; everything needed to operate the station—fuel, food, spare parts—was contained in one building. Onshore, the light station might consist of the tower with the lantern, a small house as quarters for the lighthouse keeper and his family, a separate building for the fog horn and/ or bell, and an oil house for storing the whale oil and later kerosene for maintaining the light. The keeper might maintain a garden and sheds for animals on the grounds for fresh food. If the light station was on an island, a small pier would receive occasional visits by boat from neighbors or deliveries of mail and supplies.

THE "LIGHT" OF A LIGHTHOUSE

At its heart, the lighthouse is a visual aid intended to guide a mariner toward something, such as a harbor, or away from something, including shoals, rocks, or underwater ledges. Virtually all lighthouses share one thing in common, their roofs are red with the rest of the structure painted white, sometimes paired with another hue. This color scheme helps them stand out from surrounding features, such as trees or other buildings. Towers are often painted in alternating white and a dark color ranging from red to black. Cape Lookout Lighthouse on North Carolina's Outer Banks has an unmistakable black and white diamond pattern on its tower. The St. Augustine Lighthouse in Florida has striking "barber pole" stripes along its entire 165-foot height.

Of course, stripes aren't much help at night (except perhaps in a full moon), and so lighthouse designers have tried various artificial forms of illumination over the centuries, starting with large bonfires. Starting in the 18th century, whale-oil lamps were incorporated into lighthouse lanterns, the part of the lighthouse that contained the light. Surrounded by plate glass to protect it from the wind, and focused by a parabolic mirror made of silvered glass or copper, these lights could be seen as many as 30 miles out to sea in good weather.

A revolution in lighthouse design came in 1821, when French engineer Augustin Fresnel (pronounced "freh-NEL") produced the first practical catadioptric system of glass lenses to focus and intensify the weak light of oil lamps. Commonly called Fresnel lenses, these massive objects consisted of a drum-shaped "bulls-eye" sitting between stacks of concentric glass prisms held together with a brass skeleton. While the old reflected lamps produced only a single beam of light, a Fresnel lens produced several beams of light from a single source. Fresnel lenses in lighthouses come in six sizes, called "orders," ranging from the smallest sixth-order lenses, about 18 inches tall, to the largest first-order lenses, which can be more than eight feet tall. The lens at Makapuu Light in Hawaii has over a thousand prisms and weighs 12 tons. Designed to rotate, these massive collections of glass would often float in a trough of several gallons of mercury to reduce friction to nearly zero.

Lighthouse designers also developed ways for mariners to distinguish lights at night from one another, noting these "characteristics," as they're called, on charts.

- Colors: Red, white, or green, sometimes in combination
- Flash: A flashing light is on longer than it's off.
- Occult: An occulting light is off longer than it's on.
- Equal-interval: The light is on and off equal periods.
- Sectors: Some colors show only if viewed from a certain direction, usually to mark danger. A narrow sector often marks a channel, allowing the mariner to line up properly.
- Visibility: The range or distance in miles or kilometers from which the light is visible.

The effectiveness of these characteristics, especially visibility, are affected by weather conditions, such as fog, rain, or clear weather.

Fresnel lens are still used on some lighthouses, but most have been replaced with smaller lights based on designs used at airports. All are powered by electricity; offshore stations usually include a bank of batteries recharged with solar cells.

THE LIGHTSHIP

In some areas of the world, especially the United States, lightships formed a unique cadre of navigational aids at sea. The first lightship appeared near the mouth of the Thames estuary in Great Britain in 1732, but the peak of the lightship occurred between the mid-19th and mid-20th centuries. Manned by crews of a dozen or more seamen, these self-propelled, sea-going lighthouses marked the entrance to major harbors or near-shore shoals where a lighthouse was impractical. While most ships would avoid storms, lightships were expected to stay put on their station during all weathers.

Among the most famous lightships on the east coast were the Ambrose Lightship (actually named for the station; several different vessels would serve on the station serially) at the entrance to New York Harbor and the Nantucket Lightship on Nantucket Shoals off the coast of Massachusetts. On the west coast, the Swiftsure Lightship marked Swiftsure Bank off Cape Flattery on the extreme northwest tip of the continental United States. Expensive to operate and highly stressful on crews, lightships were phased out in the 1960s, replaced by automated buoys.

LIGHTHOUSES IN THE 21ST CENTURY

Starting in the early 20th century, technological advances chipped away at the classic image of the lonely lighthouse keeper diligently caring for navigation lights on some remote shore. Electricity gradually replaced oil and kerosene as the fuel for the lights themselves, and lighthouse keepers evolved from maintenance specialists to a rescue force in some locations, although many lighthouses had long been associated with life-saving stations on the west and east coasts, and the Great Lakes. But even the rescue roles diminished as aircraft and powerful marine engines cut down on response times and labor costs. After World War II, the Coast Guard accelerated a program of automating its lighthouses, and the advent of new navigational aids based on radar and global positioning satellites made many light stations redundant.

The golden age of lighthouses in America ended in the late 20th century, when the last manned light—Boston Light—was automated in 1998. (It should be noted that more than two dozen lighthouses in Canada still have full or part-time human keepers.) But instead of entering a dark age, lighthouse culture in the United States entered a new period of public accessibility. In 2000, Congress passed the National Historic Lighthouse Preservation Act, which allows local governments, non-profit organizations, and individuals to take over maintenance and operations of lighthouse grounds and buildings. In some cases, ownership of lighthouses deemed government surplus is transferred to other entities, in return for keeping them open to the public. If the Coast Guard wants to maintain a beacon but doesn't want to maintain an expensive older structure, the government forms a partnership with another entity.

A prime example is the Grays Harbor Lighthouse in Westport, Washington on the Pacific Ocean. The lighthouse buildings are kept in good condition by the Westport South Beach Historical Society, which also operates the Westport Maritime Museum nearby in a former Coast Guard life-saving station. (Incidentally, the museum also features a special building housing the fourth-order Fresnel lens that once stood atop the Destruction Island Lighthouse.) The lighthouse has regular open hours, and visitors can climb the tower for a spectacular view from the lighthouse lantern. For its part, the Coast Guard maintains a modern optic at the lighthouse, allowing the structure to keep its historic role as a navigation aid while encouraging the public to appreciate its place in local and national maritime history.

Today, hundreds of lighthouses are open to the public for exploration. Most accessible lighthouses permit visitors to stroll the grounds, which sometimes feature beautiful gardens and scenic vistas. Some are easily reached by car; others are on remote islands accessible only by small boat. Many owners open the towers or lanterns to visitors, who are asked to donate a small fee to help maintain the building. Many lighthouses are part of larger maritime museums, such as the St. Augustine Lighthouse in Florida. A few are on military bases, such as the Pensacola Lighthouse, which is at the Pensacola Naval Air Station. Numerous lighthouses and their grounds are closed to the public due to security concerns. Use the *Fyddeye Guide to America's Lighthouses* to plan a visit to one lighthouse or a tour of many for a rewarding journey into America's maritime past.

IT'S GREEK TO THEM

The English word "lighthouse" derives from the function of the structure it describes. But in French, Spanish, Scandinavian, and other European languages, the word for "lighthouse" comes from the island where the Lighthouse of Alexandria once stood, called "Pharos" in Greek, pronounced "FARE-ohs." For example, the Castillo San Felipe del Morro Lighthouse at the San Juan National Historic Site in San Juan, Puerto Rico is more properly called the "Faro de Castillo San Felipe del Morro."

U.S. LIGHTHOUSE STATISTICS

- Oldest lighthouse: Either the St. Augustine Lighthouse (16th century) or the Boston Light (1755)

- Tallest lighthouse: Cape Hatteras Lighthouse, 207 feet.

- Newest lighthouse: Charleston Harbor, 1962.

- Remotest lighthouse: Candidates include Eldred Rock Lighthouse in Alaska, Crisp Point in Michigan, and Mount Desert, off Yarmouth, Maine.

New England and Mid-Atlantic Lighthouse Tour Itinerary

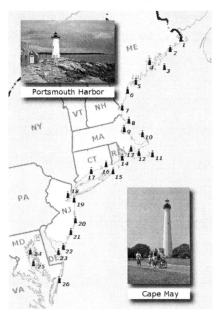

Portsmouth Harbor

Cape May

1. West Quoddy Head (Lubec, ME)	14. Beavertail (Jamestown, RI)
2. Moose Peak (Jonesport, ME)	15. Montauk (Long Island, NY)
3. Mount Desert Rock	16. New London Harbor (New London, CT)
4. Goose Rocks (North Haven, ME)	17. Five-Mile Point (New Haven, CT)
5. Seguin Island	18. Statue of Liberty (New York, NY)
6. Portland Head (Portland, ME)	19. Sandy Hook (Highlands, NJ)
7. Portsmouth Harbor (Portsmouth, NH)	20. Barnegat
8. Thacher Island (Rockport, ME)	21. Absecon (Atlantic City, NJ)
9. Boston Harbor (Boston, MA)	22. Cape May (Cape May, NJ)
10. Long Point (Provincetown, MA)	23. Harbor of Refuge (Lewes, DE)
11. Sankaty Head (Siasconset, MA)	24. Baltimore Harbor (Baltimore, MD)
12. Edgartown Harbor (Edgartown, MA)	25. Bloody Bar
13. Butler Flats (New Bedford, MA)	26. Assateague

West Quoddy Head on the Canadian border is a perfect place to start your exploration of America's lighthouse history. U.S. Highway 1 will be your main route and reference point, with side routes such as U.S. Highway 6 to Cape Cod, New York Route 27 to Montauk, and U.S. Highway 9 along the New Jersey coastline.

CONNECTICUT

AVERY POINT LIGHTHOUSE

Formerly the site of the U.S. Coast Guard Training Center, Avery Point is now the site of a University of Connecticut campus. The lighthouse operated for just 23 years, from 1944 to 1967. *Address:* Avery Point Light *State:* **CT** *Visitors welcome?* Yes *Hours:* Daily *Admission:* **FREE** *Operated by:* Avery Point Lighthouse Society *NR?* No *NHL?* No *Year established/ built:* 1944 *Latitude:* 41.31515 *Longitude:* -72.0635

BLACK ROCK HARBOR LIGHTHOUSE

Established in 1808, the current Black Rock Harbor Lighthouse, also called the Fayerweather Island Lighthouse, was constructed in 1817 and deactivated in 1932. The rehabilitated structure is now part of a district on the National Register of Historic Places. *Address:* Black Rock Harbor Light *City:* Bridgeport *State:* **CT** *Visitors welcome?* Yes *Hours:* Access to grounds only *Admission:* Access to grounds only *Operated by:* City of Bridgeport *NR?* Yes *NHL?* No *Year established/built:* 1808 *Latitude:* 41.1424 *Longitude:* -73.2167

FAULKNERS ISLAND LIGHTHOUSE

Established and built in 1802, the Faulkners Island Lighthouse was automated in 1978 and is still an active aid to navigation. The lighthouse is now part of a wildlife refuge and it is maintained by a volunteer group. *Address:* Faulkner Island Light *State:* **CT** *Visitors welcome?* No *Operated by:* Faulkner's Light Brigade *NR?* Yes *NHL?* No *Year established/built:* 1802 *Latitude:* 41.2119 *Longitude:* -72.6536

FIVE MILE POINT LIGHTHOUSE

Established in 1805, the current Five Mile Point Lighthouse, also called the Old New Haven Lighthouse, was constructed in 1845. The light was deactivated in 1877, and it was rehabilitated in 1986. *Address:* Lighthouse Point Park *City:* New Haven *State:* **CT** *Visitors welcome?* Yes *Hours:* Daily *Admission:* **FREE** *Operated by:* City of New Haven *NR?* Yes *NHL?* No *Year established/built:* 1805 *Latitude:* 41.2484 *Longitude:* -72.9036

GREAT CAPTAIN ISLAND LIGHTHOUSE

Established in 1830, the current Great Captain Island Lighthouse was constructed in 1868 and deactivated in 1970. *Address:* Great Captain Island Light *City:* Greenwich *State:* **CT** *Visitors welcome?* No *Operated by:* Town of Greenwich *NR?* Yes *NHL?* No *Year established/built:* 1830 *Latitude:* 40.9825 *Longitude:* -73.6235

GREENS LEDGE LIGHTHOUSE

Established and built in 1902, the Greens Ledge Lighthouse was automated in 1972 and is still an active aid to navigation. *Address:* Greens Ledge Light *City:* Scott Cove *State:* **CT**

Visitors welcome? No *Operated by:* U.S. Coast Guard (District 1) *NR?* Yes *NHL?* No *Year established/built:* 1902 *Latitude:* 41.0417 *Longitude:* -73.4439

LYNDE POINT LIGHTHOUSE
Established in 1803, the current Lynde Point Lighthouse, also called the Saybrook Lighthouse, was constructed in 1839. Automated in 1975, the light is still an active aid to navigation. *Address:* Lynde Point Light *City:* Fenwick *State:* CT *Visitors welcome?* No *Operated by:* U.S. Coast Guard (District 1) *NR?* Yes *NHL?* No *Year established/built:* 1803 *Latitude:* 41.27137 *Longitude:* -72.34325

MORGAN POINT LIGHTHOUSE
Established in 1831, the current Morgan Point Lighthouse was constructed in 1868 and deactivated in 1919. Renovated in 1993, it is now part of the Noank Historic District. *Address:* Morgan Point *City:* Noank *State:* CT *Visitors welcome?* No *Operated by:* Private owner *NR?* Yes *NHL?* No *Year established/built:* 1831 *Latitude:* 41.31888 *Longitude:* -71.99025

NEW LONDON HARBOR LIGHTHOUSE
Established in 1760, making it Connecticut's oldest lighthouse, the current New London Harbor Lighthouse (or more properly New London Harbor Light) was constructed in 1801. Automated in 1912, the lighthouse is still an active aid to navigation. *Address:* New London Harbor Light *City:* New London *State:* CT *Phone:* 860-447-2501 *Web:* www.nlmaritimesociety.org *Visitors welcome?* Yes *Hours:* Contact attraction directly *Admission:* Contact attraction directly *Operated by:* New London Maritime Society *NR?* Yes *NHL?* No *Year established/built:* 1760 *Latitude:* 41.3167 *Longitude:* -72.0900

NEW LONDON LEDGE LIGHTHOUSE
Established and built in 1909, the New London Ledge Lighthouse was automated in 1909 and is still an active aid to navigation. *Address:* New London Ledge Light *City:* New London *State:* CT *Visitors welcome?* Yes *Hours:* By appointment *Admission:* By appointment *Operated by:* New London Ledge Lighthouse Foundation *NR?* Yes *NHL?* No *Year established/built:* 1909 *Latitude:* 41.3061 *Longitude:* -72.0773

PECK LEDGE LIGHTHOUSE
Established and built in 1906, the Peck Ledge Lighthouse was automated in 1993 and is still an active aid to navigation. *Address:* Norwalk Harbor *City:* Norwalk *State:* CT *Visitors welcome?* No *Operated by:* U.S. Coast Guard (District 1) *NR?* Yes *NHL?* No *Year established/built:* 1906 *Latitude:* 41.07573 *Longitude:* -73.36945

PENFIELD REEF LIGHTHOUSE
Established and built in 1874, the Penfield Reef Lighthouse was automated in 1971 and is still an active aid to navigation. *Address:* Penfield Reef Light *City:* Fairfield *State:* CT *Visitors welcome?* Yes *Hours:* Contact attraction directly *Admission:* Contact attraction directly

Operated by: U.S. Coast Guard *NR?* Yes *NHL?* No *Year established/built:* 1874 *Latitude:* 41.1163 *Longitude:* -73.2218

SAYBROOK BREAKWATER LIGHTHOUSE

Established and built in 1886, the Saybrook Breakwater Lighthouse was automated in 1959 and is still an active aid to navigation. *Address:* Saybrook Breakwater Light *City:* Fenwick *State:* CT *Visitors welcome?* Yes *Hours:* No public access to tower *Admission:* No public access to tower *Operated by:* U.S. Coast Guard (District 1) *NR?* Yes *NHL?* No *Year established/built:* 1886 *Latitude:* 41.2632 *Longitude:* -72.3428

SHEFFIELD ISLAND LIGHTHOUSE

Established in 1828, the current Sheffield Island Lighthouse, also called the Norwalk Lighthouse, was constructed in 1868 and deactivated in 1902. *Address:* Sheffield Island Light *City:* South Norwalk *State:* CT *Phone:* 203-838-9444 *Web:* www.seaport.org *Email:* info@seaport.org *Visitors welcome?* Yes *Hours:* Contact attraction directly *Admission:* Contact attraction directly *Operated by:* Norwalk Seaport Association *NR?* Yes *NHL?* No *Year established/built:* 1828 *Latitude:* 41.04878 *Longitude:* -73.41914

SOUTHWEST LEDGE LIGHTHOUSE

Established and built in 1877, the Southwest Ledge Lighthouse, also called the New Haven Breakwater Lighthouse, was automated in 1973 and is still an active aid to navigation. *Address:* Southwest Ledge Light *City:* West Haven *State:* CT *Visitors welcome?* No *Operated by:* U.S. Coast Guard (District 1) *NR?* Yes *NHL?* No *Year established/built:* 1877 *Latitude:* 41.2350 *Longitude:* -72.9116

STAMFORD HARBOR LIGHTHOUSE

Established and built in 1882, the Stamford Harbor Lighthouse, also called the Chatham Rocks Lighthouse, was deactivated in 1953. It is now in private hands. *Address:* Samford Harbor *City:* Stamford *State:* CT *Visitors welcome?* No *Operated by:* Private owner *NR?* Yes *NHL?* No *Year established/built:* 1882 *Latitude:* 41.05343 *Longitude:* -73.53873

STONINGTON HARBOR LIGHTHOUSE

Established in 1823, the current Stonington Harbor Lighthouse was constructed in 1840 and deactivated in 1889. It is now a local history museum. *Address:* 7 Water Street *City:* Stonington *State:* CT *Zip:* 06378 *Phone:* 860-535-1440 *Web:* www.stoningtonhistory.org *Email:* lighthouse@stoningtonhistory.org *Visitors welcome?* Yes *Hours:* Daily, May to October, 10 a.m to 5 p.m. *Admission:* Contact attraction directly *Operated by:* Stonington Historical Society *NR?* Yes *NHL?* No *Year established/built:* 1823 *Latitude:* 41.3286 *Longitude:* -71.9059

STRATFORD POINT LIGHTHOUSE

Established in 1822, the current Stratford Point Lighthouse was constructed in 1881. Automated in 1970, the lighthouse is still an active aid to navigation. *Address:* Stratford Point

Light *City:* Bridgeport *State:* CT *Visitors welcome?* No *Operated by:* U.S. Coast Guard (District 1) *NR?* Yes *NHL?* No *Year established/built:* 1822 *Latitude:* 41.15152 *Longitude:* -73.1044

TONGUE POINT LIGHTHOUSE

Established and built in 1895, the Tongue Point Lighthouse--called locally The Bug--is still an active aid to navigation. *Address:* Tongue Point Light *City:* Bridgeport *State:* CT *Visitors welcome?* No *Operated by:* U.S. Coast Guard (District 1) *NR?* No *NHL?* No *Year established/built:* 1895 *Latitude:* 41.1667 *Longitude:* -73.1775

DELAWARE

BAKER SHOAL RANGE REAR LIGHTHOUSE

Established and built in 1904 as one of three range lights, the Baker Shoal Range Rear Lighthouse was automated in 1924 and later abandoned. *Address:* Baker Shoal Range Rear Light *City:* Port Penn *State:* DE *Visitors welcome?* No *Operated by:* U.S. Coast Guard (District 1) *NR?* No *NHL?* No *Year established/built:* 1904 *Latitude:* 39.5416 *Longitude:* -75.5701

BELLEVUE REAR RANGE LIGHTHOUSE

Established in 1834, the current Bellevue Rear Range Lighthouse was constructed in 1909. It is now deactivated. *Address:* Bellevue Rear Range Light *City:* Wilmington *State:* DE *Visitors welcome?* No *Operated by:* U.S. Coast Guard (District 1) *NR?* Yes *NHL?* No *Year established/built:* 1834 *Latitude:* 39.7201 *Longitude:* -75.5181

CHERRY ISLAND RANGE LIGHTHOUSE

Established and built in 1880, the Cherry Island Range Lighthouse was demolished in 1970, leaving a skeletal tower. *Address:* Cherry Island *City:* Edgemoor *State:* DE *Visitors welcome?* No *Operated by:* U.S. Coast Guard (District 1) *NR?* No *NHL?* No *Year established/built:* 1880 *Latitude:* 39.72956 *Longitude:* -75.51659

DELAWARE BREAKWATER LIGHTHOUSE

Established and built in 1885, the Delaware Breakwater Lighthouse was deactivated in 1996. It is now managed by a local not-for-profit organization. *Address:* Delaware Breakwater Light *City:* Lewes *State:* DE *Visitors welcome?* Yes *Hours:* By appointment *Admission:* By appointment *Operated by:* Delaware River & Bay Lighthouse Foundation *NR?* Yes *NHL?* No *Year established/built:* 1885 *Latitude:* 38.7971 *Longitude:* -75.0999

FENWICK ISLAND LIGHTHOUSE

Established and built in 1859, the Fenwick Island Lighthouse was inactive from 1978-1982, when it was relighted. It is now an active aid to navigation and a museum. *Address:* 146th Street and Lighthouse Avenue *City:* Fenwick Island *State:* DE *Phone:* 302-

436-8100 *Web:* fenwickislandlighthouse.org/ *Email:* wlewis@fenwickislandlighthouse.org *Visitors welcome?* Yes *Hours:* Daily, weather permitting *Admission:* Donation *Operated by:* New Friends of Fenwick Island Lighthouse *NR?* Yes *NHL?* No *Year established/built:* 1859 *Latitude:* 38.4512 *Longitude:* -75.0548

FOURTEEN FOOT BANK LIGHTHOUSE
Established in 1876, the Fourteen Foot Bank Lighthouse became operational in 1888 as the country's first caisson lighthouse structure. Automated in 1972, the lighthouse is still an active aid to navigation. *Address:* Fourteen Foot Bank Light *City:* Bowers Beach *State:* DE *Visitors welcome?* No *Operated by:* Private owner *NR?* Yes *NHL?* No *Year established/built:* 1876 *Latitude:* 39.0482 *Longitude:* -75.1836

HARBOR OF REFUGE LIGHTHOUSE
Established in 1896, the current Harbor of Refuge Breakwater Lighthouse, also called the South Breakwater Lighthouse, was constructed in 1926. Automated in 1973, the lighthouse is still an active aid to navigation managed by a local not-for-profit organization. *Address:* Harbor of Refuge Light *City:* Lewes *State:* DE *Visitors welcome?* Yes *Hours:* By appointment *Admission:* By appointment *Operated by:* Delaware River & Bay Lighthouse Foundation *NR?* Yes *NHL?* No *Year established/built:* 1896 *Latitude:* 38.8146 *Longitude:* -75.0924

LISTON FRONT RANGE LIGHTHOUSE
Built in 1904 to replace older range lights, the Liston Front Range Light marks the mouth of the Delaware River. The lighthouse was sold to a private party in 1954. *Address:* Liston Range Front Light *City:* Port Penn *State:* DE *Visitors welcome?* No *Operated by:* Private owner *NR?* No *NHL?* No *Year established/built:* 1904 *Latitude:* 39.4829 *Longitude:* -75.5920

LISTON REAR RANGE LIGHTHOUSE
Built in 1877, the Liston Rear Range Lighthouse once served as the Port Penn Rear Range Light and it is still an active aid to navigation. *Address:* Liston Range Rear Light *City:* Biddle's Corner *State:* DE *Visitors welcome?* No *Operated by:* Private owner *NR?* Yes *NHL?* No *Year established/built:* 1877 *Latitude:* 39.5239 *Longitude:* -75.6390

MARCUS HOOK RANGE LIGHTHOUSES
Established and built in 1918, the Marcus Hook Range Lighthouses are still active aids to navigation. The range rear light is 1.5 miles southwest of the front range light. *Address:* Marcus Hook Range Rear Light *City:* Edgemoor *State:* DE *Visitors welcome?* No *Operated by:* U.S. Coast Guard (District 1) *NR?* Yes *NHL?* No *Year established/built:* 1918 *Latitude:* 39.7621 *Longitude:* -75.5031

MISPILLION RIVER LIGHTHOUSE
Established in 1831, the current Mispillion River Lighthouse was constructed in 1873 and deactivated in 1929. *Address:* Mispillion Light *State:* DE *Visitors welcome?* No *Operated*

by: Delaware Dept. of Natural Resources & Environmental Control *NR?* Yes *NHL?* No *Year established/built:* 1831 *Latitude:* 38.94733 *Longitude:* -75.31491

NEW CASTLE RANGE LIGHTHOUSE

Built to mark Bulkhead Shoal on the Delaware River, New Castle Range Lighthouse was built around 1876 as a pair of range lights. The lights were automated around 1925, and the property sold in 1953. The original wooden tower was replaced by a steel tower. *Address:* Bulkhead Shoal *City:* New Castle *State:* DE *Visitors welcome?* No *Operated by:* Private owner *NR?* No *NHL?* No *Year established/built:* 1876 *Latitude:* 39.61678 *Longitude:* -75.59687

REEDY ISLAND RANGE REAR LIGHTHOUSE

Established in 1839, the current Reedy Island Rear Range Lighthouse was built in 1910 and is still an active aid to navigation. *Address:* Reedy Island Range Rear Light *City:* Taylor's Bridge *State:* DE *Visitors welcome?* No *Operated by:* U.S. Coast Guard (District 1) *NR?* Yes *NHL?* No *Year established/built:* 1839 *Latitude:* 39.4064 *Longitude:* -75.5898

FLORIDA

AMELIA ISLAND LIGHTHOUSE

Established in 1839, the Amelia Island Lighthouse originally stood on Cumberland Island in Georgia and was moved to its current location in 1820. The lighthouse was automated in 1956 and is still an active aid to navigation. *Address:* Amelia Island Light *City:* Fernandina Beach *State:* FL *Phone:* 904-277-7305 *Visitors welcome?* Yes *Hours:* By appointment *Admission:* Contact attraction directly *Operated by:* City of Fernandina Beach *NR?* Yes *NHL?* No *Year established/built:* 1839 *Latitude:* 30.67318 *Longitude:* -81.44244

CAPE CANAVERAL LIGHTHOUSE

The Cape Canaveral Lighthouse has witnessed more than maritime history; it has seen the launch of the space age, starting with the first rocket tests in 1950. Many of the images on the Fyddeye listing pages show the restoration of the lighthouse in 2005. *Address:* Cape Canaveral Light *City:* Cape Canaveral *State:* FL *Visitors welcome?* No *Operated by:* Cape Canaveral Lighthouse Foundation *NR?* No *NHL?* No *Year established/built:* 1848 *Latitude:* 28.4580 *Longitude:* -80.5445

CAPE FLORIDA LIGHTHOUSE

Established in 1825, the current Cape Florida Lighthouse was constructed in 1846 and automated in 1978. It still functions as a private aid to navigation. *Address:* Cape Florida Light *City:* Key Biscayne *State:* FL *Phone:* 305-361-5811 *Visitors welcome?* Yes *Hours:* Contact attraction directly *Admission:* Contact attraction directly *Operated by:* Florida Division of Recreation and Parks *NR?* Yes *NHL?* No *Year established/built:* 1825 *Latitude:* 25.6666 *Longitude:* -80.1560

CARYSFORT REEF LIGHTHOUSE

Established in 1825, the current Carysfort Reef Lighthouse was the first screwpile light-house built in on the Florida Keys in 1852. Automated in 1960, the light is still an active aid to navigation. *Address:* Carysfort Reef Light *City:* Key Largo *State:* FL *Visitors welcome?* No *Operated by:* U.S. Coast Guard (District 7) *NR?* Yes *NHL?* No *Year established/built:* 1825 *Latitude:* 25.2217 *Longitude:* -80.2117

DRY TORTUGAS LIGHTHOUSE

✝ Established and built in 1858, the Dry Tortugas Lighthouse, also known as Logger-head Key Lighthouse, is part of the Dry Tortugas National Park. It is still an active aid to navigation. *Address:* Dry Tortugas Light *City:* Key West *State:* FL *Phone:* 305-242-7700 *Visitors welcome?* Yes *Hours:* By permit *Admission:* By permit *Operated by:* Dry Tortugas National Park *NR?* No *NHL?* No *Year established/built:* 1858 *Latitude:* 24.6333 *Longitude:* -82.9200 **Accommodations for overnight and/or long-term stays available.**

FOWEY ROCKS LIGHTHOUSE

Established and built in 1878, the Fowey Rocks Lighthouse was automated in 1974 and is still an active aid to navigation. *Address:* Fowey Rocks Light *City:* Key Biscayne *State:* FL *Visitors welcome?* No *Operated by:* U.S. Coast Guard (District 7) *NR?* No *NHL?* No *Year established/built:* 1878 *Latitude:* 25.5900 *Longitude:* -80.0967

HILLSBORO INLET LIGHTHOUSE

Established and built in 1907, the Hillsboro Inlet Lighthouse was automated in 1974 and is still an active aid to navigation. *Address:* Hillsboro Inlet *City:* Pompano Beach *State:* FL *Phone:* 954-942-2102 *Web:* www.hillsborolighthouse.org *Email:* info@hillsboro-lighthouse.org *Visitors welcome?* Yes *Hours:* By appointment *Admission:* Contact attraction directly *Operated by:* Hillsboro Lighthouse Preservation Society *NR?* Yes *NHL?* No *Year established/built:* 1907 *Latitude:* 26.2598 *Longitude:* -80.0826

JUPITER INLET LIGHTHOUSE

Established and built in 1860, the Jupiter Inlet Lighthouse was automated in 1987 and is still an active aid to navigation. A museum is in the historic oil house. *Address:* 500 Captain Armour's Way *City:* Jupiter *State:* FL *Zip:* 33469 *Phone:* 561-747-8380 *Email:* visit@lrhs.org *Visitors welcome?* Yes *Hours:* Tuesday to Sunday, 10 a.m. to 5 p.m. *Admission:* $7 adults; $5 children age 6-18; FREE 5 and under *Operated by:* Loxahatchee River Historical Society *NR?* Yes *NHL?* No *Year established/built:* 1860 *Latitude:* 26.9501 *Longitude:* -80.0818

PONCE DE LEON INLET LIGHTHOUSE

Established in 1835, the Ponce de Leon Inlet Lighthouse, also called the Mosquito Inlet Lighthouse, was constructed in 1887. Automated in 1953, the light is still an active aid to navigation. *Address:* 4931 South Peninsula Drive *City:* Ponce Inlet *State:* FL *Zip:* 32127

Phone: 386-761-1821 *Web:* www.ponceinlet.org *Email:* lighthouse@ponceinlet.org *Visitors welcome?* Yes *Hours:* Daily, 10 a.m. to 6 p.m. *Admission:* $5 adults, $1.50 children 11 and under *Operated by:* Ponce de Leon Inlet Light Station Preservation Association *NR?* Yes *NHL?* Yes *Year established/built:* 1835 *Latitude:* 29.0807 *Longitude:* -80.9281

ST. AUGUSTINE LIGHTHOUSE

Established in 1823, the current St. Augustine Lighthouse was constructed in 1874 and automated in 1955. Still an active aid to navigation, the lighthouse is now part of a major museum. *Address:* 81 Lighthouse Avenue *City:* St. Augustine *State:* **FL** *Zip:* 32080 *Phone:* 904-829-0745 *Web:* www.staugustinelighthouse.com *Email:* info@staugustinelighthouse.com *Visitors welcome?* Yes *Hours:* Daily, 9 a.m. to 7 p.m. *Admission:* $9 adults; $8 seniors; $7 children 6 to 11; under six FREE *Operated by:* St. Augustine Lighthouse *NR?* Yes *NHL?* No *Year established/built:* 1823 *Latitude:* 29.8856 *Longitude:* -81.2886

ST. JOHNS LIGHTHOUSE

Replacing a lightship in 1954, St. Johns Lighthouse first housed its light inside a Plexiglas dome. Later, the lamp was modernized and the dome removed. The light was automated in 1967. *Address:* St. Johns Light *City:* East Mayport *State:* FL *Phone:* 904-270-5226 *Visitors welcome?* Yes *Hours:* Contact attraction directly *Admission:* FREE *Operated by:* U.S. Coast Guard (District 7) *NR?* No *NHL?* No *Year established/built:* 1954 *Latitude:* 30.3861 *Longitude:* -81.3981

ST. JOHNS RIVER LIGHTHOUSE

Established in 1830, the current St. Johns River Lighthouse, also known as the Mayport Lighthouse, is no longer operational. *Address:* St. Johns River Light *City:* Mayport *State:* FL *Phone:* 904-270-5226 *Visitors welcome?* Yes *Hours:* Contact attraction directly *Admission:* Contact attraction directly *Operated by:* U.S. Coast Guard (District 7) *NR?* Yes *NHL?* No *Year established/built:* 1830 *Latitude:* 30.3935 *Longitude:* -81.4260

ST. JOSEPH POINT REAR RANGE LIGHTHOUSE

Established and built in 1902, the St. Joseph Point Rear Range Lighthouse was deactivated in 1960 and is now a private residence. *Address:* 2071 County Road 30 *City:* Simmons Bayou *State:* FL *Visitors welcome?* No *Operated by:* Private owner *NR?* No *NHL?* No *Year established/built:* 1902 *Latitude:* 27.66483 *Longitude:* -81.51575

GEORGIA

COCKSPUR ISLAND LIGHTHOUSE

Established in 1772, the current Cockspur Island Lighthouse in 1857 and deactivated in 1909. It is now part of the Fort Pulaski National Monument. *Address:* Cockspur Island Light *City:* Savannah *State:* GA *Visitors welcome?* Yes *Hours:* Daily, 8:30 a.m. to 5 p.m.

(Grounds only) *Admission:* **FREE** *Operated by:* Fort Pulaski National Monument *NR?* Yes *NHL?* No *Year established/built:* 1772 *Latitude:* 32.0227 *Longitude:* -80.8799

LITTLE CUMBERLAND ISLAND LIGHTHOUSE

Established and built in 1838, the Little Cumberland Island Lighthouse is now privately owned. It was renovated by the owners in 1998. *Address:* Little Cumberland Island Light *City:* Cumberland Island *State:* GA *Visitors welcome?* No *Operated by:* Private owner *NR?* Yes *NHL?* No *Year established/built:* 1838 *Latitude:* 30.9740 *Longitude:* -81.4168

SAPELO ISLAND FRONT RANGE LIGHTHOUSE

In 1868, a wooden frame beacon was constructed about 600 feet east of the Sapelo Lighthouse to serve as a front range light at Doboy Sound. A cast-iron tower replaced it in 1878. It is now owned by the State of George Parks Department. *Address:* Sapelo Island *State:* GA *Phone:* 912-437-3224 *Visitors welcome?* Yes *Hours:* Tuesday to Friday 7:30 a.m. to 5:30 p.m.; Saturday 8 a.m. to 5:30 p.m.; Sunday 1:30 to 5 p.m. *Admission:* Contact attraction directly *Operated by:* Georgia State Parks and Historic Sites *NR?* No *NHL?* No *Year established/built:* 1868 *Latitude:* 31.39745 *Longitude:* -81.27871

SAPELO ISLAND LIGHTHOUSE

Established and built in 1820, the Sapelo Island Lighthouse was deactivated from 1899 to 1998. It is now an active aid to navigation. *Address:* Sapelo Island Light *City:* Sapelo Island *State:* GA *Phone:* 912-437-3224 *Visitors welcome?* Yes *Hours:* Tuesday to Friday 7:30 a.m. to 5:30 p.m.; Saturday 8 a.m. to 5:30 p.m.; Sunday 1:30 to 5 p.m. *Admission:* Contact attraction directly *Operated by:* Georgia State Parks and Historic Sites *NR?* Yes *NHL?* No *Year established/built:* 1820 *Latitude:* 31.3920 *Longitude:* -81.2852

SAVANNAH HARBOR LIGHT

The Savannah Harbor Light, also called the Old Harbor Light, is a cast-iron lamp was installed in 1858 to guide ships into Savannah Harbor. The light was restored in 2001. *Address:* Emmet Park *City:* Savannah *State:* GA *Visitors welcome?* Yes *Hours:* Daily *Admission:* **FREE** *Operated by:* City of Savannah *NR?* No *NHL?* No *Year established/built:* 1858 *Latitude:* 32.0796 *Longitude:* -81.0853

ST. SIMONS ISLAND LIGHTHOUSE

Established in 1811, the current St. Simons Island Lighthouse was constructed in 1872. Automated in 1954, the lighthouse is still an active aid to navigation. It is now operated as a museum by a Georgia not-for-profit group. *Address:* St. Simons Island Light *City:* St. Simons Island *State:* GA *Zip:* 31522 *Phone:* 912-638-4666 *Web:* www.saintsimonslighthouse.org *Email:* ssi1872@comcast.net *Visitors welcome?* Yes *Hours:* Monday to Saturday 10 a.m. to 5 p.m.; Sunday, 1:30 p.m. to 5 p.m. *Admission:* $6 adults; $3 children; under six **FREE** *Operated by:* Coastal Georgia Historical Society *NR?* Yes *NHL?* No *Year established/built:* 1811 *Latitude:* 31.1334 *Longitude:* -81.3933

TYBEE ISLAND LIGHTHOUSE

Established in 1736, the current Tybee Island Lighthouse was constructed in 1867. Automated in 1972, the lighthouse is still an active aid to navigation. It is now part of the Fort Screven National Historic District. *Address:* 30 Meddin Drive *City:* Tybee Island *State:* GA *Zip:* 31328 *Phone:* 912-786-5801 *Web:* www.tybeelighthouse.org *Visitors welcome?* Yes *Hours:* Daily, except Tuesday, from 9 a.m. to 5:30 p.m. *Admission:* $6 adults; $5 seniors, children, active military; children under five, FREE *Operated by:* Tybee Island Light Station *NR?* Yes *NHL?* No *Year established/built:* 1736 *Latitude:* 32.0225 *Longitude:* -80.8448

MAINE

BAKER ISLAND LIGHTHOUSE

Established in 1828, the original tower was replaced by the current tower in 1855. The light was automated in 1957. *Address:* Baker Island *City:* Seal Harbor *State:* **ME** *Visitors welcome?* Yes *Hours:* Grounds only *Admission:* **FREE** *Operated by:* U.S. Coast Guard (District 1) *NR?* Yes *NHL?* No *Year established/built:* 1828 *Latitude:* 44.2413 *Longitude:* -68.2018

BASS HARBOR HEAD LIGHTHOUSE

Built to guide ships into Blue Hill Bay, Bass Harbor Lighthouse was first lit in 1858. The light was automated in 1974 and was incorporated in Acadia National Park. *Address:* Bass Harbor Head Light *City:* Bass Harbor *State:* **ME** *Visitors welcome?* Yes *Hours:* Grounds only *Admission:* **FREE** *Operated by:* U.S. Coast Guard (District 1) *NR?* Yes *NHL?* No *Year established/built:* 1858 *Latitude:* 44.2219 *Longitude:* -68.3372

BEAR ISLAND LIGHTHOUSE

The Bear Island Lighthouse was established in 1839. The present structure was built in 1889. The light was discontinued in 1989 and transferred to the National Park Service, which leases the light station property to a private individual. *Address:* Bear Island *City:* Northeast Harbor *State:* **ME** *Visitors welcome?* No *Operated by:* Private owner *NR?* Yes *NHL?* No *Year established/built:* 1839 *Latitude:* 44.28425 *Longitude:* -68.26779

BLUE HILL BAY LIGHTHOUSE

Originally established in 1856, Blue Hill Bay Lighthouse on Green Island was once known as Eggemogin Lighthouse for nearby Eggemogin Reach. Deactivated in 1933, the structure was replaced by an automated beacon on a steel tower, which is still in use. *Address:* Green Island *State:* **ME** *Visitors welcome?* No *Operated by:* Private owner *NR?* No *NHL?* No *Year established/built:* 1856 *Latitude:* 44.5623 *Longitude:* -67.44388

BOON ISLAND LIGHTHOUSE

The light station was established in 1799 with a daymark, and the first lighthouse was built in 1811. The present structure was constructed in 1855. The lighthouse was automated in 1978 and is now maintained by the American Lighthouse Foundation. *Address:* Boon Island Light *City:* York *State:* ME *Visitors welcome?* No *Operated by:* American Lighthouse Foundation *NR?* Yes *NHL?* No *Year established/built:* 1799 *Latitude:* 43.12167 *Longitude:* -70.47667

BROWNS HEAD LIGHTHOUSE

Located on Vinalhaven Island, the Browns Head Lighthouse was established in 1832, with the present structure built in 1857. The light was discontinued and the keeper's dwelling is now occupied by the Vinalhaven town manager. *Address:* Browns Head *City:* Vinalhaven *State:* ME *Visitors welcome?* No *Operated by:* Town of Vinalhaven *NR?* Yes *NHL?* No *Year established/built:* 1832 *Latitude:* 44.11175 *Longitude:* -68.91059

BURNT COAT HARBOR LIGHTHOUSE

The lighthouse, built in 1872 at Hockamock Head, marks the entrance to Burnt Coat Harbor, one of the best protected harbors on the Maine coast. Originally two range lights, the front range light was shut down in 1884. The light was automated in 1974. *Address:* Burnt Coat Harbor Light *City:* Swan's Island *State:* ME *Zip:* 04685 *Visitors welcome?* Yes *Hours:* Grounds only *Admission:* FREE *Operated by:* Swan's Island Lighthouse Committee *NR?* Yes *NHL?* No *Year established/built:* 1872 *Latitude:* 44.13411 *Longitude:* -68.44717

BURNT ISLAND LIGHTHOUSE

Built in 1821, the lighthouse is still an active aid to navigation, though it is now owned by the Maine Department of Marine Resources. The historic buildings at this lighthouse station have been carefully restored and transformed. *Address:* Burnt Island Light *City:* Boothbay Harbor *State:* ME *Phone:* 207-633-9559 *Web:* www.maine.gov/dmr/burntisland/ *Visitors welcome?* Yes *Hours:* Contact attraction directly *Admission:* Contact attraction directly *Operated by:* Maine Department of Marine Resources *NR?* Yes *NHL?* No *Year established/built:* 1821 *Latitude:* 43.8252 *Longitude:* -69.6402

CAPE ELIZABETH LIGHTHOUSE

The Cape Elizabeth Lighthouse enjoys the distinction of having two towers, first constructed in 1828. In 1873, the rubblestone structures were replaced with cast-iron towers. The west tower was decommissioned in 1924, and the east tower still shows a light. *Address:* Cape Elizabeth Lights *City:* Cape Elizabeth *State:* ME *Visitors welcome?* No *Operated by:* American Lighthouse Foundation *NR?* No *NHL?* No *Year established/built:* 1828 *Latitude:* 43.56607 *Longitude:* -70.20006

CAPE NEDDICK LIGHTHOUSE

Lit in 1879 on a tiny island off the mainland called the Nubble Cape Neddick Lighthouse is now part of a park owned by the Town of York. The light still serves as an active aid to navigation. *Address:* Cape Neddick Light *City:* York *State:* ME *Zip:* 03909 *Phone:* 207-363-1000 *Visitors welcome?* Yes *Hours:* Daily, early May to Columbus Day *Admission:* Contact attraction directly *Operated by:* Friends of Nubble Light *NR?* Yes *NHL?* No *Year established/ built:* 1879 *Latitude:* 43.16528 *Longitude:* -70.59111

CUCKOLDS ISLAND LIGHTHOUSE

The Cuckolds Island Light Station was established in 1892, though the lighthouse itself was built in 1907. Automated in 1974, the station is now undergoing restoration. *Address:* Southport Island *City:* Boothbay Harbor *State:* ME *Web:* www.cuckoldslight.org/ *Visitors welcome?* No *Operated by:* Cuckolds Island Fog Signal and Light Station Council *NR?* Yes *NHL?* No *Year established/built:* 1892 *Latitude:* 43.82119 *Longitude:* -69.66449

CURTIS ISLAND LIGHTHOUSE

The Curtis Island Lighthouse was established in 1835, and the present structure was constructed in 1896. The station was automated in 1972 and the grounds are now a public park. *Address:* Curtis Island Light *City:* Camden *State:* ME *Zip:* 04843 *Phone:* 207-236-3353 *Visitors welcome?* Yes *Hours:* Grounds only *Admission:* FREE *Operated by:* Town of Camden *NR?* Yes *NHL?* No *Year established/built:* 1835 *Latitude:* 44.20137 *Longitude:* -69.04886

DEER ISLAND THOROFARE LIGHTHOUSE

The Deer Island Thorofare Lighthouse was established in 1858 and the present structure was constructed the same year. The station was automated in 1958 and is now privately owned. *Address:* Mark Island *City:* Stonington *State:* ME *Visitors welcome?* Yes *Hours:* Grounds only *Admission:* FREE *Operated by:* Island Heritage Trust *NR?* No *NHL?* No *Year established/built:* 1858 *Latitude:* 44.13369 *Longitude:* -68.70225

DICE HEAD LIGHTHOUSE

Constructed in 1829 at the mouth of the Penobscot River, the lighthouse stands near places that changed hands between the French and British numerous times in the 17th century. Now inactive, the lighthouse is undergoing restoration. *Address:* Dice Head Light *City:* Castine *State:* ME *Visitors welcome?* Yes *Hours:* Grounds only *Admission:* FREE *Operated by:* Town of Castine *NR?* No *NHL?* No *Year established/built:* 1829 *Latitude:* 44.38267 *Longitude:* -68.81885

DOUBLING POINT LIGHTHOUSE

Doubling Point Lighthouse was built in 1898 on Arrowsic Island on the Kennebec River in Maine. It was one of four lighthouses built that year to provide navigational aid for ships on their way to Bath. The lighthouse is now owned by a not-for-profit group. *Address:* Doubling Point Light *City:* Arrowsic *State:* **ME** *Zip:* 04530 *Web:* www.doubling-point.org *Email:* mspencer@student.uchc.edu *Visitors welcome?* **Yes** *Hours:* Contact attraction directly *Admission:* Contact attraction directly *Operated by:* Friends of the Doubling Point Light *NR?* **Yes** *NHL?* No *Year established/built:* 1898 *Latitude:* 43.88251 *Longitude:* -69.80677

EAGLE ISLAND LIGHTHOUSE

The Eagle Island Lighthouse is located on one of several islands along the Maine coast named after the majestic birds. This Eagle Island is at East Penobscot Bay. The lighthouse was established in 1839 and the current tower was built the same year. *Address:* Eagle Island Light *City:* Eagle Island *State:* **ME** *Visitors welcome?* **Yes** *Hours:* Grounds only *Admission:* **FREE** *Operated by:* Eagle Light Caretakers *NR?* No *NHL?* No *Year established/built:* 1839 *Latitude:* 44.50397 *Longitude:* -67.75527

EGG ROCK LIGHTHOUSE

Egg Rock Lighthouse was constructed in 1875. It was automated in 1976 and is an active aid to navigation. *Address:* Frenchman's Bay *City:* Bar Harbor *State:* **ME** *Visitors welcome?* No *Operated by:* Maine Coastal Islands National Wildlife Refuge *NR?* **Yes** *NHL?* No *Year established/built:* 1875 *Latitude:* 44.38758 *Longitude:* -68.2039

FORT POINT LIGHTHOUSE

The Fort Point Lighthouse was established in 1836 and the current structure built in 1857. The lighthouse was automated in 1988 and is now within a state park. *Address:* Fort Point State Park *City:* Stockton Springs *State:* **ME** *Phone:* 207-567-3356 *Visitors welcome?* **Yes** *Hours:* Grounds only *Admission:* **FREE** *Operated by:* Maine Bureau of Parks and Lands *NR?* **Yes** *NHL?* No *Year established/built:* 1836 *Latitude:* 44.4668 *Longitude:* -68.8253

FRANKLIN ISLAND LIGHTHOUSE

The Franklin Island Lighthouse was established in 1807 and the current structure was built in 1855. The light was automated in 1933, and the facility is maintained by a local not-for-profit. *Address:* Franklin Island *State:* **ME** *Visitors welcome?* **Yes** *Hours:* Grounds only *Admission:* **FREE** *Operated by:* Franklin Light Preservation Inc. *NR?* No *NHL?* No *Year established/built:* 1807 *Latitude:* 43.89175 *Longitude:* -69.37366

GOAT ISLAND LIGHTHOUSE

The Goat Island Lighthouse was established in 1833 and the present structure built in 1859. It was automated in 1990 and is an active aid to navigation. *Address:* Goat Island Light *City:* Cape Porpoise *State:* **ME** *Visitors welcome?* **Yes** *Hours:* Grounds only *Admission:* **FREE** *Operated by:* Kennebunkport Conservation Trust *NR?* **Yes** *NHL?* No *Year established/built:* 1833 *Latitude:* 43.3578 *Longitude:* -70.4250

GOOSE ROCKS LIGHTHOUSE

✛ The cast-iron Goose Rocks Lighthouse was established and built in 1890. The U.S. Coast Guard automated it in 1964. *Address:* Goose Rocks Light *City:* North Haven *State:* ME *Phone:* 203-736-9300 *Web:* www.beaconpreservation.org *Email:* info@beaconpreservation.org *Visitors welcome?* Yes *Hours:* By appointment *Admission:* Contact attraction directly *Operated by:* Beacon Preservation *NR?* Yes *NHL?* No *Year established/built:* 1890 *Latitude:* 44.1354 *Longitude:* -68.8307 **Accommodations for overnight and/or long-term stays available.**

GREAT DUCK ISLAND LIGHTHOUSE

The Great Duck Island Lighthouse was established and built in 1890. The U.S. Coast Guard automated it in 1986. *Address:* Great Duck Island Light *City:* Frenchboro *State:* ME *Visitors welcome?* No *Operated by:* College of the Atlantic *NR?* Yes *NHL?* No *Year established/built:* 1890 *Latitude:* 44.1420 *Longitude:* -68.2458

GRINDLE POINT LIGHTHOUSE

The Gringle Point Lighthouse was established in 1851 and the current structure built in 1874. The station was closed in 1934 and relit by the Town of Islesboro in 1987. *Address:* Grindle Point Light *City:* Islesboro *State:* ME *Zip:* 04848 *Phone:* 207-734-2253 *Visitors welcome?* Yes *Hours:* Summer, Saturday and Sunday, 9 a.m. to 4:30 p.m. *Admission:* Contact attraction directly *Operated by:* Town of Islesboro *NR?* Yes *NHL?* No *Year established/built:* 1851 *Latitude:* 44.2814 *Longitude:* -68.9431

HALFWAY ROCK LIGHTHOUSE

Halfway Rock is located near the midpoint between Cape Elizabeth and Cape Small in Casco Bay, and it received its lighthouse in 1871 after a series of disastrous shipwrecks. The light was automated in 1975 and the tower was leased to the American Lighthouse Foundation. *Address:* Casco Bay *City:* Portland *State:* ME *Visitors welcome?* No *Operated by:* American Lighthouse Foundation *NR?* Yes *NHL?* No *Year established/built:* 1871 *Latitude:* 43.6555 *Longitude:* -70.0375

HENDRICKS HEAD LIGHTHOUSE

The Hendricks Head Lighthouse was established in 1829, and the current structure was built in 1875. The light was decommissioned in 1933, but after electrical cables were strung to the island in 1951, the U.S. Coast Guard relit the light. *Address:* Hendricks Head *City:* Hendricks Harbor *State:* ME *Visitors welcome?* No *Operated by:* Private owner *NR?* Yes *NHL?* No *Year established/built:* 1829 *Latitude:* 43.82286 *Longitude:* -69.69115

HERON NECK LIGHTHOUSE

Address: Heron Neck Light *City:* Vinalhaven *State:* ME *Visitors welcome?* Yes *Hours:* Grounds only *Admission:* FREE *Operated by:* Island Institute *NR?* Yes *NHL?* No *Year established/built:* 1854 *Latitude:* 44.02511 *Longitude:* -68.86217

INDIAN ISLAND LIGHTHOUSE

The Indian Island Lighthouse was established in 1850 and the current structure put up in 1875. The light was deactivated in 1934 and the property has remained in private hands since. *Address:* Rockport Harbor *City:* Rockport *State:* ME *Visitors welcome?* No *Operated by:* Private owner *NR?* Yes *NHL?* No *Year established/built:* 1850 *Latitude:* 44.1748 *Longitude:* -69.06892

ISLE AU HAUT LIGHTHOUSE

✚ Built of granite the same year it was established, 1907, the Isle au Haut Lighthouse was automated in 1934. It is currently operated as part of a bed and breakfast. *Address:* The Keepers House *City:* Isle au Haut *State:* ME *Phone:* 207-460-0257 *Visitors welcome?* Yes *Hours:* Contact attraction directly *Admission:* Contact attraction directly *Operated by:* Keeper's House Inn *NR?* Yes *NHL?* No *Year established/built:* 1907 *Latitude:* 44.07536 *Longitude:* -68.63336 **Accommodations for overnight and/or long-term stays available.**

KENNEBEC RIVER RANGE LIGHTHOUSE

Also known as the Doubling Point Range Lights, the Kennebec River Range Lights guide mariners along a long stretch of the Kennebec River with two sharp turns. Constructed in 1898, the lights were transferred to a not-for-profit group exactly 100 years later. *Address:* Doubling Point Range Lights *City:* Arrowsic *State:* ME *Visitors welcome?* Yes *Hours:* Grounds only *Admission:* FREE *Operated by:* Range Light Keepers *NR?* Yes *NHL?* No *Year established/built:* 1898 *Latitude:* 43.88479 *Longitude:* -69.79567

LADIES DELIGHT LIGHTHOUSE

Located on an island in the northern end of Lake Cobbosseecontee, the Ladies Delight Lighthouse was established and built in 1908. *Address:* Lake Cobbosseecontee *City:* Manchester *State:* ME *Visitors welcome?* No *Operated by:* Cobbosseecontee Yacht Club *NR?* No *NHL?* No *Year established/built:* 1908 *Latitude:* 44.31402 *Longitude:* -69.89159

LIBBY ISLAND LIGHTHOUSE

The Libby Island Lighthouse was established in 1823, with the current struction at the site built the following year. The station was automated in 1974, and it is now part of a national wildlife refuge. *Address:* Machias Bay *City:* Machiasport *State:* ME *Visitors welcome?* Yes *Hours:* Grounds only *Admission:* FREE *Operated by:* Maine Coastal Islands National Wildlife Refuge *NR?* Yes *NHL?* No *Year established/built:* 1823 *Latitude:* 44.64924 *Longitude:* -67.3410

LITTLE RIVER ISLAND LIGHTHOUSE

*** The Little River Lighthouse was established in 1847 and the present structure was built in 1876. The light was moved to a steel tower in 1975, but the lighthouse was relit in 2001. Overnight visitors are allowed in the former keeper's quarters. *Address:* Little River Island *City:* Cutler *State:* ME *Phone:* 207-259-3833 *Web:* www.littleriverlight.org *Email:* LittleRiverLight@LighthouseFoundation.org *Visitors welcome?* Yes *Hours:* Grounds only after July 15 *Admission:* FREE *Operated by:* Friends of Little River Lighthouse *NR?* Yes *NHL?* No *Year established/built:* 1847 *Latitude:* 44.6509 *Longitude:* -67.1933 **Accommodations for overnight and/or long-term stays available.**

LUBEC CHANNEL LIGHTHOUSE

The Lubec Channel Lighthouse is a cast-iron structure of the coffee pot type built in 1890. The station was automated in 1939. *Address:* Lubec Channel Light *City:* Lubec *State:* ME *Visitors welcome?* No *Operated by:* U.S. Coast Guard (District 1) *NR?* Yes *NHL?* No *Year established/built:* 1890 *Latitude:* 44.8421 *Longitude:* -66.9766

MARSHALL POINT LIGHTHOUSE

The first lighthouse at Marshall Point, made of rubblestone, was built in 1832. In 1858 a new tower was built at its present site, at water's edge. The lighthouse was automated in 1971. A not-for-profit now operates a museum and gift shop on the property. *Address:* Marshall Point Road *City:* Port Clyde *State:* ME *Web:* www.marshallpoint.org *Visitors welcome?* Yes *Hours:* May, Saturday and Sunday, 1 p.m. to 5 p.m.; Memorial Day to Columbus Day, Sunday to Friday, 1 p.m. to 5 p.m., Saturday, 10 a.m. to 5 p.m. *Admission:* Contact attraction directly *Operated by:* Marshall Point Lighthouse Museum *NR?* Yes *NHL?* No *Year established/built:* 1832 *Latitude:* 43.92128 *Longitude:* -69.25501

MATINICUS ROCK LIGHTHOUSE

The two-lighthouse Matinicus Rock Light Station was established in 1827, and both current lighthouses were built in 1857. The north light was shut down in 1924, and the south light was automated in 1983. The station is now part of a wildlife refuge. *Address:* Matinicus Rock Light *City:* Matinicus Island *State:* ME *Visitors welcome?* Yes *Hours:* Grounds only *Admission:* FREE *Operated by:* Maine Coastal Islands National Wildlife Refuge *NR?* Yes *NHL?* No *Year established/built:* 1827 *Latitude:* 43.7835 *Longitude:* -68.8550

MONHEGAN ISLAND LIGHTHOUSE

The legendary Monhegan Island Lighthouse holds a prominent place in maritime history; it may have been visited by Phoenicians and Vikings. Local Penobscot Indians also used the island. The lighthouse was established in 1824. *Address:* 1 Lighthouse *City:* Monhegan Island *State:* ME *Email:* museum@monheganmuseum.org *Visitors welcome?* Yes *Hours:* Daily, July 1 to August 31, 11:30 a.m. to 3:30 p.m.; Sept. 1 to Sept. 30, 1:30 p.m. to 3:30 p.m. *Admission:* Contact attraction directly *Operated by:* Monhegan Historical and Cultural Museum Association *NR?* Yes *NHL?* No *Year established/built:* 1824 *Latitude:* 43.7660 *Longitude:* -69.3116

MOOSE PEAK LIGHTHOUSE

Established in 1826 on Mistake Island, the current tower was constructed in 1851. It was automated in 1972. *Address:* Mistake Island *City:* Jonesport *State:* ME *Visitors welcome?* No *Operated by:* U.S. Coast Guard (District 1) *NR?* No *NHL?* No *Year established/built:* 1826 *Latitude:* 44.4748 *Longitude:* -67.5350

Monhegan Island Lighthouse, Maine

MOUNT DESERT LIGHTHOUSE

Mount Desert Rock is a tiny, rock strewn island 26 miles off Bar Harbor, making it one of the desolate lighthouses on the Atlantic shoreline. First built in 1829, the lighthouse had a reputation for driving lighthouse keepers insane. *Address:* Mount Desert Light *City:* Yarmouth *State:* ME *Visitors welcome?* No *Operated by:* College of the Atlantic *NR?* Yes *NHL?* No *Year established/built:* 1829 *Latitude:* 43.9686 *Longitude:* -68.1283

NARRAGUAGUS ISLAND LIGHTHOUSE

Also known as Pond Island Lighthouse, the Narraguagus Lighthouse was established in 1853, and the current structure was built the same year. The light was discontinued in 1934, though a buoy marks the entrance to Narraguagus Bay formerly marked by the light. *Address:* Pond Island Light *City:* Milbridge *State:* ME *Visitors welcome?* No *Operated by:* Private owner *NR?* Yes *NHL?* No *Year established/built:* 1853 *Latitude:* 43.7400 *Longitude:* -69.7703

NASH ISLAND LIGHTHOUSE

The Nash Island Light Station was established in 1838, and the present structure was built in 1874. The station is now part of the Petit Manan National Wildlife Refuge. *Address:* Nash Island *City:* Addison *State:* ME *Visitors welcome?* Yes *Hours:* Grounds only, September to March *Admission:* FREE *Operated by:* Friends of Nash Island Light *NR?* No *NHL?* No *Year established/built:* 1838 *Latitude:* 44.4640 *Longitude:* -67.7458

OWLS HEAD LIGHTHOUSE

The Owls Head Lighthouse was established and built in 1825. It was automated in 1989. *Address:* Owls Head State Park *City:* Owls Head *State:* ME *Zip:* 04854 *Phone:* 207-941-4014 *Visitors welcome?* Yes *Hours:* Grounds only *Admission:* FREE *Operated by:* American Lighthouse Foundation *NR?* Yes *NHL?* No *Year established/built:* 1825 *Latitude:* 44.09202 *Longitude:* -69.04564

PEMAQUID POINT LIGHTHOUSE

✛ Constructed in 1827, the original structure was replaced in 1835. In 1934, the light was the first in the U.S. to be automated. *Address:* Pemaquid Point Light *City:* Pemaquid *State:* ME *Visitors welcome?* Yes *Hours:* By appointment *Admission:* Contact attraction directly *Operated by:* Friends of Pemaquid Point Lighthouse *NR?* Yes *NHL?* No *Year established/built:* 1827 *Latitude:* 43.8370 *Longitude:* -69.5061 **Accommodations for overnight and/or long-term stays available.**

PERKINS ISLAND LIGHTHOUSE

The Perkins Island Lighthouse was established and built in 1898. The station was automated in 1959. *Address:* Perkins Island *City:* Georgetown *State:* ME *Email:* perkinslight@hotmail.com *Visitors welcome?* Yes *Hours:* Grounds only *Admission:* FREE *Operated by:* Friends of Perkins Island Lighthouse *NR?* Yes *NHL?* No *Year established/built:* 1898 *Latitude:* 43.78675 *Longitude:* -69.78365

PETIT MANAN LIGHTHOUSE

The Petit Manan Lighthouse was established in 1817 and the current tower was built in 1855. The station was automated in 1972 and the island is part of a national wildlife refuge. *Address:* Petit Manan Island *City:* Steuben *State:* ME *Visitors welcome?* Yes *Hours:* Grounds only *Admission:* FREE *Operated by:* Maine Coastal Islands National Wildlife Refuge *NR?* No *NHL?* No *Year established/built:* 1817 *Latitude:* 44.3673 *Longitude:* -67.8653

POND ISLAND LIGHTHOUSE

The Pond Island Lighthouse was established in 1821, and the current structure was built in 1855. The light was automated in 1960, and the grounds are now part of the Pond

Island National Wildlife Refuge. *Address:* Pond Island Light *City:* Phippsburg *State:* ME *Visitors welcome?* Yes *Hours:* Grounds only *Admission:* FREE *Operated by:* Pond Island National Wildlife Refuge *NR?* No *NHL?* No *Year established/built:* 1820 *Latitude:* 43.7400 *Longitude:* -69.7703

PORTLAND BREAKWATER LIGHTHOUSE
The Portland Breakwater Lighthouse was constructed in 1854 to mark the end of a breakwater constructed eighteen years before. The brick lighthouse was replaced in 1875 with a cast-iron structure said to mimic a fourth-century B.C. Greek temple. *Address:* Portland Breakwater Light *City:* South Portland *State:* ME *Phone:* 207-767-3201 *Email:* COSP@southportland.org *Visitors welcome?* Yes *Hours:* Grounds only *Admission:* FREE *Operated by:* City of South Portland *NR?* Yes *NHL?* No *Year established/built:* 1854 *Latitude:* 43.65556 *Longitude:* -70.23473

Portland Head Lighthouse, Cape Elizabeth, Maine

PORTLAND HEAD LIGHTHOUSE

Originally established in 1791, Portland Head Lighthouse tower has stood for more than two hundred years guarding the entrance to Portland Harbor. The property is now leased to the town of Cape Elizabeth, which operates the facility as a museum and public park. *Address:* Portland Head Light *City:* Cape Elizabeth *State:* ME *Zip:* 04107 *Phone:* 207-799-2661 *Web:* www.portlandheadlight.com *Email:* cephl@aol.com *Visitors welcome?* Yes *Hours:* Daily, Memorial Day to the Friday following Columbus Day, 10 a.m. to 4 p.m. *Admission:* $2 adults; $1 children 6-18 *Operated by:* Portland Head Light *NR?* Yes *NHL?* No *Year established/built:* 1791 *Latitude:* 43.6231 *Longitude:* -70.2078

PROSPECT HARBOR LIGHTHOUSE

Established in 1850, the Prospect Harbor Lighthouse dwelling now standing was built in 1891. The light was automated in 1951, and the grounds are owned by the U.S. Navy. *Address:* Prospect Harbor Light *City:* Prospect Harbor *State:* ME *Visitors welcome?* No *Operated by:* American Lighthouse Foundation *NR?* No *NHL?* No *Year established/built:* 1850 *Latitude:* 44.40336 *Longitude:* -68.0130

PUMPKIN ISLAND LIGHTHOUSE

The Pumpkin Island Lighthouse was established in 1855, although the keeper's house was built the year before. The station was decommissioned by the U.S. Coast Guard in 1933. *Address:* Little Deer Isle *City:* Little Deer Isle *State:* ME *Visitors welcome?* No *Operated by:* Private owner *NR?* No *NHL?* No *Year established/built:* 1855 *Latitude:* 44.2906 *Longitude:* -68.7161

RAM ISLAND LEDGE LIGHTHOUSE

An underwater ledge runs from Ram Island at the entrance to Portland Harbor, and the Ram Island Ledge Lighthouse was built in 1905 to mark the hazard. Several ships have been lost on this rocky outcropping. *Address:* Ram Island Ledge Light *City:* Portland *State:* ME *Visitors welcome?* No *Operated by:* Private owner *NR?* Yes *NHL?* No *Year established/built:* 1905 *Latitude:* 43.6317 *Longitude:* -70.1867

RAM ISLAND LIGHTHOUSE

The Ram Island Lighthouse was established in 1883 and the current structures were built the same year. The station was automated in 1965, and the facility is owned by the Grand Banks Maritime Museum Trust, which also owns the *F/V Sherman Zwicker*. *Address:* Ram Island Light *City:* Boothbay *State:* ME *Phone:* 207-882-9721 *Web:* www.schoonermuseum.org *Email:* staff@schoonermuseum.org *Visitors welcome?* Yes *Hours:* Grounds only *Admission:* Contact attraction directly *Operated by:* Grand Banks Schooner Museum Trust *NR?* Yes *NHL?* No *Year established/built:* 1883 *Latitude:* 43.80375 *Longitude:* -69.5992

ROCKLAND BREAKWATER LIGHTHOUSE

The Rockland Breakwater Lighthouse was built in 1902 and automated in 1965. It is now maintained by a community not-for-profit. *Address:* Rockland Breakwater Light *City:*

Rockland *State:* ME *Zip:* 04841 *Phone:* 207-785-4609 *Web:* www.rocklandlighthouse.com *Email:* brkwater@midcoast.com *Visitors welcome?* Yes *Hours:* Saturdays, Sundays, and holidays, Memorial Day weekend to Columbus Day *Admission:* Contact attraction directly *Operated by:* Friends of the Rockland Breakwater Lighthouse *NR?* No *NHL?* No *Year established/built:* 1902 *Latitude:* 44.10417 *Longitude:* -69.0775

ROCKLAND HARBOR SOUTHWEST LIGHTHOUSE
The Rockland Harbor Southwest Lighthouse was built by a private party in 1987. *Address:* Rockland Harbor *City:* Owls Head *State:* ME *Visitors welcome?* No *Operated by:* Private owner *NR?* No *NHL?* No *Year established/built:* 1987 *Latitude:* 44.10036 *Longitude:* -69.09057

SADDLEBACK LEDGE LIGHTHOUSE
Constructed in 1839 on a bare, windswept island, Saddleback Ledge Lighthouse is considered one of the most isolated light stations in New England. The light was automated in 1954. *Address:* Saddleback Ledge Light *City:* Vinalhaven *State:* ME *Visitors welcome?* No *Operated by:* U.S. Coast Guard (District 1) *NR?* Yes *NHL?* No *Year established/built:* 1839 *Latitude:* 44.01436 *Longitude:* -68.72645

Seguin Island Lighthouse, Maine

SEGUIN ISLAND LIGHTHOUSE

✦ Commissioned by George Washington in 1795, the Sequin Island Lighthouse was established the next year. The current granite lighthouse was built in 1857 and automated in 1985. Tours are conducted by a not-for-profit organization based in Bath. *Address:* Seguin Island Light *City:* Seguin Island *State:* **ME** *Phone:* 207-443-4808 *Web:* www.seguinisland. org *Email:* keeper@seguinisland.org *Visitors welcome?* Yes *Hours:* **By** appointment *Admission:* Contact attraction directly *Operated by:* Friends Of Seguin Island Lighthouse *NR?* Yes *NHL?* No *Year established/built:* 1796 *Latitude:* 44.5176 *Longitude:* -67.5325 **Accommodations for overnight and/or long-term stays available.**

SPRING POINT LEDGE LIGHTHOUSE

Spring Point Ledge Lighthouse was constructed in 1897 to mark a dangerous ledge which is now covered by the breakwater. It was automated in the 1980s and is now owned by a not-for-profit organization. *Address:* Spring Point Ledge Light *City:* Portland *State:* **ME** *Phone:* 207-699-2676 *Web:* www.springpointlight.org *Email:* info@springpointlight.org *Visitors welcome?* Yes *Hours:* Selected days, contact attraction *Admission:* Contact attraction directly *Operated by:* Spring Point Ledge Light Trust *NR?* Yes *NHL?* No *Year established/built:* 1897 *Latitude:* 43.65222 *Longitude:* -70.22361

SQUIRREL POINT LIGHTHOUSE

The Kennebec River has been an important maritime thoroughfare since the 17th century. Arrowsic Island was one of the first areas settled, and ships moved goods up and down the river. The Squirrel Point Lighthouse was built in 1898. *Address:* Squirrel Point Light *City:* Arrowsic *State:* **ME** *Visitors welcome?* No *Operated by:* Chewonki Foundation *NR?* Yes *NHL?* No *Year established/built:* 1898 *Latitude:* 43.81652 *Longitude:* -69.80238

TENANTS HARBOR LIGHTHOUSE

The Tenants Harbor Lighthouse was established in 1858 and discontinued in 1933. At that time, it was purchased by the Andrew Wyeth family, and the artist's son, Jamie Wyeth, now lives there. *City:* Tenants Harbor *State:* **ME** *Visitors welcome?* No *Operated by:* Private owner *NR?* Yes *NHL?* No *Year established/built:* 1858 *Latitude:* 43.9673 *Longitude:* -69.2081

TWO BUSH ISLAND LIGHTHOUSE

The Two Bush Island Lighthouse was established and built in 1897. It was automated in 1964 and is now part of a wildlife refuge. *Address:* Two Bush Island *State:* **ME** *Visitors welcome?* Yes *Hours:* Grounds only *Admission:* **FREE** *Operated by:* Maine Coastal Islands National Wildlife Refuge *NR?* No *NHL?* No *Year established/built:* 1897 *Latitude:* 43.75286 *Longitude:* -69.93588

WEST QUODDY HEAD LIGHTHOUSE

Built in 1808, West Quoddy Head Lighthouse marks the Lubec Channel at the easternmost point of the United States. It also has a unique red and white bands, one of only two lighthouse with these marks. *Address:* West Quoddy Head Light *City:* Lubec *State:* ME *Visitors welcome?* Yes *Hours:* Daily, mid-May to mid-October *Admission:* FREE *Operated by:* West Quoddy Head Light Keepers Association *NR?* Yes *NHL?* No *Year established/built:* 1808 *Latitude:* 44.8150 *Longitude:* -66.9506

WHALEBACK LEDGE LIGHTHOUSE

Established in 1830 at the mouth of Piscataqua River just east of the Maine / New Hampshire border, a second structure replaced the original in 1872. The station was automated in 1963. The station is owned by the American Lighthouse Foundation, and managed by its chapter, Friends of Portsmouth Lighthouse. *Address:* Whaleback Light *City:* Kittery *State:* ME *Email:* info@portsmouthharborlighthouse.com *Visitors welcome?* No *Operated by:* Friends of Portsmouth Harbor Lighthouse *NR?* Yes *NHL?* No *Year established/built:* 1830 *Latitude:* 43.0588 *Longitude:* -70.6963

WHITEHEAD ISLAND LIGHTHOUSE

✦ Commissioned by President Thomas Jefferson in 1803, the light marks the entrance to Penobscot Bay. The lighthouse is now owned by Pine Island Camp as a recreational and educational facility, although the light itself is still an active aid to navigation. *Address:* Whitehead Island Light *State:* ME *Zip:* 04011 *Phone:* 207-729-7714 *Web:* www.whiteheadlightstation.org *Email:* info@whiteheadlightstation.org *Visitors welcome?* Yes *Hours:* Contact attraction directly *Admission:* Contact attraction directly *Operated by:* Whitehead Light Station *NR?* Yes *NHL?* No *Year established/built:* 1803 *Latitude:* 43.97871 *Longitude:* -69.12428 **Accommodations for overnight and/or long-term stays available.**

WHITLOCKS MILL LIGHTHOUSE

In 1892, the U.S. Coast Guard asked a mill operator named Whitlock to place a red lighted lantern on a post at this dog leg in the St. Croix River because of the heavy traffic. In 1909 the last lighthouse to be built in Maine was erected here. *Address:* Whitlocks Mill Light *City:* Whitlocks Mill *State:* ME *Web:* www.stcroixhistorical.org/whitlock/ *Email:* schs@stcroixhistorical.org *Visitors welcome?* Yes *Hours:* Contact attraction directly *Admission:* Contact attraction directly *Operated by:* St. Croix Historical Society *NR?* Yes *NHL?* No *Year established/built:* 1909 *Latitude:* 45.1628 *Longitude:* -67.2273

WINTER HARBOR LIGHTHOUSE

The Winter Harbor lighthouse was established and built in 1857. Shut down by the U.S. Coast Guard in 1933, the property was sold to a private owner. *Address:* Mark Island *City:* Winter Harbor *State:* ME *Visitors welcome?* No *Operated by:* Private owner *NR?* Yes *NHL?* No *Year established/built:* 1857 *Latitude:* 44.36203 *Longitude:* -68.08667

WOOD ISLAND LIGHTHOUSE

Established in 1808, the current Wood Island Lighthouse was built in 1858. The station was automated by the U.S. Coast Guard in 1986. *Address:* Wood Island Light *City:*

Biddeford Pool *State:* ME *Zip:* 04006 *Web:* www.woodislandlighthouse.org *Email:* Brad@ woodislandlighthouse.org *Visitors welcome?* Yes *Hours:* Contact attraction directly *Admission:* Contact attraction directly *Operated by:* Friends of Wood Island Light Station *NR?* Yes *NHL?* No *Year established/built:* 1808 *Latitude:* 43.45667 *Longitude:* -70.32833

MARYLAND

BALTIMORE HARBOR LIGHTHOUSE
Established and built in 1908, the Baltimore Harbor Lighthouse was automated in 1964 and is still an active aid to navigation. *Address:* Baltimore Harbor Light *State:* MD *Web:* www.baltimorelight.org *Email:* keeper@baltimorelight.org *Visitors welcome?* Yes *Hours:* By appointment *Admission:* Contact attraction directly *Operated by:* Baltimore Harbor Light *NR?* Yes *NHL?* No *Year established/built:* 1908 *Latitude:* 39.0592 *Longitude:* -76.3990

BETHEL BRIDGE LIGHTHOUSE
The Bethel Bridge Lighthouse is a replica of a small number of wooden lighthouses meant to guide rivercraft on the Chesapeake & Delaware Canal. *Address:* 815 Bethel Rd *City:* Chesapeake City *State:* MD *Phone:* 215-656-6515 *Web:* www.nap.usace.army.mil/sb/c&d. htm *Email:* edward.c.voigt@usace.army.mil *Visitors welcome?* Yes *Hours:* Monday to Friday, 8 a.m. to 4 p.m. *Admission:* FREE *Operated by:* U.S. Army Corps of Engineers (Philadelphia District) *NR?* No *NHL?* No *Latitude:* 39.5210 *Longitude:* -75.7936

BLOODY POINT BAR LIGHTHOUSE
Established and built in 1882, the spark plug-style Bloody Bar Lighthouse was automated in 1960 and is still an active aid to navigation. *Address:* Kent Island *City:* Romancoke *State:* MD *Visitors welcome?* No *Operated by:* Private owner *NR?* No *NHL?* No *Year established/ built:* 1882 *Latitude:* 38.88123 *Longitude:* -76.33634

CONCORD POINT LIGHTHOUSE
Established in 1827, the current Concord Point Lighthouse, also known as the Havre de Grace Lighthouse, was constructed in 1875. Deactivated in 1975, the lighthouse is the second oldest on Chesapeake Bay. *Address:* Concord and Lafayette Streets *City:* Havre de Grace *State:* MD *Zip:* 21078 *Phone:* 410-939-3213 *Email:* directorcpt@verizon.net *Visitors welcome?* Yes *Hours:* April to October, Saturdays and Sundays, 1 p.m. to 5 p.m. *Admission:* Contact attraction directly *Operated by:* Friends of Concord Point Lighthouse *NR?* Yes *NHL?* No *Year established/built:* 1827 *Latitude:* 39.5407 *Longitude:* -76.0854

COVE POINT LIGHTHOUSE
Established and built in 1828, the Cove Point Lighthouse was automated in 1986 and is still an active aid to navigation. *Address:* Cove Point Light *City:* Cove Point *State:* MD

Phone: 410-326-2042 *Web:* www.calvertmarinemuseum.com/cove_point.htm *Visitors welcome?* Yes *Hours:* Daily, June to August, 1 p.m. to 4 p.m.; May and September, Saturday and Sunday, 1 p.m. to 4 p.m. *Admission:* Contact attraction directly *Operated by:* Calvert Marine Museum *NR?* Yes *NHL?* No *Year established/built:* 1828 *Latitude:* 38.3863 *Longitude:* -76.3817

CRAIGHILL CHANNEL LOWER RANGE FRONT LIGHT
Range lights working in pairs allowed mariners to know their position in channels relative to their destination. The Craighill Channel Lower Front Range Lighthouse marks the channel from Chesapeake Bay to the Patapsco River and Baltimore Harbor. *City:* Fort Howard *State:* MD *Phone:* 703-967-8118 *Web:* www.craighillrange.org *Visitors welcome?* Yes *Hours:* By appointment *Admission:* Contact attraction directly *Operated by:* Historical Place Preservation *NR?* Yes *NHL?* No *Year established/built:* 1873 *Latitude:* 39.2073 *Longitude:* -76.4450

CRAIGHILL CHANNEL LOWER REAR RANGE LIGHTHOUSE
Range lights working in pairs allowed mariners to know their position in channels relative to their destination. The Craighill Channel Lower Rear Range Lighthouse marks the channel from Chesapeake Bay to the Patapsco River and Baltimore Harbor. *City:* Ramona Beach *State:* MD *Phone:* 703-967-8118 *Web:* www.craighillrange.org *Visitors welcome?* Yes *Hours:* By appointment *Admission:* Contact attraction directly *Operated by:* Historical Place Preservation *NR?* Yes *NHL?* No *Year established/built:* 1873 *Latitude:* 39.2291 *Longitude:* -76.3942

CRAIGHILL CHANNEL UPPER FRONT RANGE LIGHTHOUSE
Range lights working in pairs allowed mariners to know their position in channels relative to their destination. The Craighill Channel Upper Front Range Lighthouse marks the channel from Chesapeake Bay to the Patapsco River and Baltimore Harbor. *City:* Fort Howard *State:* MD *Phone:* 703-967-8118 *Web:* www.craighillrange.org *Visitors welcome?* No *Operated by:* U.S. Coast Guard (District 5) *NR?* Yes *NHL?* No *Year established/built:* 1886 *Latitude:* 39.1971 *Longitude:* -76.4482

CRAIGHILL CHANNEL UPPER REAR RANGE LIGHTHOUSE
Range lights working in pairs allowed mariners to know their position in channels relative to their destination. The Craighill Channel Upper Front Range Lighthouse marks the channel from Chesapeake Bay to the Patapsco River and Baltimore Harbor. *City:* Sparrows Point *State:* MD *Web:* www.craighillrange.org *Visitors welcome?* No *Operated by:* U.S. Coast Guard (District 5) *NR?* Yes *NHL?* No *Year established/built:* 1886 *Latitude:* 39.2162 *Longitude:* -76.4627

DRUM POINT LIGHTHOUSE
Established and built in 1883, the Drum Point Lighthouse was moved from its original location on the Patuxent River to Solomons, Maryland, where it is used as a museum.

Address: Calvert Marine Museum *City:* Solomons *State:* MD *Zip:* 20688 *Phone:* 410-326-2042 *Web:* www.calvertmarinemuseum.com *Email:* mccormmj@co.cal.md.us *Visitors welcome?* Yes *Hours:* Daily, 10 a.m to 5 p.m. *Admission:* $7 adults, $6 seniors, $2 children 5 to 12; under five FREE *Operated by:* Calvert Marine Museum *NR?* Yes *NHL?* No *Year established/built:* 1883 *Latitude:* 38.3433 *Longitude:* -76.4650

FISHING BATTERY LIGHTHOUSE

Built on an artificial island at the mouth of the Susquehanna River, Fishing Battery Island Lighthouse was built in 1853. The island was intended to aid local fishermen as a point to anchor nets and site a fish hatchery. The island is now part of a wildlife refuge. *Address:* Fishing Battery Light *City:* Oakington *State:* MD *Visitors welcome?* Yes *Hours:* Grounds only *Admission:* FREE *Operated by:* U.S. Fish and Wildlife Service *NR?* No *NHL?* No *Year established/built:* 1853 *Latitude:* 39.4950 *Longitude:* -76.0830

FORT CARROLL LIGHTHOUSE

Built in 1854 on Fort Carroll, the Fort Carroll Lighthouse, the original light was replaced by a wooden tower in 1898. The lighthouse was automated in 1920 and the fort abandoned by the Army, except for the years of World War II. The property is now privately owned. *Address:* Fort Carroll Light *State:* MD *Visitors welcome?* No *Operated by:* Struever Bros., Eccles & Rouse *NR?* No *NHL?* No *Year established/built:* 1854 *Latitude:* 39.2147 *Longitude:* -76.5199

FORT WASHINGTON LIGHTHOUSE

Built at Fort Washington, which guards the mouth of the Potomac River, the Fort Washington Lighthouse is now within the grounds of Fort Washington Park. *Address:* Fort Washington Light *City:* Fort Washington *State:* MD *Zip:* 20744 *Phone:* 301-763-4600 *Web:* www.nps.gov/fowa/ *Visitors welcome?* Yes *Hours:* Daily, 8 a.m. to sunset *Admission:* $5 vehicle, $3 individual *Operated by:* Fort Washington Park *NR?* No *NHL?* No *Year established/built:* 1857 *Latitude:* 38.7120 *Longitude:* -77.0370

HOOPER ISLAND LIGHTHOUSE

Established and built in 1902, the spark-plug style Hooper Island Lighthouse was automated in 1961 and is still an active aid to navigation. *Address:* Hooper Island Light *City:* Hoopersville *State:* MD *Visitors welcome?* No *Operated by:* U.S. Coast Guard (District 5) *NR?* Yes *NHL?* No *Year established/built:* 1902 *Latitude:* 38.2560 *Longitude:* -76.2500

HOOPER STRAIT LIGHTHOUSE

✛ Established and built in 1879, the Hooper Strait Lighthouse was deactivated in 1966 and moved to its current location in Talbot for use as a museum. *Address:* 213 N. Talbot Street *City:* St. Michaels *State:* MD *Zip:* 21663 *Phone:* 410-745-2916 *Web:* www.cbmm.org *Email:* cbland@cbmm.org *Visitors welcome?* Yes *Hours:* Daily, hours vary by season *Admission:* $13 adults; $10 seniors over 62; $6 kids 6 to 17; kids under 6 FREE *Operated by:*

Chesapeake Bay Maritime Museum *NR?* Yes *NHL?* No *Year established/built:* 1879 *Latitude:* 38.7876 *Longitude:* -76.2249 **Accommodations for overnight and/or long-term stays available.**

LAZARETTO POINT LIGHTHOUSE

The Lazaretto Lighthouse is a replica of an 1863 structure that was torn down in 1954. The replica, built by the owner of a Baltimore port services company, is on private property. *Address:* Lazaretto Point Light *City:* Baltimore *State:* MD *Zip:* 21061 *Visitors welcome?* No *Operated by:* Rukert Terminals Corp. *NR?* No *NHL?* No *Year established/built:* 1831 *Latitude:* 39.2622 *Longitude:* -76.5715

POINT LOOKOUT LIGHTHOUSE

Established in 1830, the original Point Lookout Lighthouse was near the site of a notorious prisoner of war camp for Confederate soldiers. The lighthouse received a major upgrade in 1927, and it was transferred to the U.S. Navy in the 1960s. *Address:* Point Lookout Light *City:* St. Leonard *State:* MD *Web:* www.ptlookoutlighthouse.com *Email:* admin@ptlookoutlighthouse.com *Visitors welcome?* Yes *Hours:* By appointment *Admission:* Contact attraction directly *Operated by:* Point Lookout Lighthouse Preservation Society *NR?* No *NHL?* No *Year established/built:* 1830 *Latitude:* 38.0387 *Longitude:* -76.3221

POINT NO POINT (MARYLAND) LIGHTHOUSE

Established and built in 1905, the Point No Point (Maryland) Lighthouse was automated in 1962 and is still an active aid to navigation. *Address:* Point No Point Light *City:* Airdele *State:* MD *Visitors welcome?* No *Operated by:* U.S. Coast Guard (District 5) *NR?* No *NHL?* No *Year established/built:* 1905 *Latitude:* 38.1280 *Longitude:* -76.2900

POOLES ISLAND LIGHTHOUSE

The Pooles Island Lighthouse was established in 1824 to mark the entrance to the Bush and Gunpowder rivers. The lighthouse and the island was handed over to the U.S. Army in 1917, and it became part of the Aberdeen Proving Ground. *Address:* Pooles Island Light *City:* Aberdeen *State:* MD *Phone:* 410-278-5201 *Visitors welcome?* No *Operated by:* Aberdeen Proving Ground *NR?* Yes *NHL?* No *Year established/built:* 1824 *Latitude:* 39.2790 *Longitude:* -76.2700

SANDY POINT SHOAL LIGHTHOUSE

Established and built in 1882, the Sandy Point Shoal Lighthouse was automated in 1963 and is now in the hands of a private owner. *Address:* Sandy Point Shoal Light *City:* Cape St. Clair *State:* MD *Visitors welcome?* No *Operated by:* Private owner *NR?* Yes *NHL?* No *Year established/built:* 1882 *Latitude:* 39.0160 *Longitude:* -76.3850

SEVEN FOOT KNOLL LIGHTHOUSE

Built in 1856, Seven Foot Knoll Lighthouse is the oldest screw-pile lighthouse in Maryland. The lighthouse marked the mouth of Baltimore's Harbor for 133 years before being moved to the Inner Harbor for restoration. The lighthouse was built at the mouth of the Patapsco River, marking the shoal known as Seven Foot Knoll. It was built on cast iron pilings with corkscrew-like bases that were screwed into the mud on the bottom of the Bay, eliminating the need for a masonry foundation. *Address:* Pier 5, Baltimore Inner Harbor (301 E. Pratt St.) *City:* Baltimore *State:* MD *Zip:* 21202 *Phone:* 410-539-1797 *Web:* www.historicships.org/ *Email:* administration@historicships.org *Visitors welcome?* Yes *Hours:* Contact attraction directly *Admission:* Contact attraction directly *Operated by:* Historic Ships in Baltimore *NR?* Yes *NHL?* No *Year established/built:* 1856 *Latitude:* 39.2866 *Longitude:* -76.6087

SHARPS ISLAND LIGHTHOUSE

The Sharps Island Lighthouse marks shoals off Poplar Island and Black Island Point in Chesapeake Bay. The current 1881 caisson structure replaced a screw-pile lighthouse damaged by moving ice fields. *Address:* Sharps Island Light *City:* Fairbank *State:* MD *Visitors welcome?* No *Operated by:* Private owner *NR?* Yes *NHL?* No *Year established/built:* 1865 *Latitude:* 38.6391 *Longitude:* -76.3757

SOLOMONS LUMP LIGHTHOUSE

Solomons Lump Lighthouse marks a shoal extending from Smith Island in Chesapeake Bay. Replacing a light at Fog Point, the 1875 screwpile lighthouse was destroyed by ice and replaced in 1895 caisson-style structure. *Address:* Solomons Lump Light *City:* Smith Island *State:* MD *Visitors welcome?* No *Operated by:* U.S. Coast Guard (District 5) *NR?* Yes *NHL?* No *Year established/built:* 1875 *Latitude:* 38.0480 *Longitude:* -76.0150

THOMAS POINT SHOAL LIGHTHOUSE

First located on land in 1825, the lighthouse was moved offshore onto pilings in 1875. The lighthouse was the last manned station in Chesapeake Bay before it was automated in 1986. It is now owned and operated by a consortium of local governments and not-for-profit organizations. *Address:* Thomas Point Shoal Light *City:* Highland Beach *State:* MD *Web:* www.thomaspointlighthouse.org *Visitors welcome?* Yes *Hours:* Contact attraction directly *Admission:* Contact attraction directly *Operated by:* Thomas Point Shoal Lighthouse *NR?* Yes *NHL?* Yes *Year established/built:* 1825 *Latitude:* 38.8990 *Longitude:* -76.4360

TURKEY POINT LIGHTHOUSE

Established and built in 1833, the Turkey Point Lighthouse sits on a bluff overlooking Chesapeake Bay. It marks the course for ship masters into the Chesapeake & Delaware Canal. In 2008, the lighthouse was decommissioned. *Address:* Turkey Point Light *State:* MD *Phone:* 410-287-8170 *Web:* www.tpls.org *Visitors welcome?* Yes *Hours:* Saturday and Sunday, 11 a.m. to 4 p.m. *Admission:* Contact attraction directly *Operated by:* Turkey Point Light Station *NR?* Yes *NHL?* No *Year established/built:* 1833 *Latitude:* 39.4500 *Longitude:* -76.0090

MASSACHUSETTS

ANNISQUAM HARBOR LIGHTHOUSE

Established in 1801, the current Annisquam Harbor Lighthouse was constructed in 1897 and automated in 1974. The dwelling is now used by the U.S. Coast Guard as housing. *Address:* Annisquam Harbor Light *City:* Annisquam *State:* MA *Visitors welcome?* No *Operated by:* U.S. Coast Guard (District 1) *NR?* Yes *NHL?* No *Year established/built:* 1801 *Latitude:* 42.6619 *Longitude:* -70.6815

BAKER'S ISLAND LIGHTHOUSE

Established in 1791, the current Baker's Island Lighthouse tower was built in 1821. The light was automated in 1971. It is owned by the Essex National Heritage Commission. *Address:* Baker's Island Light *State:* MA *Visitors welcome?* No *Operated by:* Essex National Heritage Commission *NR?* Yes *NHL?* No *Year established/built:* 1791 *Latitude:* 42.53645 *Longitude:* -70.78592

BASS RIVER LIGHTHOUSE

✦ Established and built in 1855, the Bass River Lighthouse is now a prominent hotel and restaurant on Cape Cod known as the Lighthouse Inn. *Address:* 1 Lighthouse Inn Road *City:* West Dennis *State:* MA *Zip:* 02670 *Phone:* 508-398-2244 *Web:* www.lighthouseinn. com *Email:* inquire@lighthouseinn.com *Visitors welcome?* Yes *Hours:* Contact attraction directly *Admission:* Contact attraction directly *Operated by:* Lighthouse Inn *NR?* No *NHL?* No *Year established/built:* 1855 *Latitude:* 41.65202 *Longitude:* -70.16917 **Accommodations for overnight and/or long-term stays available.**

BIRD ISLAND LIGHTHOUSE

Bird Island Lighthouse was established and built by the government in 1819, and the orginal tower still stands. The station was inactive from 1933 to 1997, when the light was re-lit by the Town of Marion as a civic landmark. *Address:* Bird Island Light *City:* Marion *State:* MA *Phone:* 508-748-3500 *Visitors welcome?* Yes *Hours:* Grounds only *Admission:* FREE *Operated by:* Town of Marion *NR?* Yes *NHL?* No *Year established/built:* 1819 *Latitude:* 41.66943 *Longitude:* -70.71735

BISHOP AND CLERKS LIGHTHOUSE

The Bishop and Clerks Lighthouse was established in 1858 and discontinued in 1928. The tower was demolished in 1952 and replaced by a daymark and light. *Address:* Point Gammon *City:* Yarmouth *State:* MA *Visitors welcome?* No *Operated by:* U.S. Coast Guard (District 1) *NR?* No *NHL?* No *Year established/built:* 1858 *Latitude:* 41.6098 *Longitude:* -70.2661

BORDEN FLATS LIGHTHOUSE

The Borden Flats Lighthouse, established and built in 1881, warns mariners of submerged hazards at the mouth of the Taunton River. The light was automated in 1963 and is privately owned. *City:* Fall River *State:* MA *Visitors welcome?* No *Operated by:* Private owner *NR?* Yes *NHL?* No *Year established/built:* 1881 *Latitude:* 41.70149 *Longitude:* -71.15505

BOSTON HARBOR LIGHTHOUSE

Considered an iconic American lighthouse, Boston Harbor Lighthouse was established in 1716, and the 1783 tower still stands. The light is an active aid to navigation, though it was automated in 1998. It marks the entrance to Boston Harbor. *Address:* Little Brewster Island *City:* Boston *State:* MA *Visitors welcome?* Yes *Hours:* Grounds only *Admission:* FREE *Operated by:* U.S. Coast Guard (District 1) *NR?* Yes *NHL?* Yes *Year established/built:* 1716 *Latitude:* 42.3279 *Longitude:* -70.8903

BRANT POINT LIGHTHOUSE

The Brant Point Lighthouse was established in 1746. The current wooden tower was constructed in 1901 and automated in 1965. *Address:* Brant Point Light *City:* Nantucket *State:* MA *Visitors welcome?* Yes *Hours:* Grounds only *Admission:* FREE *Operated by:* U.S. Coast Guard (District 1) *NR?* Yes *NHL?* No *Year established/built:* 1746 *Latitude:* 41.2900 *Longitude:* -70.0903

BUTLER FLATS LIGHTHOUSE

Established in 1804, the current cast-iron, caisson-style Butler Flats Lighthouse was established and built in 1898 at the entrance to New Bedford Harbor and automated in 1978. *Address:* Butler Flats Light *City:* New Bedford *State:* MA *Visitors welcome?* No *Operated by:* City of New Bedford *NR?* Yes *NHL?* No *Year established/built:* 1804 *Latitude:* 41.60361 *Longitude:* -70.89445

Cape Ann Lighthouses, Rockport, Massachusetts

CAPE ANN LIGHTHOUSE

✦ Established in 1771, two lighthouse were built together on Thacher Island, also known as Cape Ann. Two new towers were constructed of granite in 1961. The light on the northeast tower was shut down in 1932. The lighthouse is now owned by the City of Rockport. *Address:* Cape Ann Light *City:* Rockport *State:* MA *Zip:* 01966 *Phone:* 617-599-2590 *Web:* www.thacherisland.org *Email:* info@thacherisland.org *Visitors welcome?* Yes *Hours:* Contact attraction directly *Admission:* Contact attraction directly *Operated by:* Thacher Island Association *NR?* Yes *NHL?* Yes *Year established/built:* 1771 *Latitude:* 42.6368 *Longitude:* -70.5749 **Accommodations for overnight and/or long-term stays available.**

CAPE COD LIGHTHOUSE

Established in 1797, the current Cape Cod Lighthouse, also called the Highland Lighthouse, was constructed in 1857. In 1996, it was moved further from the beach due to erosion concerns. *Address:* Cape Cod Light *City:* Truro *State:* MA *Zip:* 02666 *Phone:* 608-487-1121 *Web:* www.capecodlight.org *Visitors welcome?* Yes *Hours:* Mid-May to mid-October, 10 a.m. to 5:30 p.m. *Admission:* $4, children must be 48 inches tall *Operated by:* Truro Historical Society *NR?* Yes *NHL?* No *Year established/built:* 1797 *Latitude:* 42.0395 *Longitude:* -70.0609

CAPE POGE LIGHTHOUSE

Established in 1801, the Cape Poge (also spelled Pogue) Lighthouse's current tower was constructed in 1893 and automated in 1943. *Address:* Cape Poge Light *City:* Martha's Vineyard *State:* MA *Phone:* 508-627-7689 *Email:* islands@ttor.org *Visitors welcome?* Yes *Hours:* By appointment *Admission:* Contact attraction directly *Operated by:* Trustees of Reservations *NR?* Yes *NHL?* No *Year established/built:* 1801 *Latitude:* 41.4188 *Longitude:* -70.4518

CHATHAM LIGHTHOUSE

Established in 1808, the current Chatham Lighthouse tower was built in 1877 and automated in 1982. The local U.S. Coast Guard Auxiliary offers tours during the summer months. *Address:* Main Street and Water Street *City:* Chatham *State:* MA *Phone:* 508-430-0628 *Visitors welcome?* Yes *Hours:* Contact attraction directly *Admission:* Contact attraction directly *Operated by:* U.S. Coast Guard (District 1) *NR?* Yes *NHL?* No *Year established/built:* 1808 *Latitude:* 41.6714 *Longitude:* -69.9503

CLARK'S POINT LIGHTHOUSE

The Clark's Point Lighthouse was established in 1797 on the ground of Fort Taber, now a city park. The current lighthouse tower was constructed in 1869 and deactivated in 1898. The light was relit in 2001. *Address:* Fort Taber Park *City:* New Bedford *State:* MA *Visitors welcome?* Yes *Hours:* Grounds only *Admission:* FREE *Operated by:* City of New Bedford *NR?* Yes *NHL?* No *Year established/built:* 1797 *Latitude:* 41.63622 *Longitude:* -70.9342

CLEVELAND LEDGE LIGHTHOUSE

Established and built in 1943, the Cleveland Ledge Lighthouse is a relative latecomer to the nation's lighthouse inventory. Built in the Art Moderne style, the lighthouse was automated in 1978. *City:* Buzzards Bay *State:* MA *Visitors welcome?* No *Operated by:* U.S. Coast Guard (District 1) *NR?* Yes *NHL?* No *Year established/built:* 1943 *Latitude:* 41.6226 *Longitude:* -70.6956

CUTTYHUNK LIGHTHOUSE

The Cuttyhunk Lighthouse was established in 1803 and deactivated in 1947. A steel skeletal tower now stands at the site. *Address:* Cuttyhunk Island *City:* Cuttyhunk Island *State:* MA *Visitors welcome?* Yes *Hours:* Grounds only *Admission:* FREE *Operated by:* U.S. Coast Guard (District 1) *NR?* No *NHL?* No *Year established/built:* 1823 *Latitude:* 41.41678 *Longitude:* -70.93559

DEER ISLAND LIGHTHOUSE

Established in 1890, the original cast-iron tower of the Deer Island Lighthouse was replaced in 1982 with a fiberglass tower. *Address:* Deer Island Light *City:* Boston *State:* MA *Visitors welcome?* No *Operated by:* U.S. Coast Guard (District 1) *NR?* No *NHL?* No *Year established/built:* 1890 *Latitude:* 42.3399 *Longitude:* -70.9545

DERBY WHARF LIGHTHOUSE

The Derby Wharf Lighthouse was established in 1871 and built the same year. It was deactivated in 1977, but reactivated in 1983. The lighthouse is now part of the Salem National Maritime Historic Site. *Address:* Derby Wharf Light *City:* Salem *State:* MA *Zip:* 01970 *Phone:* 978-740-1650 *Fax:* 978-740-1655 *Web:* www.nps.gov/sama/ *Visitors welcome?* Yes *Hours:* Grounds only, daily, 9 a.m. to 5 p.m. *Admission:* Contact attraction directly *Operated by:* Salem National Maritime Historic Site *NR?* Yes *NHL?* No *Year established/built:* 1871 *Latitude:* 42.51656 *Longitude:* -70.88358

DOG BAR BREAKWATER LIGHTHOUSE

The Dog Bar Breakwater Lighthouse is an auxiliary light to the Eastern Point Lighthouse in Gloucester, Mass. *Address:* Eastern Point Light *City:* Gloucester *State:* MA *Visitors welcome?* Yes *Hours:* Grounds only *Admission:* FREE *Operated by:* U.S. Coast Guard (District 1) *NR?* No *NHL?* No *Latitude:* 42.58017 *Longitude:* -70.66444

DUXBURY PIER LIGHTHOUSE

Duxbury Pier Lighthouse was built in 1871 in the main channel in Plymouth Harbor to mark a shoal off Saquish Head. Known locally as The Bug, the lighthouse was constructed in the distinctive coffee pot style. *Address:* Duxbury Pier Light *City:* Duxbury *State:* MA *Zip:* 02331 *Web:* www.buglight.org *Email:* info@buglight.org *Visitors welcome?* No *Operated by:* Project Gurnet & Bug Lights *NR?* No *NHL?* No *Year established/built:* 1871 *Latitude:* 41.9874 *Longitude:* -70.6485

EAST CHOP LIGHTHOUSE
The East Chop Lighthouse, also known as the Telegraph Hill Lighthouse, on Martha's Vineyard was established in 1869 and built in 1878. The station was automated in 1933 and is now cared for by the Martha's Vineyard Historical Society. *Address:* East Chop Light *City:* Martha's Vineyard *State:* MA *Zip:* 02539 *Phone:* 508-627-4441 *Visitors welcome?* Yes *Hours:* Contact attraction directly *Admission:* Contact attraction directly *Operated by:* Martha's Vineyard Historical Society *NR?* Yes *NHL?* No *Year established/built:* 1869 *Latitude:* 41.47022 *Longitude:* -70.5674

EASTERN POINT LIGHTHOUSE
Established in 1832, the current Eastern Point Lighthouse was built in 1890. The station was automated in 1985. *Address:* Eastern Point Light *City:* Gloucester *State:* MA *Visitors welcome?* Yes *Hours:* Grounds only *Admission:* FREE *Operated by:* U.S. Coast Guard (District 1) *NR?* Yes *NHL?* No *Year established/built:* 1832 *Latitude:* 42.58017 *Longitude:* 70.66444

EDGARTOWN HARBOR LIGHTHOUSE
Established in 1828, the current cast-iron tower was built in 1881. The lighthouse was automated in 1939 and is now operated by the Martha's Vineyard Historical Society. *Address:* Edgartown Harbor Light *City:* Martha's Vineyard *State:* MA *Phone:* 508-627-4441 *Email:* KGorman@mvmuseum.org *Visitors welcome?* Yes *Hours:* Grounds only *Admission:* FREE *Operated by:* Martha's Vineyard Historical Society *NR?* Yes *NHL?* No *Year established/built:* 1828 *Latitude:* 41.3909 *Longitude:* 70.5031

FORT PICKERING LIGHTHOUSE
The Fort Pickering Lighthouse, also known as the Winter Island Lighthouse, was established and built in 1871. Now part of a public park, the light was deactivated in 1983. *Address:* 50 Winter Island Road *City:* Salem *State:* MA *Zip:* 01970 *Phone:* 978-745-9595 *Visitors welcome?* Yes *Hours:* Grounds only *Admission:* FREE *Operated by:* City of Salem *NR?* Yes *NHL?* No *Year established/built:* 1871 *Latitude:* 42.5310 *Longitude:* -70.8689

GAY HEAD LIGHTHOUSE
The Gay Head Lighthouse was established in 1799, with the current tower built in 1856. The lighthouse was automated in 1960. *Address:* Gay Head Light *City:* Martha's Vineyard *State:* MA *Phone:* 508-627-4441 *Visitors welcome?* Yes *Hours:* By appointment *Admission:* Contact attraction directly *Operated by:* Martha's Vineyard Historical Society *NR?* Yes *NHL?* No *Year established/built:* 1799 *Latitude:* 41.3484 *Longitude:* -70.8350

GRAVES LIGHTHOUSE
The Graves Lighthouse, named for the underwater ledges it marks, was built in 1905 and is still an operational, though automated, navigation aid. *Address:* The Graves *City:* Boston *State:* MA *Visitors welcome?* No *Operated by:* U.S. Coast Guard (District 1) *NR?* Yes *NHL?* No *Year established/built:* 1905 *Latitude:* 42.3654 *Longitude:* -70.8689

GREAT POINT LIGHTHOUSE

The Great Point Lighthouse was established on the northeast tip of Nantucket Island in 1784. The current structure is a replica of the 1818 tower, which was destroyed in a storm in 1984. The structure is now part of a wildlife refuge. *Address:* Great Point Light *City:* Nantucket *State:* MA *Phone:* 508-228-5646 *Email:* islands@ttor.org *Visitors welcome?* Yes *Hours:* Contact attraction directly *Admission:* Contact attraction directly *Operated by:* Trustees of Reservations *NR?* No *NHL?* No *Year established/built:* 1784 *Latitude:* 41.3887 *Longitude:* -70.0481

HOSPITAL POINT RANGE FRONT LIGHTHOUSE

The Hospital Point Front Range Lighthouse was established and constructed in 1872. It was automated in 1947. *Address:* Hospital Point Light *City:* Beverly *State:* MA *Visitors welcome?* No *Operated by:* U.S. Coast Guard (District 1) *NR?* Yes *NHL?* No *Year established/built:* 1872 *Latitude:* 42.54649 *Longitude:* -70.85596

HOSPITAL POINT RANGE REAR LIGHTHOUSE

The Hospital Point Rear Range Lighthouse is located in the steeple of the First Baptist Church in Beverly, Mass. *Address:* 221 Cabot Street *City:* Beverly *State:* MA *Visitors welcome?* No *Operated by:* Private owner *NR?* No *NHL?* No *Year established/built:* 1872 *Latitude:* 42.5487 *Longitude:* -70.8785

HYANNIS REAR RANGE LIGHTHOUSE

Established and built in 1849, the Hyannis Rear Range Lighthouse was deactivated in 1929 and is now part of a private residence. *Address:* Hyannis Harbor *City:* Hyannis *State:* MA *Visitors welcome?* No *Operated by:* Private owner *NR?* No *NHL?* No *Year established/built:* 1849 *Latitude:* 41.6315 *Longitude:* -70.28696

LONG ISLAND HEAD LIGHTHOUSE

Established in 1819, the Long Island Head Lighthouse on Long Island in Boston Harbor was reconstructed in 1901. Deactivated in 1982, it was relit with an automated mechanism in 1985. *Address:* Long Island Head Light *City:* Boston *State:* MA *Visitors welcome?* No *Operated by:* U.S. Coast Guard (District 1) *NR?* Yes *NHL?* No *Year established/built:* 1819 *Latitude:* 42.33028 *Longitude:* -70.95778

LONG POINT LIGHTHOUSE

Established in 1827, the current Long Point Lighthouse was constructed in 1875 and automated in 1952. It is now located within the Cape Cod National Seashore. *Address:* Long Point Light *City:* Provincetown *State:* MA *Visitors welcome?* Yes *Hours:* Grounds only *Admission:* FREE *Operated by:* Cape Cod Chapter, ALF *NR?* Yes *NHL?* No *Year established/built:* 1827 *Latitude:* 42.0331 *Longitude:* -70.1687

MARBLEHEAD LIGHTHOUSE

Established in 1835, the current Marblehead Lighthouse tower was constructed of cast-iron in 1896 and automated in 1960. *City:* Marblehead *State:* MA *Visitors welcome?* Yes *Hours:* Grounds only *Admission:* FREE *Operated by:* U.S. Coast Guard (District 1) *NR?* Yes *NHL?* No *Year established/built:* 1835 *Latitude:* 42.50539 *Longitude:* -70.83881

MAYO'S BEACH LIGHTHOUSE

Established in 1838, the Mayo's Beach Lighthouse was discontinued in 1922 and the cast-iron tower moved to serve as the Point Montaro light in California. The keeper's dwelling remained in Wellfleet. *Address:* Kendrick Avenue *City:* Wellfleet *State:* MA *Visitors welcome?* No *Operated by:* Private owner *NR?* No *NHL?* No *Year established/built:* 1838 *Latitude:* 41.9307 *Longitude:* -70.0372

MINOT'S LEDGE LIGHTHOUSE

Established in 1850, the current Minot's Ledge Lighthouse tower was constructed in 1860 and automated in 1947. An original iron tower constructed in 1851 collapsed, killing two keepers. Remnants of the tower were discovered in 2007 by divers at the site. *Address:* Minot's Ledge Light *State:* MA *Visitors welcome?* No *Operated by:* U.S. Coast Guard (District 1) *NR?* Yes *NHL?* No *Year established/built:* 1850 *Latitude:* 42.2698 *Longitude:* -70.7593

MONOMOY POINT LIGHTHOUSE

Established in 1823, Monomoy Point Lighthouse is located off Chatham on Cape Cod. The current tower was built in 1849 and deactivated in 1923. The island is now a wildlife refuge. *Address:* Monomoy Point Light *State:* MA *Phone:* 508-945-0594 *Visitors welcome?* Yes *Hours:* Grounds only *Admission:* FREE *Operated by:* Monomoy National Wildlife Refuge *NR?* Yes *NHL?* No *Year established/built:* 1823 *Latitude:* 41.5592 *Longitude:* -69.9942

NANTUCKET CLIFF RANGE LIGHTHOUSE

The Nantucket Cliff Range Lighthouse is a range light designed to work in conjunction with the Brant Point Lighthouse. *City:* Nantucket *State:* MA *Visitors welcome?* No *Operated by:* Private owner *NR?* No *NHL?* No *Latitude:* 41.2835 *Longitude:* -70.0995

NAUSET BEACH LIGHTHOUSE

Established in 1838, the current Nauset Lighthouse was constructed in 1877, although it was moved 300 feet away from the shore in 1996 to save it from erosion. It is now a private aid to navigation. *Address:* Nauset Beach Light, Cape Cod National Seashore *City:* Eastham *State:* MA *Zip:* 02642 *Phone:* 508-240-2612 *Email:* nausetlight@capecod.net *Visitors welcome?* Yes *Hours:* Open May to October; check lighthouse website for details *Admission:* Donation *Operated by:* Nauset Light Preservation Society *NR?* Yes *NHL?* No *Year established/built:* 1838 *Latitude:* 41.8600 *Longitude:* -69.9533

NED'S POINT LIGHTHOUSE

Ned's Point Lighthouse was built in 1838 with the lamps first lit in March of that year. The station was automated in 1923 and deactivated in 1952. The light was reactivated in 1961 and continues to be an active aid to navigation. The light is a 6-second osophase light; three seconds on, three seconds off. Contact: Bert Theriault, Aids to Navigation Officer, CGAux Flotilla 63 at nedspointlight@comcast.net. Please note that the tower is not opened for weddings or pre-wedding photography. *Address:* Ned Point Light *City:* Mattapoisett *State:* MA *Email:* nedspointlight@comcast.net *Visitors welcome?* Yes *Hours:* Grounds open daily; Tower: July 10 a.m to noon; August 4 p.m. to 6 p.m. *Admission:* FREE *Operated by:* U.S. Coast Guard; Open to public by the Coast Guard Auxiliary Flotilla 63 *NR?* Yes *NHL?* No *Year established/built:* 1838 *Latitude:* 1.6509 *Longitude:* -70.7956

NEWBURYPORT HARBOR LIGHTHOUSE

The Newburyport Harbor Lighthouse, sometimes called the Plum Island Lighthouse, was established in 1788. The current tower was built in 1898 and automated in 1951. *Address:* Newburyport Harbor Light *City:* Newburyport *State:* MA *Visitors welcome?* Yes *Hours:* Grounds only *Admission:* FREE *Operated by:* Friends of Plum Island Light *NR?* Yes *NHL?* No *Year established/built:* 1788 *Latitude:* 42.81523 *Longitude:* -70.81894

NEWBURYPORT HARBOR RANGE FRONT LIGHTHOUSE

The Newburyport Range Lighthouses were established in 1873 and deactivated in 1961. The front range light is under the care of the New Hampshire-based Lighthouse Preservation Society. *Address:* Newburyport Harbor Front Range Light *City:* Newburyport *State:* MA *Visitors welcome?* Yes *Hours:* Grounds only *Admission:* FREE *Operated by:* Lighthouse Preservation Society *NR?* Yes *NHL?* No *Year established/built:* 1873 *Latitude:* 42.81153 *Longitude:* -70.86486

NEWBURYPORT HARBOR RANGE REAR LIGHTHOUSE

The Newburyport Range Lighthouses were established in 1873 and deactivated in 1961. The rear range light is privately owned. *Address:* Newburyport Harbor Rear Range Light *City:* Newburyport *State:* MA *Visitors welcome?* No *Operated by:* Private owner *NR?* Yes *NHL?* No *Year established/built:* 1873 *Latitude:* 42.81126 *Longitude:* -70.86608

NOBSKA POINT LIGHTHOUSE

The Nobska Point Lighthouse was established in 1829, and the current tower was built in 1876. Automated in 1985, the station is now the home for the regional U.S. Coast Guard commandant. *Address:* Nobska Point Light *City:* Woods Hole *State:* MA *Visitors welcome?* No *Operated by:* U.S. Coast Guard (District 1) *NR?* Yes *NHL?* No *Year established/built:* 1829 *Latitude:* 41.5158 *Longitude:* -70.6551

PALMER ISLAND LIGHTHOUSE

Established and built in 1849, the Palmer Island Lighthouse in New Bedford Harbor was automated in 1941 and deactivated in 1963. The Coast Guard relit the light in 1999.

Address: Palmer Island *City:* New Bedford *State:* MA *Visitors welcome?* Yes *Hours:* Grounds only *Admission:* FREE *Operated by:* City of New Bedford *NR?* Yes *NHL?* No *Year established/built:* 1849 *Latitude:* 41.6251 *Longitude:* -70.91003

PLYMOUTH LIGHTHOUSE

✦ Established in 1768, the current Plymouth Lighthouse, also known as the Gurnet Lighthouse, was constructed in 1843. Automated in 1986, the light is still an active aid to navigation. *Address:* Plymouth Light *City:* Duxbury *State:* MA *Zip:* 02331 *Web:* www. buglight.org *Email:* info@buglight.org *Visitors welcome?* Yes *Hours:* Grounds only *Admission:* Contact attraction directly *Operated by:* Project Gurnet & Bug Lights *NR?* Yes *NHL?* No *Year established/built:* 1768 *Latitude:* 42.0037 *Longitude:* -70.6006 **Accommodations for overnight and/or long-term stays available.**

POINT GAMMON LIGHTHOUSE

Established in 1816, the Point Gammon Lighthouse was built the same year. The lighthouse was discontinued in 1858, though it is maintained by the private owner. *Address:* Hyannis Harbor *City:* West Yarmouth *State:* MA *Visitors welcome?* No *Operated by:* Private owner *NR?* No *NHL?* No *Year established/built:* 1816 *Latitude:* 41.6479 *Longitude:* -70.26265

RACE POINT LIGHTHOUSE

✦ Established in 1816, the current Race Point Lighthouse was built in 1876 and automated in 1872. The lighthouse is now cared for by a volunteer group. The nearby keeper's house is available for overnight stays. *Address:* Race Point Light *City:* Provincetown *State:* MA *Phone:* 508-487-9930 *Email:* racepointlighthouse@comcast.net *Visitors welcome?* Yes *Hours:* Some Saturdays, May to October *Admission:* Contact attraction directly *Operated by:* Cape Cod Chapter, ALF *NR?* Yes *NHL?* No *Year established/built:* 1816 *Latitude:* 42.0623 *Longitude:* -70.2430 **Accommodations for overnight and/or long-term stays available.**

SANDY NECK LIGHTHOUSE

Established in 1827, the current tower of Sandy Neck Lighthouse was rebuilt in 1857. The station was deactivated in 1931 and relit in 2007. It is privately owned. *Address:* Barnstable Harbor *City:* Cape Cod *State:* MA *Visitors welcome?* No *Operated by:* Private owner *NR?* Yes *NHL?* No *Year established/built:* 1827 *Latitude:* 41.70846 *Longitude:* -70.29261

SANKATY HEAD LIGHTHOUSE

Established and built in 1850, the current Sankaty Head Lighthouse was automated in 1965. In 2008, the lighthouse was moved to the west to avoid cliff erosion. *Address:* Sankaty Head Light *City:* Siasconset *State:* MA *Visitors welcome?* Yes *Hours:* Grounds only *Admission:* FREE *Operated by:* Sconset Trust *NR?* Yes *NHL?* No *Year established/built:* 1850 *Latitude:* 41.28361 *Longitude:* -69.9652

SCITUATE LIGHTHOUSE

Established and built in 1811, the Scituate Lighthouse was deactivated in 1860 and relit in 1990 as a private aid to navigation. *Address:* Scituate Light *City:* Scituate *State:* MA *Visitors welcome?* Yes *Hours:* Grounds only daily, some tours *Admission:* Contact attraction directly *Operated by:* Scituate Historical Society *NR?* Yes *NHL?* No *Year established/built:* 1811 *Latitude:* 42.2032 *Longitude:* -70.7131

STAGE HARBOR LIGHTHOUSE

The Stage Harbor Lighthouse was established and constructed in 1880. Built of cast-iron, the tower was deactivated in 1933. It is now privately owned. *Address:* Stage Harbor *City:* Chatham *State:* MA *Visitors welcome?* No *Operated by:* Private owner *NR?* No *NHL?* No *Year established/built:* 1880 *Latitude:* 41.66039 *Longitude:* -69.97446

STRAITSMOUTH ISLAND LIGHTHOUSE

The lighthouse at Straitsmouth Island was established in 1835, and the current tower was constructed in 1896. The lighthouse was automated in 1967. *Address:* Straitsmouth Island Light *City:* Rockport *State:* MA *Visitors welcome?* No *Operated by:* U.S. Coast Guard (District 1) *NR?* Yes *NHL?* No *Year established/built:* 1835 *Latitude:* 42.66226 *Longitude:* -70.58807

TARPAULIN COVE LIGHTHOUSE

Established in 1759, the current structure of the Tarpaulin Cove Lighthouse was built in 1891, and it was automated in 1941. *Address:* Tarpaulin Cove Light *City:* Naushon Island *State:* MA *Visitors welcome?* No *Operated by:* Cuttyhunk Historical Society *NR?* Yes *NHL?* No *Year established/built:* 1759 *Latitude:* 41.46881 *Longitude:* -70.7575

TEN POUND ISLAND LIGHTHOUSE

The Ten Pound Island Lighthouse in Gloucester Harbor was established in 1821. The current structure was built in 1881. The light was deactivated by the U.S. Coast Guard in 1956 and relighted in 1989. *Address:* Ten Pound Island Light *City:* Gloucester *State:* MA *Visitors welcome?* Yes *Hours:* Grounds only *Admission:* FREE *Operated by:* City of Gloucester *NR?* Yes *NHL?* No *Year established/built:* 1821 *Latitude:* 42.60186 *Longitude:* -70.66556

THREE SISTERS OF NAUSET LIGHTHOUSE

Established in 1838 and originally the only light station in the U.S. with three towers, only one tower remains of the Three Sisters Lighthouse, sometimes called Twin Lights. Two of the towers were discontinued in 1911 and taken down. *Address:* Nauset Light *City:* Wellfleet *State:* MA *Visitors welcome?* Yes *Hours:* By appointment *Admission:* FREE *Operated by:* Cape Cod National Seashore *NR?* Yes *NHL?* No *Year established/built:* 1838 *Latitude:* 41.8600 *Longitude:* -69.9533

WEST CHOP LIGHTHOUSE

Established in 1818, the current West Chop Lighthouse was built in 1891, and it was automated in 1976. *City:* West Chop *State:* MA *Visitors welcome?* No *Operated by:* U.S. Coast Guard (District 1) *NR?* Yes *NHL?* No *Year established/built:* 1818 *Latitude:* 41.48011 *Longitude:* -70.60281

WINGS NECK LIGHTHOUSE

✦ Wings Neck Light was established and built in 1849 because of heavy marine traffic traveling in Buzzards Bay to ports in Wareham and Sandwich. *Address:* Wings Neck Light *State:* MA *Phone:* 617-899-5063 *Email:* admin@wingsnecklighthouse.com *Visitors welcome?* Yes *Hours:* Contact attraction directly *Admission:* Contact attraction directly *Operated by:* Wings Neck Lighthouse Trust *NR?* Yes *NHL?* No *Year established/built:* 1849 *Latitude:* 41.68222 *Longitude:* -70.66028 **Accommodations for overnight and/or long-term stays available.**

WOOD END LIGHTHOUSE

Established in 1864, the Wood End Lighthouse marks the entrance to Provincetown Harbor on Cape Cod. The current tower was built in 1872 and automated in 1961. The structure is located with the Cape Cod National Seashore. *Address:* Wood End Light *City:* Provincetown *State:* MA *Visitors welcome?* Yes *Hours:* Grounds only *Admission:* **FREE** *Operated by:* Cape Cod Chapter, ALF *NR?* Yes *NHL?* No *Year established/built:* 1864 *Latitude:* 42.0213 *Longitude:* -70.1935

NEW HAMPSHIRE

BURKEHAVEN LIGHTHOUSE

The Burkehaven Lighthouse on Lake Sunapee is a replica of a lighthouse built in 1989 and destroyed by ice in 1935. *Address:* Lake Sunapee *City:* Sunapee *State:* NH *Visitors welcome?* No *Operated by:* Lake Sunapee Protective Association *NR?* No *NHL?* No *Year established/built:* 1898 *Latitude:* 43.38025 *Longitude:* -72.05274

HERRICK COVE LIGHTHOUSE

Built in 1893, the Herrick Cove Lighthouse deteriorated over the years until a local family sponsored a renovation in 2003. *Address:* Herrick Cove, Lake Sunapee *City:* Sunapee *State:* NH *Visitors welcome?* No *Operated by:* Lake Sunapee Protective Association *NR?* No *NHL?* No *Year established/built:* 1893 *Latitude:* 43.38025 *Longitude:* -72.05274

ISLE OF SHOALS LIGHTHOUSE

Established in 1822, the current Isle of Shoals Lighthouse, also called the White Island Lighthouse, was built in 1855. Still an active aid to navigation, the station is cared for by a local not-for-profit organization. *Address:* White Island Light *State:* NH *Visitors welcome?* Yes *Hours:* Grounds only *Admission:* FREE *Operated by:* Lighthouse Kids *NR?* No *NHL?* No *Year established/built:* 1822 *Latitude:* 42.96833 *Longitude:* -70.62583

LOON ISLAND LIGHTHOUSE

Constructed in 1893 by a steamship company, the Loon Island Lighthouse is still an active aid to navigation. *Address:* Loon Island, Lake Sunapee *City:* Sunapee *State:* NH *Visitors welcome?* No *Operated by:* Lake Sunapee Protective Association *NR?* No *NHL?* No *Year established/built:* 1893 *Latitude:* 43.38025 *Longitude:* -72.05274

Portsmouth Harbor Lighthouse, New Castle, New Hampshire

PORTSMOUTH HARBOR LIGHTHOUSE

Established in 1771, the current Portsmouth Harbor Lighthouse was constructed in 1878. Still an active aid to navigation, the lighthouse is operated by a not-for-profit organization, which offers occasional guided tours. *Address:* Portsmouth Harbor Light *City:* New Castle *State:* NH *Web:* www.portsmouthharborlighthouse.org *Email:* info@portsmouthharborlighthouse.com *Visitors welcome?* Yes *Hours:* Contact attraction directly *Admission:* Contact attraction directly *Operated by:* Friends of Portsmouth Harbor Lighthouse *NR?* Yes *NHL?* No *Year established/built:* 1771 *Latitude:* 43.0710 *Longitude:* -70.7086

Absecon Lighthouse, Atlantic City, New Jersey

NEW JERSEY

ABSECON LIGHTHOUSE

Established and built in 1857, the Absecon Lighthouse is the tallest in New Jersey and the third tallest masonry lighthouse in the U.S. Decommissioned in 1933, the light is kept lit as a visitor attraction. The keepers house and light are also a museum. *Address:* 31 S. Rhode Island Ave. *City:* Atlantic City *State:* NJ *Zip:* 08401 *Phone:* 609-449-1360 *Web:* www.abseconlighthouse.org *Email:* jean@abseconlighthouse.org *Visitors welcome?* Yes *Hours:* September to June, Thursday to Monday, 11 a.m. to 4 p.m.; July and August, daily, 10 a.m. to 5 p.m. *Admission:* $7 adults, $5 seniors, $4 children 4-12, under four **FREE** *Operated by:* Absecon Lighthouse *NR?* Yes *NHL?* No *Year established/built:* 1857 *Latitude:* 39.3672 *Longitude:* -74.4155

Barnegat Lighthouse, New Jersey

BARNEGAT LIGHTHOUSE

Established in 1835, the current Barnegat Lighthouse tower was built in 1857. The lighthouse was run by the government until 1926, when the light was placed offshore on the Barnegat Lightship. The lighthouse was discontinued in 1944, and a public outcry led to restoration of the lighthouse. *Address:* Barnegat Lighthouse State Park *City:* Barnegat Light *State:* NJ *Zip:* 08006 *Phone:* 609-494-2016 *Web:* www.bl-hs.org *Visitors welcome?* Yes *Hours:* Daily, April 1 to Oct. 1, 9 a.m. to 4:30 p.m.; Wednesday to Sunday, Oct. 1 to April 1, 9 a.m. to 3:30 p.m. *Admission:* $1 all visitors *Operated by:* Barnegat Light Historical Society *NR?* Yes *NHL?* No *Year established/built:* 1835 *Latitude:* 39.7584 *Longitude:* -74.1012

BRANDYWINE SHOAL LIGHTHOUSE

Established in 1823, the Brandywine Shoal Lighthouse was first a lightship. The vessel was replaced in 1850 with the first screwpile lighthouse, in which the structure rests on pilings literally screwed into the bottom. *Address:* Brandywine Shoal Light *City:* Cape May *State:* NJ *Visitors welcome?* No *Operated by:* U.S. Coast Guard (District 5) *NR?* No *NHL?* No *Year established/built:* 1823 *Latitude:* 38.9864 *Longitude:* -75.1135

CAPE MAY LIGHTHOUSE

Established in 1823, the current Cape May Lighthouse was built in 1859, and it marks the northern entrance to Delaware Bay. The light was automated in 1933, and the property was turned over to the state of New Jersey, which sub-leases it to the Mid-Atlantic Center for the Arts and Humanities. *Address:* Cape May Light *City:* Cape May *State:* NJ *Zip:* 08204 *Phone:* 609-884-5404 *Web:* www.capemaymac.org *Email:* mac4arts@capemaymac.org *Visitors welcome?* Yes *Hours:* Contact attraction directly *Admission:* To climb the lighthouse: $7 adults, $3 children three to 12; Visitors center: FREE *Operated by:* Mid-Atlantic Center for the Arts and Humanities *NR?* Yes *NHL?* No *Year established/built:* 1823 *Latitude:* 38.9331 *Longitude:* -74.9603

CHAPEL HILL REAR RANGE LIGHTHOUSE

Established and built in 1856, the Chapel Hill Lighthouse served until 1957, when the light was moved to the south. The structure is now a private residence. *Address:* Chapel Hill Rear Range Light *City:* Leonardo *State:* NJ *Visitors welcome?* No *Operated by:* Private owner *NR?* No *NHL?* No *Year established/built:* 1856 *Latitude:* 40.3983 *Longitude:* -74.0587

CONOVER BEACON LIGHTHOUSE

Established in 1856, the current skeletal tower Conover Beacon Lighthouse was constructed in 1941. The beacon, also called Chapel Hill Front Range Lightouse, is no longer active. It was the companion to the Chapel Hill Rear Range Lighthouse. *Address:* Beach Avenue and North Leonard Avenue *City:* Leonardo *State:* NJ *Visitors welcome?* Yes *Hours:* Grounds only *Admission:* FREE *Operated by:* Monmouth County *NR?* No *NHL?* No *Year established/built:* 1856 *Latitude:* 40.4218 *Longitude:* -74.05636

CROSS LEDGE LIGHTHOUSE

Established and built in 1875, the Cross Ledge Lighthouse was discontinued in 1910, and only the foundation of the lighthouse remains. *City:* Fortescue *State:* NJ *Visitors welcome?* No *Operated by:* U.S. Coast Guard (District 5) *NR?* No *NHL?* No *Year established/built:* 1875 *Latitude:* 39.23761 *Longitude:* -75.17158

EAST POINT LIGHTHOUSE

Established and built in 1849, the East Point Lighthouse was first called the Maurice River Lighthouse for the river mouth it marks. It operated until 1941, when the U.S. Coast Guard discontinued it. It is now undergoing restoration by the Maurice River Historical Society. *Address:* East Point Light *City:* Heislerville *State:* NJ *Phone:* 856-785-1120 *Visitors welcome?* Yes *Hours:* Grounds open, tours by appointment *Admission:* Contact attraction directly *Operated by:* Maurice River Township *NR?* Yes *NHL?* No *Year established/built:* 1849 *Latitude:* 39.1958 *Longitude:* -75.0272

ELBOW OF CROSS LEDGE LIGHTHOUSE

Built in 1907 on an extension of Cross Ledge in Delaware Bay, the Elbow of Cross Ledge Lighthouse features a cast-iron design common around the turn of the 20th century.

Address: Elbow of Cross Ledge Light *City:* Fortescue *State:* NJ *Visitors welcome?* No *Operated by:* U.S. Coast Guard (District 5) *NR?* No *NHL?* No *Year established/built:* 1907 *Latitude:* 39.1816 *Longitude:* -75.2683

FINNS POINT RANGE LIGHTHOUSE

Established and built in 1877, the Finns Point Range Light was one of a series of range lights that guided mariners up the Delaware River. The lights were closed down in 1950, though the wrought iron tower of the Finns Point light remains. *Address:* 197 Lighthouse Road *City:* Pennsville *State:* NJ *Zip:* 08070 *Phone:* 609-463-0994 *Visitors welcome?* Yes *Hours:* Grounds only *Admission:* FREE *Operated by:* Supawna Meadows Wildlife Refuge *NR?* Yes *NHL?* No *Year established/built:* 1877 *Latitude:* 39.6150 *Longitude:* -75.5285

GREAT BEDS LIGHTHOUSE

Established in 1880, the Great Beds Lighthouse marks an area known for its rich oyster beds. The lighthouse is still an active aid to navigation. *Address:* Great Beds Light *City:* South Amboy *State:* NJ *Visitors welcome?* No *Operated by:* U.S. Coast Guard (District 5) *NR?* No *NHL?* No *Year established/built:* 1880 *Latitude:* 40.4867 *Longitude:* -74.2533

HEREFORD INLET LIGHTHOUSE

Established and built in 1874, the Hereford Inlet Lighthouse was manned until 1964, when the light was automated. The buildings were taken over by the state of New Jersey and the City of North Wildwood and converted to a museum in 1988. *Address:* Central Avenue and East First Avenue *City:* Rio Grande *State:* NJ *Zip:* 08242 *Phone:* 609-522-4520 *Web:* www.herefordlighthouse.org *Visitors welcome?* Yes *Hours:* Mid-October to Mid-May, Wednesday to Sunday, 10 a.m. to 4 p.m.; Mid-May to Mid-October, daily, 9 a.m. to 4 p.m. *Admission:* $4 adults, $1 children *Operated by:* Friends of Hereford Lighthouse *NR?* Yes *NHL?* No *Year established/built:* 1874 *Latitude:* 40.8478 *Longitude:* -73.9968

LUDLUM BEACH LIGHTHOUSE

Established in 1885, the Ludlum Beach Lighthouse is now a summer rental house. *Address:* 3414 Landis Avenue *City:* Sea Isle City *State:* NJ *Visitors welcome?* No *Operated by:* Private owner *NR?* No *NHL?* No *Year established/built:* 1885 *Latitude:* 39.15978 *Longitude:* -74.68807

MIAH MAULL SHOAL LIGHTHOUSE

Built in 1913, the cast-iron Miah Maull Shoal Lighthouse is atop an underwater feature named for an 18th century citizen, Nehemiah Maull, who died in a shipwreck on the site. The lighthouse was automated in 1973. *Address:* Miah Maull Shoal Light *City:* Fortescue *State:* NJ *Visitors welcome?* No *Operated by:* U.S. Coast Guard (District 5) *NR?* Yes *NHL?* No *Year established/built:* 1913 *Latitude:* 39.12643 *Longitude:* -75.20966

NAVESINK LIGHTHOUSE

Established in 1828, the current brownstone Navesink Lighthouse with its twin light towers was constructed in 1862. Also called Twin Lights, the lighthouse was decommissioned in 1949 and turned over to the State of New Jersey. A not-for-profit operates a museum at the site. *Address:* Navesink Twin Lights *City:* Highlands *State:* NJ *Zip:* 07732 *Phone:* 732-872-1814 *Web:* twin-lights.org *Email:* info@twin-lights.org *Visitors welcome?* Yes *Hours:* Daily, Memorial Day to Labor, 10 a.m to 4:30 p.m.; Wednesday to Sunday, Labor Day to Memorial Day, 10 a.m. to 4:30 p.m. *Admission:* Donation *Operated by:* Twin Lights Historical Society *NR?* Yes *NHL?* Yes *Year established/built:* 1828 *Latitude:* 40.3962 *Longitude:* -73.9858

ROBBINS REEF LIGHTHOUSE

Established in 1839, the current coffee pot-style Robbins Reef Lighthouse was constructed in 1883. The light is still an active aid to navigation. *Address:* Robbins Reef Light *City:* Bayonne *State:* NJ *Visitors welcome?* No *Operated by:* U.S. Coast Guard (District 5) *NR?* Yes *NHL?* No *Year established/built:* 1839 *Latitude:* 40.6574 *Longitude:* -74.0656

ROMER SHOAL LIGHTHOUSE

Established by a daymark in 1838, the current Romer Shoal Lighthouse was constructed in 1898 using the coffee pot design. It is still an active aid to navigation. *Address:* Romer Shoal *City:* Keansburg *State:* NJ *Visitors welcome?* No *Operated by:* Private owner *NR?* No *NHL?* No *Year established/built:* 1838 *Latitude:* 40.5068 *Longitude:* -74.0021

SANDY HOOK LIGHTHOUSE

Established in 1764, the original Sandy Hook Lighthouse was called the New York Lighthouse, because it marked the entrance to New York Harbor. The original tower still stands, though it was reinforced with brick in the 19th century, and it is no longer an active aid to navigation. *Address:* Sandy Hook *City:* Highlands *State:* NJ *Phone:* 732-872-5970 *Visitors welcome?* Yes *Hours:* Contact attraction directly *Admission:* Contact attraction directly *Operated by:* Gateway National Recreation Area *NR?* Yes *NHL?* Yes *Year established/built:* 1764 *Latitude:* 40.4432 *Longitude:* -73.9899

SEA GIRT LIGHTHOUSE

Established and built in 1896, the Sea Girt Lighthouse marks a harbor of refuge at the resort community of Sea Girt. The light fell into disuse during World War II, although it was revived in the 1990s by a local not-for-profit. *Address:* Sea Girt Light *City:* Sea Girt *State:* NJ *Zip:* 08750 *Phone:* 732-974-0514 *Web:* www.seagirtboro.com/lighthouse.html *Visitors welcome?* Yes *Hours:* Sunday, April to November, 2 p.m. to 4 p.m. *Admission:* Contact attraction directly *Operated by:* Sea Girt Lighthouse Citizens Committee *NR?* No *NHL?* No *Year established/built:* 1896 *Latitude:* 40.1367 *Longitude:* -74.0275

SHIP JOHN SHOAL LIGHTHOUSE

Established in 1854 and constructed in 1874, the Ship John Shoal Lighthouse was placed above an underwater feature named for a ship called John which had wrecked on the future in the 18th century. The light was automated in 1973 and it is still an active aid to navigation. *Address:* Ship John Shoal Light *City:* Woodland Beach *State:* NJ *Visitors welcome?* No *Operated by:* U.S. Coast Guard (District 5) *NR?* No *NHL?* No *Year established/built:* 1854 *Latitude:* 39.3053 *Longitude:* -75.3767

TINICUM ISLAND REAR RANGE LIGHTHOUSE

The Tinicum Island Rear Range Lighthouse is one of a series of four range lights built along the Delaware River in the late 19th century. Still in operation after a century and a quarter, the Tinicum light is now located within a baseball field complex. *Address:* Tinicum Island Rear Range Light *City:* Paulsboro *State:* NJ *Zip:* 08066 *Phone:* 856-423-1500 *Visitors welcome?* Yes *Hours:* Contact attraction directly *Admission:* Contact attraction directly *Operated by:* U.S. Coast Guard (District 5) *NR?* Yes *NHL?* No *Year established/built:* 1880 *Latitude:* 39.8475 *Longitude:* -75.2398

NEW YORK

BARBER'S POINT LIGHTHOUSE

Established and built in 1873, the Barber's Point Lighthouse was deactivated in 1935 and is now a private residence. *Address:* Barber Point Light *City:* Westport *State:* NY *Visitors welcome?* No *Operated by:* Private owner *NR?* Yes *NHL?* No *Year established/built:* 1873 *Latitude:* 44.1543 *Longitude:* -73.4045

BLACKWELL ISLAND LIGHTHOUSE

Built by the city of New York in 1872 at aid ships in the East River, the Blackwell Island Lighthouse stands in a park on what is today called Roosevelt Island. *Address:* Lighthouse Park *City:* New York *State:* NY *Zip:* 10038 *Visitors welcome?* Yes *Hours:* Daily *Admission:* FREE *Operated by:* New York City Department of Parks & Recreation *NR?* No *NHL?* No *Year established/built:* 1872 *Latitude:* 40.7715 *Longitude:* -73.9413

BLUFF POINT LIGHTHOUSE

Established and built in 1874, the Bluff Point Lighthouse was automated in 1930 and is still an active aid to navigation. *Address:* Bluff Point Light *City:* Valcour *State:* NY *Visitors welcome?* Yes *Hours:* Contact attraction directly *Admission:* Contact attraction directly *Operated by:* Clinton County Historical Association *NR?* Yes *NHL?* No *Year established/built:* 1874 *Latitude:* 44.6233 *Longitude:* -73.4319

BREWERTON RANGE REAR LIGHTHOUSE

The 85-foot Brewerton Range Rear Lighthouse marks the junction of the western end of Lake Oneida with the Oneida River, part of the New York State Barge Canal complex. *Address:* Oneida River *City:* Brewerton *State:* NY *Visitors welcome?* Yes *Hours:* Daily *Admission:* FREE *Operated by:* New York State Canals *NR?* No *NHL?* No *Year established/built:* 1916 *Latitude:* 43.2362 *Longitude:* -76.1174

CAYUGA INLET LIGHTHOUSE

The Cayuga Inlet Lighthouse was constructed in 1917 as part of a series of improvements to the Cayuga and Seneca Canal and other waterways. Now located at Alan Treman State Park, the lighthouse has a companion called the Cayuga Inlet Breakwater Lighthouse. *Address:* Cayuga Inlet *City:* Ithaca *State:* NY *Visitors welcome?* Yes *Hours:* No tower access *Admission:* FREE *Operated by:* New York State Office of Parks, Recreation and Historic Preservation *NR?* No *NHL?* No *Year established/built:* 1917 *Latitude:* 42.4595 *Longitude:* -76.5122

CEDAR ISLAND LIGHTHOUSE

Established in 1839, the current Cedar Island Lighthouse was constructed in 1868 and deactivated in 1934. The lighthouse is in the process of being preserved. *Address:* Cedar Point County Park *City:* Sag Harbor *State:* NY *Visitors welcome?* Yes *Hours:* Daily *Admission:* Grounds open, tower closed *Operated by:* Suffolk County, New York *NR?* Yes *NHL?* No *Year established/built:* 1839 *Latitude:* 40.99678 *Longitude:* -72.26154

COLD SPRING HARBOR LIGHTHOUSE

Address: Cold Spring Harbor Light *City:* Cold Spring Harbor *State:* NY *Visitors welcome?* No *Operated by:* Private owner *NR?* No *NHL?* No *Year established/built:* 1890 *Latitude:* 40.9061 *Longitude:* -73.4366

CONEY ISLAND LIGHTHOUSE

Established in 1890, the current Coney Island Lighthouse, also called the Nortons Point Lighthouse, was constructed in 1920. Still an active aid to navigation, the lighthouse is near one of the most famous resort areas in the country. *Address:* Coney Island Light *City:* Coney Island *State:* NY *Visitors welcome?* No *Operated by:* U.S. Coast Guard (District 1) *NR?* No *NHL?* No *Year established/built:* 1890 *Latitude:* 40.5767 *Longitude:* -74.0117

CUMBERLAND HEAD LIGHTHOUSE

Established in 1838, the current Cumberland Head Lighthouse was built in 1868 and deactivated in 1934. It is now a private residence. *Address:* Cumberland Head Light *City:* Plattsburgh *State:* NY *Visitors welcome?* No *Operated by:* U.S. Coast Guard (District 1) *NR?* No *NHL?* No *Year established/built:* 1838 *Latitude:* 44.6914 *Longitude:* -73.3853

DUNKIRK LIGHTHOUSE

Established in 1826, the current Dunkirk Lighthouse, also called the Point Gratiot Lighthouse, was constructed in 1875 and is still an active aid to navigation. It is operated by a local not-for-profit organization. *Address:* 1 Lighthouse Point Drive *City:* Dunkirk *State:* NY *Zip:* 14048 *Phone:* 716-366-5050 *Email:* LST551@juno.com *Visitors welcome?* Yes *Hours:* May to June, 10 a.m. to 2 p.m. (closed Wednesday and Sunday); July to August, 10 a.m. to 4 p.m. (closed Wednesday and Sunday); September to October, 10 a.m. to 2 p.m. (closed Wednesday and Sunday) *Admission:* $6 adults; $2.50 children 4 to 12; under 4, FREE *Operated by:* Dunkirk Lighthouse & Veterans Park Museum *NR?* Yes *NHL?* No *Year established/built:* 1826 *Latitude:* 42.48849 *Longitude:* -79.3514

EATONS NECK LIGHTHOUSE

Established and built in 1799, the Eatons Neck Lighthouse is still an active aid to navigation. *Address:* Eatons Neck Light *City:* Asharoken *State:* NY *Visitors welcome?* No *Operated by:* U.S. Coast Guard (District 1) *NR?* Yes *NHL?* No *Year established/built:* 1799 *Latitude:* 40.9540 *Longitude:* -73.3951

ELM TREE BEACON LIGHTHOUSE

Elm Tree Lighthouse got its name from a large elm tree which once served as a beacon for early Dutch sailors. The lighthouse itself was built in 1856. It is located at Miller Field. *Address:* Elm Tree Beacon Light *City:* New Dorp *State:* NY *Visitors welcome?* Yes *Hours:* Grounds open *Admission:* FREE *Operated by:* Gateway National Recreation Area *NR?* No *NHL?* No *Year established/built:* 1856 *Latitude:* 40.5639 *Longitude:* -74.0953

ESOPUS MEADOWS LIGHTHOUSE

Established in 1839, the Esopus Meadows Lighthouse, also called the Middle Hudson Lighthouse, was automated in 1965 and is still an active aid to navigation. It is now operated by a local not-for-profit organization. *Address:* Esopus Meadows Light *City:* Esopus *State:* NY *Visitors welcome?* No *Operated by:* Save Esopus Lighthouse Commission *NR?* Yes *NHL?* No *Year established/built:* 1839 *Latitude:* 41.86861 *Longitude:* -73.94139

EXECUTION ROCKS LIGHTHOUSE

Established and built in 1850, the Execution Rocks Lighthouse was automated in 1979 and is still an active aid to navigation. *Address:* Execution Rocks Light *City:* Sands Point *State:* NY *Visitors welcome?* No *Operated by:* U.S. Coast Guard (District 1) *NR?* No *NHL?* No *Year established/built:* 1850 *Latitude:* 40.8783 *Longitude:* -73.7374

FIRE ISLAND LIGHTHOUSE

Established in 1827, the current Fire Island Lighthouse was built in 1858 and automated in 1986. Still an active aid to navigation, the lighthouse is operated by a local not-for-profit. The lighthouse is located within the Fire Island National Seashore. *Address:* Fire Island Light *City:* Saltaire *State:* NY *Phone:* 631-661-4876 *Visitors welcome?* Yes *Hours:*

Daily *Admission:* Contact attraction directly *Operated by:* Fire Island Lighthouse Preservation Society *NR?* Yes *NHL?* No *Year established/built:* 1827 *Latitude:* 40.6324 *Longitude:* -73.2186

FORT WADSWORTH LIGHTHOUSE

Established and built in 1903, the Fort Wadsworth Lighthouse was deactivated in 1963. It is now part of the Gateway National Recreation Area. *Address:* Fort Wadsworth Light *City:* Staten Island *State:* NY *Visitors welcome?* Yes *Hours:* Fort Wadsworth is open Wednesday through Sunday, 10 a.m. to 5 p.m. *Admission:* Free admission to Fort Wadsworth, tower closed *Operated by:* Gateway National Recreation Area *NR?* No *NHL?* No *Year established/built:* 1828 *Latitude:* 40.6058 *Longitude:* -74.0539

HORTON POINT LIGHTHOUSE

Established and built in 1857, the Horton Point Lighthouse was automated in 1933 and is still an active aid to navigation. *Address:* Horton Point Light *City:* Southold *State:* NY *Phone:* 631-765-5500 *Visitors welcome?* Yes *Hours:* Grounds open daily 8 a.m. to dusk Memorial Day to Columbus Day *Admission:* FREE *Operated by:* East End Lighthouses *NR?* Yes *NHL?* No *Year established/built:* 1857 *Latitude:* 41.08349 *Longitude:* -72.44659

HUDSON-ATHENS LIGHTHOUSE

Established and built in 1874, the Hudson-Athens Lighthouse, also called the Hudson City Lighthouse, was automated in 1949 and is still an active aid to navigation. It is operated by a local not-for-profit. *Address:* Hudson-Athens Light *City:* Athens *State:* NY *Phone:* 518-828-5294 *Web:* www.hudsonathenslighthouse.org *Visitors welcome?* Yes *Hours:* Contact attraction directly *Admission:* Contact attraction directly *Operated by:* Hudson-Athens Lighthouse Preservation Society *NR?* Yes *NHL?* No *Year established/built:* 1874 *Latitude:* 42.26247 *Longitude:* -73.81048

HUNTINGTON HARBOR LIGHTHOUSE

Established in 1857, the current Huntington Harbor Lighthouse, once known as the Lloyd Harbor Lighthouse, was automated in 1949 and is still an active aid to navigation. *Address:* Huntington Harbor Light *City:* Huntington Harbor *State:* NY *Visitors welcome?* Yes *Hours:* By appointment *Admission:* By appointment *Operated by:* Huntington Lighthouse Preservation Society *NR?* Yes *NHL?* No *Year established/built:* 1912 *Latitude:* 40.9108 *Longitude:* -73.4317

JEFFREYS HOOK LIGHTHOUSE

Jeffreys Hook Lighthouse is also known as the Little Red Lighthouse. *Address:* Riverside Drive & W 181st St *City:* New York *State:* NY *Phone:* 212-304-2365 *Visitors welcome?* Yes *Hours:* Dawn to dusk *Admission:* Tower closed *Operated by:* New York City Department of Parks & Recreation *NR?* Yes *NHL?* No *Year established/built:* 1921 *Latitude:* 40.85192 *Longitude:* -73.94191

LATIMER REEF LIGHTHOUSE

Established in 1804, the current Latimer Reef Lighthouse was constructed in 1884 and automated in 1974. It is currently an active aid to navigation. *City:* Fishers Island *State:* NY *Visitors welcome?* No *Operated by:* U.S. Coast Guard (District 1) *NR?* No *NHL?* No *Year established/built:* 1804 *Latitude:* 41.2570 *Longitude:* -72.0240

LITTLE GULL ISLAND LIGHTHOUSE

Established in 1806, the current Little Gull Island Lighthouse was built in 1869, and it is still an active aid to navigation. *Address:* Plum Island *State:* NY *Visitors welcome?* No *Operated by:* U.S. Coast Guard (District 1) *NR?* No *NHL?* No *Year established/built:* 1806 *Latitude:* 41.1792 *Longitude:* -72.2056

Montauk Point Lighthouse, Montauk, New York

MONTAUK POINT LIGHTHOUSE

Authorized by President George Washington in 1796 and built the next year, the Montauk Point Lighthouse is an iconic American lighthouse. Automated in 1987, the lighthouse is now a museum. *Address:* Montauk Point Light *City:* Montauk *State:* NY *Zip:* 11954 *Phone:* 631-668-2544 *Web:* www.montauklighthouse.com *Email:* keeper@montauklighthouse. com *Visitors welcome?* Yes *Hours:* Daily during the summer, else weekends *Admission:* $8 adults, $6 seniors, $4 children *Operated by:* Montauk Historical Society *NR?* Yes *NHL?* Yes *Year established/built:* 1796 *Latitude:* 41.0710 *Longitude:* -71.8571

NEW DORP LIGHTHOUSE

Established and built in 1856, the New Dorp Lighthouse, also called the Swash Channel Rear Range Lighthouse, was deactivated in 1964 and is now a private residence. *Address:* New Dorp Light *City:* Staten Island *State:* NY *Visitors welcome?* No *Operated by:* Private owner *NR?* Yes *NHL?* No *Year established/built:* 1856 *Latitude:* 40.58083 *Longitude:* -74.1200

NORTH BROTHER ISLAND LIGHTHOUSE

Constructed in 1869, North Brother Island Lighthouse marks a treacherous area of the Narrows in Long Island Sound. The lighthouse has famous neighbors, including Riverside Hospital, home to Typhoid Mary and other quarantined patients, and Rikers Island. *Address:* North Brother Island Light *City:* New York *State:* NY *Visitors welcome?* No *Operated by:* City of New York *NR?* No *NHL?* No *Year established/built:* 1869 *Latitude:* 40.80121 *Longitude:* -73.89764

NORTH DUMPLING LIGHTHOUSE

Established in 1849, the current North Dumpling Lighthouse was constructed in 1871. Deactivated in 1959, it is now a private residence. *Address:* North Dumpling Island *City:* Fishers Island *State:* NY *Visitors welcome?* No *Operated by:* Private owner *NR?* No *NHL?* No *Year established/built:* 1849 *Latitude:* 41.2829 *Longitude:* -72.0162

OLD FIELD POINT LIGHTHOUSE

Established in 1823, the current Old Field Point Lighthouse was constructed in 1868 and automated in 1933. It is still an active aid to navigation and also serves as offices for the local municipality. *Address:* Old Field Point Light *City:* Village of Old Field *State:* NY *Zip:* 11733 *Phone:* 631-941-9412 *Email:* villageclerk@oldfieldny.org *Visitors welcome?* Yes *Hours:* Contact attraction directly *Admission:* Contact attraction directly *Operated by:* Village of Old Field *NR?* No *NHL?* No *Year established/built:* 1823 *Latitude:* 40.9770 *Longitude:* -73.1186

OLD ORCHARD SHOAL LIGHTHOUSE

Established and built in 1893, the Old Orchard Shoal Lighthouse is still an active aid to navigation. *Address:* Old Orchard Shoal Light *City:* Staten Island *State:* NY *Visitors welcome?* No *Operated by:* U.S. Coast Guard (District 1) *NR?* No *NHL?* No *Year established/built:* 1893 *Latitude:* 40.5122 *Longitude:* -74.0986

ORIENT LONG BEACH BAR LIGHTHOUSE

Known as Bug Light because of its perch on piles sunk into the sand, the Long Beach Bar Lighthouse was constructed in 1871 to mark the opening to Peconic Bay. Frequently damaged by ice during the winter, the station was taken out of service in 1948. *Address:* Orient Long Beach Bar Light *City:* Greenport *State:* NY *Zip:* 11944 *Phone:* 631-477-2100 *Email:* eseaport@verizon.net *Visitors welcome?* No *Operated by:* East End Seaport Museum & Marine Foundation *NR?* No *NHL?* No *Year established/built:* 1871 *Latitude:* 41.10889 *Longitude:* -72.30639

ORIENT POINT LIGHTHOUSE

Established and built in 1899, the Orient Point Lighthouse was automated in 1954 and is still an active aid to navigation. *Address:* Orient Point Light *City:* Orient Point *State:* NY *Visitors welcome?* No *Operated by:* U.S. Coast Guard (District 1) *NR?* No *NHL?* No *Year established/built:* 1899 *Latitude:* 41.1633 *Longitude:* -72.2233

PLUM ISLAND LIGHTHOUSE

Established in 1827, the current Plum Island Lighthouse, also called the Plum Gut Lighthouse, was built in 1870 and deactivated in 1978. The island is now the site of a USDA research facility. *Address:* Plum Island Light *City:* Plum Island *State:* NY *Visitors welcome?* No *Operated by:* U.S. Animal Disease Center *NR?* No *NHL?* No *Year established/built:* 1827 *Latitude:* 41.1737 *Longitude:* -72.2115

POINT AUX ROCHES LIGHTHOUSE

Established and built in 1858, the Point aux Roches Lighthouse was deactivated in 1989. *Address:* Point Au Roches Light *City:* Plattsburg *State:* NY *Visitors welcome?* No *Operated by:* Private owner *NR?* No *NHL?* No *Year established/built:* 1858 *Latitude:* 44.7994 *Longitude:* -73.3606

PRINCES BAY LIGHTHOUSE

Established and built in 1828, the Princes Bay Lighthouse was deactivated in 1922. *Address:* Mt. Loretto Unique Area *City:* Staten Island *State:* NY *Visitors welcome?* No *Operated by:* Mt. Loretto Unique Area *NR?* No *NHL?* No *Year established/built:* 1828 *Latitude:* 40.58344 *Longitude:* -74.14959

RACE ROCK LIGHTHOUSE

Established and built in 1828, the Race Rock Lighthouse was automated in 1978 and is still an active aid to navigation. *Address:* Race Rock Light *City:* Fishers Island *State:* NY *Visitors welcome?* No *Operated by:* U.S. Coast Guard (District 1) *NR?* Yes *NHL?* No *Year established/built:* 1878 *Latitude:* 41.2436 *Longitude:* -72.0469

RONDOUT CREEK LIGHTHOUSE

Established in 1838, the current Rondout Creek Lighthouse was built in 1915 and automated in 1954. Now owned by the local municipality, the lighthouse is still an active aid to navigation. *Address:* Rondout Light *City:* Kingston *State:* NY *Visitors welcome?* Yes *Hours:* Contact attraction directly *Admission:* Contact attraction directly *Operated by:* Hudson River Maritime Museum *NR?* Yes *NHL?* No *Year established/built:* 1838 *Latitude:* 41.92056 *Longitude:* -73.96222

SANDS POINT LIGHTHOUSE

Established and built in 1809, the Sands Point Lighthouse was deactivated in 1922. *Address:* Sands Point Light *City:* Sands Point *State:* NY   *Visitors welcome?* No *Operated by:* Private owner *NR?* No *NHL?* No *Year established/built:* 1809 *Latitude:* 40.8659 *Longitude:* -73.7295

SAUGERTIES LIGHTHOUSE

✦ Established in 1836, the current Saugerties Lighthouse was built in 1869 and automated in 1954. It is still an active aid to navigation. *Address:* Saugerties Light *City:* Saugerties *State:* NY *Zip:* 12477 *Phone:* 845-247-0656 *Web:* www.saugertieslighthouse. com *Email:* info@saugertieslighthouse.com *Visitors welcome?* Yes *Hours:* Contact attraction directly *Admission:* Contact attraction directly *Operated by:* Saugerties Lighthouse Conservancy *NR?* Yes *NHL?* No *Year established/built:* 1836 *Latitude:* 42.07195 *Longitude:* -73.93028 **Accommodations for overnight and/or long-term stays available.**

SHINNECOCK LIGHTHOUSE

Constructed in 1858, Shinnecock Lighthouse, also called Great West Bay Lighthouse, was one of the tallest lights on the eastern seaboard at 150 feet. The U.S. Coast Guard replaced the brick tower with a steel skeleton tower in 1931. *City:* Shinnecock Bay *State:* NY *Visitors welcome?* No *Operated by:* U.S. Coast Guard (District 1) *NR?* No *NHL?* No *Year established/built:* 1858 *Latitude:* 40.8408 *Longitude:* -72.4741

SPLIT ROCK POINT LIGHTHOUSE

Established in 1838, the current Split Rock Point Lighthouse was built in 1867 and deactivated in 1928. It is now a private residence. *Address:* Split Rock Point, Adirondack Park Preserve *City:* Essex *State:* NY *Visitors welcome?* No *Operated by:* Private owner *NR?* No *NHL?* No *Year established/built:* 1838 *Latitude:* 44.3101 *Longitude:* -73.3526

STATEN ISLAND REAR RANGE LIGHTHOUSE

Established in 1909, the current Staten Island Rear Range Lighthouse was constructed in 1912 and is still an active aid to navigation. *Address:* Latourette Park *City:* Staten Island *State:* NY *Visitors welcome?* No *Operated by:* U.S. Coast Guard (District 1) *NR?* No *NHL?* No *Year established/built:* 1909 *Latitude:* 40.5659 *Longitude:* -74.1680

STATUE OF LIBERTY

Known as one of the greatest American icons, the Statue of Liberty was also a working lighthouse in the first few years of her operation after the statue was installed in 1886. It ceased being an official navigation aid in 1902. *Address:* Statue of Liberty *State:* NY *Zip:* 10004 *Phone:* 212-363-3200 *Web:* www.nps.gov/stli/ *Visitors welcome?* Yes *Hours:* Daily, 9 a.m. to 5 p.m. *Admission:* FREE *Operated by:* Statue of Liberty National Monument *NR?* Yes *NHL?* No *Year established/built:* 1886 *Latitude:* 40.6891 *Longitude:* -74.0446

STEPPING STONES LIGHTHOUSE

Established in 1866, the current Stepping Stones Lighthouse was constructed in 1877. Automated in 1967, it is still an active aid to navigation. *Address:* Stepping Stones Light *City:* Kings Point *State:* NY *Visitors welcome?* No *Operated by:* U.S. Coast Guard (District 1) *NR?* Yes *NHL?* No *Year established/built:* 1866 *Latitude:* 40.8244 *Longitude:* -73.7747

STONY POINT LIGHTHOUSE

Established and built in 1826, the Stony Point Lighthouse on the Hudson River is now a private aid to navigation. *Address:* Stony Point Light *City:* Stony Point *State:* NY *Visitors welcome?* Yes *Hours:* Daily *Admission:* FREE *Operated by:* Palisades Interstate Parks Commission *NR?* Yes *NHL?* No *Year established/built:* 1826 *Latitude:* 41.2414 *Longitude:* -73.9722

STRATFORD SHOAL LIGHTHOUSE

Established in 1837, the current Stratford Shoal Lighthouse was constructed in 1877. Automated in 1970, the light is still an active aid to navigation. *Address:* Stratford Shoal Light *State:* NY *Visitors welcome?* No *Operated by:* U.S. Coast Guard (District 1) *NR?* Yes *NHL?* No *Year established/built:* 1837 *Latitude:* 41.0597 *Longitude:* -73.1014

TARRYTOWN LIGHTHOUSE

Established and built in 1883, the Tarrytown Lighthouse, also called the Kingsland Point Lighthouse, was deactivated in 1961. *Address:* Tarrytown Light *City:* Sleepy Hollow *State:* NY *Visitors welcome?* Yes *Hours:* Contact attraction directly *Admission:* Contact attraction directly *Operated by:* Westchester County Dept. of Parks *NR?* Yes *NHL?* No *Year established/built:* 1883 *Latitude:* 41.08417 *Longitude:* -73.87417

THROGS NECK LIGHTHOUSE

The State of New York decided in the 1820s that a lighthouse was needed at Throgs Neck, which juts out in the East River, and the structure was finished in 1827. The lighthouse was replaced in 1835 by temporary structures that lasted almost 50 years. *Address:* Throgs Neck Light *City:* Throggs Neck *State:* NY *Zip:* 10465 *Phone:* 718-409-7200 *Visitors welcome?* Yes *Hours:* Contact attraction directly *Admission:* Contact attraction directly *Operated by:* State University of New York Maritime College *NR?* No *NHL?* No *Year established/built:* 1827 *Latitude:* 40.80444 *Longitude:* -73.79056

VERONA BEACH LIGHTHOUSE

The Verona Beach Lighthouse was one of three constructed on Lake Oneida to mark the entrance to the Wood Creek Canal on the east end of the lake. The light was lit in 1917, and is now cared for by the not-for-profit Verona Beach Lighthouse Association. *Address:* Verona Beach State Park *City:* Verona Beach *State:* NY *Visitors welcome?* Yes *Hours:* Daily *Admission:* **FREE** *Operated by:* Verona Beach Lighthouse Association *NR?* No *NHL?* No *Year established/built:* 1917 *Latitude:* 43.18092 *Longitude:* -75.7168

WEST BANK LIGHTHOUSE

Established and constructed in 1901, the West Bank Lighthouse is the front range light for the Staten Island Lighthouse, both of which are still active aids to navigation. *Address:* West Bank Light *City:* Staten Island *State:* NY *Visitors welcome?* No *Operated by:* U.S. Coast Guard (District 1) *NR?* No *NHL?* No *Year established/built:* 1901 *Latitude:* 40.5381 *Longitude:* -74.0428

Bald Head Island (Old Baldy) Lighthouse, North Carolina

NORTH CAROLINA

BALD HEAD ISLAND LIGHTHOUSE

The Bald Head Island Lighthouse, often called Old Baldy Lighthouse, was built in 1817, making it North Carolina's oldest standing tower. This lighthouse replaced the first Bald Head Light (1795) that was destroyed due to beach erosion around 1813. *City:* Bald Head Island *State:* NC *Zip:* 28461 *Phone:* 910-457-7481 *Web:* www.oldbaldy.org *Email:* info@oldbaldy.org *Visitors welcome?* Yes *Hours:* Summer: Tuesday through Saturday, 10 a.m. to 4 p.m.;

Winter (Dec. 1 to March 15): Friday to Saturday, 10 a.m. to 4 p.m.; Sunday, 11 a.m. to 4 p.m. *Admission:* $5 age 12 and up, $3 under 12, age 2 and under **FREE** *Operated by:* Old Baldy Foundation *NR?* Yes *NHL?* No *Year established/built:* 1795 *Latitude:* 33.9900 *Longitude:* -78.0424

BODIE ISLAND LIGHTHOUSE

✢ Established in 1837, the current Bodie Island Lighthouse is the third on the island, built in 1872. Still an active aid to navigation, the light is now owned by the National Park Service, which operates a visitors center in the keepers house. *Address:* Bodie Island Light Station *City:* Whalebone *State:* NC *Phone:* 252-441-5711 *Web:* www.nps.gov/caha/ *Visitors welcome?* Yes *Hours:* Grounds only *Admission:* **FREE** *Operated by:* Cape Hatteras National Seashore *NR?* Yes *NHL?* No *Year established/built:* 1837 *Latitude:* 35.8185 *Longitude:* -75.5633 **Accommodations for overnight and/or long-term stays available.**

CAPE FEAR LIGHTHOUSE

Established in 1794 by the federal government, the Cape Fear Lighthouse was a series of three structures, the last of which was a skeletal tower that was torn down in 1958 in favor of the Oak Island Lighthouse. All that remains are the large concrete footings. *City:* Bald Head Island *State:* NC *Zip:* 28461 *Phone:* 910-457-0089 *Web:* www.bhic.org *Email:* email@bhic.org *Visitors welcome?* Yes *Hours:* Grounds only *Admission:* **FREE** *Operated by:* Bald Head Island Conservancy *NR?* Yes *NHL?* No *Year established/built:* 1794 *Latitude:* 33.9900 *Longitude:* -78.0424

Cape Hatteras Lighthouse, Buxton, North Carolina

CAPE HATTERAS LIGHTHOUSE

✦ Established in 1803, the current Cape Hatteras Lighthouse, perhaps the most famous lighthouse in the United States, was constructed in 1870. Still an active aid to navigation, the lighthouse is near the site where the Wright Brothers first demonstrated powered flight. *Address:* Cape Hatteras Light *City:* Buxton *State:* NC *Zip:* 27959 *Phone:* 252-473-2111 *Web:* www.nps.gov/caha/ *Visitors welcome?* Yes *Hours:* Grounds only *Admission:* **FREE** *Operated by:* Cape Hatteras National Seashore *NR?* Yes *NHL?* Yes *Year established/built:* 1803 *Latitude:* 35.2506 *Longitude:* -75.5288 **Accommodations for overnight and/or long-term stays available.**

CAPE LOOKOUT LIGHTHOUSE

Established in 1812, the current Cape Lookout Lighthouse was constructed in 1859 and automated in 1950. Now owned by the National Park Service, the light is an active aid to navigation. *Address:* Cape Lookout Light *City:* Harkers Island *State:* NC *Zip:* 28531 *Phone:* 252-728-2250 *Web:* www.nps.gov/calo/ *Visitors welcome?* Yes *Hours:* Grounds only *Admission:* **FREE** *Operated by:* Cape Lookout National Seashore *NR?* Yes *NHL?* No *Year established/built:* 1812 *Latitude:* 34.6053 *Longitude:* -76.5361

CURRITUCK BEACH LIGHTHOUSE

Established in 1875, the Currituck Beach Lighthouse completed a string of lighthouses along the Outer Banks. It was automated in 1939, and in the 1970s, the grounds and light were taken over by a local group of preservationists, which have restored the grounds and light. *Address:* 1101 Corolla Village Road *City:* Corolla *State:* NC *Zip:* 27927 *Phone:* 252-453-8152 *Web:* www.currituckbeachlight.com *Email:* info@currituckbeachlight.com *Visitors welcome?* Yes *Hours:* Daily, Easter through Thanksgiving, 9 a.m to 5 p.m.; until 8 p.m. Thursdays *Admission:* Parking and grounds free; $7 to climb the tower *Operated by:* Outer Banks Conservationists *NR?* Yes *NHL?* No *Year established/built:* 1875 *Latitude:* 36.3789 *Longitude:* -75.8322

OAK ISLAND LIGHTHOUSE

Established in 1849, the current Oak Island Lighthouse was constructed of concrete in 1958. The lighthouse is one of the few owned by the Coast Guard in which visitors are allowed to climb to the top. *Address:* Caswell Beach Road *City:* Caswell Beach *State:* NC *Zip:* 28465 *Web:* www.oakislandlighthouse.org *Email:* lighthouse@caswellbeach.org *Visitors welcome?* Yes *Hours:* Memorial Day to Labor Day, Wednesdays and Saturdays, 10 a.m. to 2 p.m. *Admission:* Contact attraction directly *Operated by:* Friends of Oak Island Lighthouse *NR?* Yes *NHL?* No *Year established/built:* 1849 *Latitude:* 33.8964 *Longitude:* -78.0494

OCRACOKE LIGHTHOUSE

✦ Established in 1822 on a cove reportedly a favorite for the 18th-century pirate Blackbeard, the Ocracoke Lighthouse is still an active aid to navigation as the second oldest lighthouse in the U.S.. It is now owned by the National Park Service. *Address:* Lighthouse Road and Silverlark Drive *City:* Ocracoke *State:* NC *Phone:* 252-473-2111 *Web:* www.nps.gov/caha/ *Visitors welcome?* Yes *Hours:* Grounds only *Admission:* FREE *Operated by:* Cape Hatteras National Seashore *NR?* No *NHL?* No *Year established/built:* 1822 *Latitude:* 35.1146 *Longitude:* -75.9810 **Accommodations for overnight and/or long-term stays available.**

PRICE'S CREEK LIGHTHOUSE

The Price's Creek Lighthouse was one of a number of range lights along the Cape Fear River. *Address:* Price's Creek *City:* Southport *State:* NC *Visitors welcome?* No *Operated by:* Private owner *NR?* No *NHL?* No *Latitude:* 33.93552 *Longitude:* -78.0088

ROANOKE MARSHES LIGHTHOUSE

A replica of the last Roanake Marshes Lighthouse, which was lost in the 1950s, sits in the harbor at Manteo. It is operated by a local maritime museum. *Address:* Roanoke Marshes Light *City:* Manteo *State:* NC *Zip:* 27954 *Phone:* 252-475-1750 *Web:* www.obxmaritime.org *Visitors welcome?* Yes *Hours:* Contact attraction directly *Admission:* Contact attraction directly *Operated by:* North Carolina Maritime Museum on Roanoke Island *NR?* No *NHL?* No *Year established/built:* 1831 *Latitude:* 35.8111 *Longitude:* -75.7006

ROANOKE RIVER LIGHTHOUSE

Established by a lightship in 1832, the current Roanoke River Lighthouse was constructed on screwpiles in 1887. The U.S. Coast Guard deactivated the lighthouse in 1941. The lighthouse was eventually sold to the Edenton Historical Commission and moved to Colonial Park in Edenton. *Address:* Colonial Park *City:* Edenton *State:* NC *Zip:* 27932 *Phone:* 252-482-7800 *Web:* edentonhistoricalcommission.org *Email:* becky.winslow@edentonhistoricalcommission.org *Visitors welcome?* Yes *Hours:* Grounds only *Admission:* Contact attraction directly *Operated by:* Edenton Historical Commission *NR?* No *NHL?* No *Year established/built:* 1832 *Latitude:* 36.0579 *Longitude:* -76.6077

PENNSYLVANIA

TURTLE ROCK LIGHTHOUSE

The Turtle Rock Lighthouse is a private aid to navigation owned by a Philadelphia boat club. *Address:* 15 Kelly Drive *City:* Philadelphia *State:* PA *Visitors welcome?* Yes *Hours:* Grounds only *Admission:* FREE *Operated by:* Private owner *NR?* No *NHL?* No *Year established/built:* 1887 *Latitude:* 39.9694 *Longitude:* -75.18484

PUERTO RICO

ARECIBO LIGHTHOUSE
Established and built in 1898, the Arecibo Lighthouse, also called the Faro de Arecibo Lighthouse, was automated in 1964 and is still an active aid to navigation. It is now located with in a private park. *Address:* Carr #655 Bo. Islote, Sector El Muelle *City:* Arecibo *State:* PR *Phone:* 787-880-7540 *Web:* www.arecibolighthouse.com *Email:* mail@arecibolighthouse.com *Visitors welcome?* Yes *Hours:* Monday to Friday: 9 a.m. to 6 p.m.; Saturday and Sunday, 10 a.m. to 7 p.m. *Admission:* $10 adults, $8 children 2-12 and seniors *Operated by:* Arecibo Lighthouse & Historical Park *NR?* Yes *NHL?* No *Year established/built:* 1898 *Latitude:* 18.4724 *Longitude:* -66.7157

CABRAS ISLAND LIGHTHOUSE
Established in 1902, the original lighthouse structure was destroyed in 1965. The light is now on a skeletal metal tower. *Address:* Isla de Cabras National Park *City:* San Juan *State:* PR *Visitors welcome?* No *Operated by:* U.S. Coast Guard (District 7) *NR?* No *NHL?* No *Year established/built:* 1902 *Latitude:* 18.46633 *Longitude:* -66.10572

CAPE ROJO LIGHTHOUSE
Established and built in 1882, the Cape Rojo Lighthouse was automated in 1967 and is still an active aid to navigation. *Address:* Cabo Rojo National Wildlife Refuge *City:* Cabo Rojo *State:* PR *Visitors welcome?* Yes *Hours:* Daily, Wednesday through Sunday *Admission:* FREE *Operated by:* City of Cabo Rojo *NR?* Yes *NHL?* No *Year established/built:* 1882 *Latitude:* 17.9747 *Longitude:* -67.1760

CAPE SAN JUAN LIGHTHOUSE
Established and constructed in 1880, the Cape San Juan Lighthouse was automated in 1975 and is still an active aid to navigation. *City:* Fajardo *State:* PR *Phone:* 787-722-5834 *Email:* fideicomiso@fideicomiso.org *Visitors welcome?* Yes *Hours:* By appointment *Admission:* Contact attraction directly *Operated by:* Conservation Trust of Puerto Rico *NR?* Yes *NHL?* No *Year established/built:* 1880 *Latitude:* 18.3258 *Longitude:* -65.6524

CARDONA ISLAND LIGHTHOUSE
Established and built in 1889, the Cardona Island Lighthouse was automated in 1962. It is still an active aid to navigation. *Address:* Cardono Island *City:* Ponce *State:* PR *Visitors welcome?* No *Operated by:* U.S. Coast Guard (District 7) *NR?* Yes *NHL?* No *Year established/built:* 1889 *Latitude:* 17.95719 *Longitude:* -66.6349

CASTILLO SAN FELIPE DEL MORRO LIGHTHOUSE

Four lighthouses have stood on Castillo San Felipe del Morro 6th level in its long history. The first one was built in 1846. A second one replaced it in 1876 but took a direct hit during the 1898 bombardment of the Spanish-American War. However, its brick foundation was salvaged in 1899 to erect the first American lighthouse. The current lighthouse was built between 1908 and 1909. Restoration of the El Morro lighthouse was completed in August 2009. It has since been opened to visitors on a regular daily basis from 9 a.m. to 6 p.m. (weather allowing). *Address:* Castillo San Felipe del Morro *City:* San Juan *State:* PR *Phone:* 787-729-6754 *Web:* www.nps.gov/saju/ *Visitors welcome?* Yes *Hours:* 9 a.m. to 6 p.m. *Admission:* $3 adults, children 15 and under FREE *Operated by:* National Park Service, San Juan National Historic Site *NR?* Yes *NHL?* No *Year established/built:* 1846 *Latitude:* 18.4711 *Longitude:* -66.1242

CULEBRITA ISLAND LIGHTHOUSE

Established and built in 1886, the Culebrita Island Lighthouse was automated in 1964 and is still an active aid to navigation. *Address:* Culebrita Island *City:* Culebra *State:* PR *Visitors welcome?* No *Operated by:* City of Culebrita *NR?* Yes *NHL?* No *Year established/built:* 1886 *Latitude:* 18.31468 *Longitude:* -65.22877

GUANICA LIGHTHOUSE

Established and built in 1893, the Guanica Lighthouse was deactivated in 1950. *City:* Guanica *State:* PR *Visitors welcome?* Yes *Hours:* Grounds only *Admission:* FREE *Operated by:* Puerto Rico Dept. of Natural Resources *NR?* Yes *NHL?* No *Year established/built:* 1893 *Latitude:* 17.9750 *Longitude:* -66.9100

MONA ISLAND LIGHTHOUSE

Established and built in 1900, the Mona Island Lighthouse was deactivated in 1976. *Address:* Mona Island *City:* Mayaguez *State:* PR *Visitors welcome?* Yes *Hours:* Grounds only *Admission:* FREE *Operated by:* Puerto Rico Dept. of Natural Resources *NR?* Yes *NHL?* No *Year established/built:* 1900 *Latitude:* 18.0897 *Longitude:* -67.8777

MUERTOS ISLAND LIGHTHOUSE

Established and built in 1887, the Muertos Island Lighthouse, or Isla Caja de Muertos Lighthouse, was automated in 1945 and is still an active aid to navigation. It is now within a wildlife refuge. *Address:* Muertos Island *City:* Ponce *State:* PR *Visitors welcome?* Yes *Hours:* Grounds only *Admission:* FREE *Operated by:* Puerto Rico Dept. of Natural Resources *NR?* Yes *NHL?* No *Year established/built:* 1887 *Latitude:* 17.89469 *Longitude:* -66.51989

NAVASSA ISLAND LIGHTHOUSE

Established and built in 1917, the Navassa Island Lighthouse off Jamaica was deactivated in 1996 and is now part of a wildlife refuge. *City:* Boqueron *State:* PR *Phone:* 787-851-7258 *Visitors welcome?* Yes *Hours:* Grounds only *Admission:* FREE *Operated by:* Navassa Island National Wildlife Refuge *NR?* No *NHL?* No *Year established/built:* 1917 *Latitude:* 18.0267 *Longitude:* -67.1733

NEW POINT BORINQUEN LIGHTHOUSE

Established in 1889, the New Point Borinquen Lighthouse was built in 1920 is now used for U.S. Coast Guard housing. *City:* Aquadilla *State:* PR *Visitors welcome?* No *Operated by:* U.S. Coast Guard (District 7) *NR?* Yes *NHL?* No *Year established/built:* 1889 *Latitude:* 18.4274 *Longitude:* -67.1541

OLD POINT BORINQUEN LIGHTHOUSE

Established in 1889, the Old Point Borinquen Lighthouse was nearly destroyed by a 1918 tsunami and is now in ruins. *City:* Aquadilla *State:* PR *Visitors welcome?* Yes *Hours:* Grounds only *Admission:* FREE *Operated by:* U.S. Coast Guard (District 7) *NR?* Yes *NHL?* No *Year established/built:* 1889 *Latitude:* 18.42744 *Longitude:* -67.15407

POINT FIGURAS LIGHTHOUSE

Established and built in 1893, the Point Figuras Lighthouse was deactivated in 1938. *City:* Guayama *State:* PR *Visitors welcome?* Yes *Hours:* Contact attraction directly *Admission:* Contact attraction directly *Operated by:* Puerto Rico Dept. of Natural Resources *NR?* Yes *NHL?* No *Year established/built:* 1893 *Latitude:* 17.98413 *Longitude:* -66.11378

POINT JIGUERO LIGHTHOUSE

Established in 1892, the current Point Jiguero Lighthouse, or Point Higuero Lighthouse, was constructed in 1922 and is still an active aid to navigation. *City:* Rincon *State:* PR *Visitors welcome?* Yes *Hours:* Grounds only *Admission:* FREE *Operated by:* City of Rincon *NR?* Yes *NHL?* No *Year established/built:* 1892 *Latitude:* 18.34095 *Longitude:* -67.25264

POINT MULAS LIGHTHOUSE

Established in 1885 and built the following year, the Point Mulas Lighthouse was automated in 1949, but is no longer an active aid to navigation. It is now home to a small marine museum. *City:* Vieques *State:* PR *Visitors welcome?* Yes *Hours:* Daily *Admission:* Contact attraction directly *Operated by:* City of Vieques *NR?* Yes *NHL?* No *Year established/built:* 1885 *Latitude:* 18.14746 *Longitude:* -65.44488

POINT TUNA LIGHTHOUSE

Established and built in 1892, the Point Tuna Lighthouse was automated in 1989. *City:* Maunabo *State:* PR *Visitors welcome?* No *Operated by:* U.S. Coast Guard (District 7) *NR?* Yes *NHL?* No *Year established/built:* 1892 *Latitude:* 18.00719 *Longitude:* -65.89933

PUERTO FERRO LIGHTHOUSE

Established and built in 1896, the Puerto Ferro Lighthouse was deactivated in 1926 and is now abandoned. *City:* Vieques *State:* PR *Visitors welcome?* Yes *Hours:* Grounds only *Admis-*

sion: **FREE** *Operated by:* U.S. Coast Guard (District 7) *NR?* No *NHL?* No *Year established/built:* 1896 *Latitude:* 18.14746 *Longitude:* -65.44488

RHODE ISLAND

BEAVERTAIL LIGHTHOUSE

Established in 1749, the current Beavertail Lighthouse was constructed in 1856 and automated in 1972. Still an active aid to navigation, the lighthouse is now a museum. *Address:* Beavertail State Park *City:* Jamestown *State:* RI *Zip:* 02835 *Phone:* 401-423-3270 *Web:* www.beavertaillight.org *Email:* info@BeavertailLight.org *Visitors welcome?* Yes *Hours:* Memorial Day weekend to mid-June: Saturday and Sunday, noon to 3 p.m.; Mid-June to Labor Day, 10 a.m. to 4 p.m.; Labor Day to Columbus Day, noon to 3 p.m. *Admission:* Contact attraction directly *Operated by:* Beavertail Lighthouse Museum Association *NR?* Yes *NHL?* No *Year established/built:* 1749 *Latitude:* 41.4490 *Longitude:* -71.4000

BLOCK ISLAND NORTH LIGHTHOUSE

Established in 1829, the current Block Island North Lighthouse was built in 1867 and automated in 1955. It is still an active aid to navigation located within a wildlife refuge. *Address:* Block Island North Light *City:* Block Island *State:* RI *Visitors welcome?* Yes *Hours:* Grounds only *Admission:* **FREE** *Operated by:* Town of New Shoreham *NR?* Yes *NHL?* No *Year established/built:* 1829 *Latitude:* 41.2275 *Longitude:* -71.57611

BLOCK ISLAND SOUTHEAST LIGHTHOUSE

Established and built in 1875, the brick lighthouse was deactivated in 1990 and re-lighted in 1994. It is now operated by a local foundation. *Address:* Block Island Southeast Light *City:* Block Island *State:* RI *Zip:* 02807 *Phone:* 401-466-5009 *Email:* selight@verizon.net *Visitors welcome?* Yes *Hours:* Contact attraction directly *Admission:* Contact attraction directly *Operated by:* Block Island Southeast Lighthouse Foundation *NR?* Yes *NHL?* Yes *Year established/built:* 1875 *Latitude:* 41.1526 *Longitude:* -71.5553

BRISTOL FERRY LIGHTHOUSE

Established in 1846 and built in 1855, the Bristol Ferry Lighthouse operated until 1927 when the Mount Hope Bridge was under construction. It is now a private residence. *Address:* Bristol Ferry Light *City:* Bristol *State:* RI *Visitors welcome?* No *Operated by:* Private owner *NR?* Yes *NHL?* No *Year established/built:* 1846 *Latitude:* 41.6431 *Longitude:* -71.2603

CASTLE HILL LIGHTHOUSE

Established and built in 1890, the stone Castle Hill Lighthouse lights the entrance to Narrangansett Bay. The light was automated in 1957. *Address:* Castle Hill Light *City:*

Newport *State:* RI *Visitors welcome?* Yes *Hours:* Grounds only *Admission:* **FREE** *Operated by:* U.S. Coast Guard (District 1) *NR?* Yes *NHL?* No *Year established/built:* 1890 *Latitude:* 41.46195 *Longitude:* -71.36334

CONANICUT ISLAND LIGHTHOUSE
Established and built in 1886, the Conanicut Lighthouse was discontinued in 1933. It is now a private residence. *Address:* Conanicut Island Light *City:* Jamestown *State:* RI *Visitors welcome?* No *Operated by:* Private owner *NR?* Yes *NHL?* No *Year established/built:* 1886 *Latitude:* 41.57333 *Longitude:* -71.3725

CONIMICUT SHOAL LIGHTHOUSE
Established on a shoal in 1868, the current Conimicut Shoal Lighthouse in the coffee pot style was built in 1883 and automated in 1960. *Address:* Providence River *City:* Warwick *State:* RI *Visitors welcome?* No *Operated by:* City of Warwick *NR?* Yes *NHL?* No *Year established/built:* 1868 *Latitude:* 41.7663 *Longitude:* -71.4038

DUTCH ISLAND LIGHTHOUSE
Dutch Island Lighthouse, in the west passage of Rhode Island's Narragansett Bay, is a 42-foot brick tower built in 1857. It was built to replace a lighthouse established in 1826. The lighthouse was restored in 2007 and is an active aid to navigation. *Address:* Dutch Island Light *City:* Saunderstown *State:* RI *Visitors welcome?* No *Operated by:* Dutch Island Lighthouse Society *NR?* Yes *NHL?* No *Year established/built:* 1826 *Latitude:* 41.49556 *Longitude:* -71.40444

HOG ISLAND SHOAL LIGHTHOUSE
Established in 1886 by a lightship, the current cast-iron coffee pot structure was built in 1901 and automated in 1964. It is now owned by a private party. *Address:* Hog Island *City:* Portsmouth *State:* RI *Visitors welcome?* No *Operated by:* Private owner *NR?* Yes *NHL?* No *Year established/built:* 1886 *Latitude:* 41.6440 *Longitude:* -71.2801

IDA LEWIS ROCK LIGHTHOUSE
Established and built in 1854 as Lime Rock Lighthouse, the station was renamed the Ida Lewis Rock Lighthouse in honor of a famous female lighthouse keeper who maintained the facility after her husband was incapacitated by a stroke. *Address:* Ida Lewis Rock Lighthouse *City:* Newport *State:* RI *Visitors welcome?* No *Operated by:* Private owner *NR?* Yes *NHL?* No *Year established/built:* 1854 *Latitude:* 41.4775 *Longitude:* -71.3260

NAYATT POINT LIGHTHOUSE
Established in 1828, the current Nayatt Point Lighthouse was constructed in 1856. The light was discontinued in 1868 and the facility is now a private residence. *Address:* Nayatt Point Light *City:* Barrington *State:* RI *Visitors welcome?* No *Operated by:* Private owner *NR?* Yes *NHL?* No *Year established/built:* 1828 *Latitude:* 41.7250 *Longitude:* -71.33972

NEWPORT HARBOR LIGHTHOUSE

Established in 1824, the current Newport Harbor Lighthouse was built in 1842 and automated in 1923. Still an active aid to navigation, a local not-for-profit raised money to fund restoration of the structure in 2006. *Address:* Newport Harbor Light *City:* Newport *State:* RI *Visitors welcome?* Yes *Hours:* Grounds only *Admission:* FREE *Operated by:* Friends of Newport Harbor Light *NR?* Yes *NHL?* No *Year established/built:* 1824 *Latitude:* 41.49333 *Longitude:* -71.32694

PLUM BEACH LIGHTHOUSE

Established in 1897 and built in 1899 as a coffee pot lighthouse on a caisson, the Plum Beach Lighthouse was decommissioned in 1941 after the completion of the Jamestown Bridge. *Address:* Plum Beach Light *City:* North Kingstown *State:* RI *Visitors welcome?* No *Operated by:* Friends of Plum Beach Lighthouse *NR?* Yes *NHL?* No *Year established/built:* 1897 *Latitude:* 41.5300 *Longitude:* -71.4056

POINT JUDITH LIGHTHOUSE

Established in 1810, the current Point Judith Lighthouse was constructed of brownstone in 1857. It was automated in 1854 and is located on the grounds of the Point Judith Coast Guard Station. *Address:* Point Judith Light *City:* Point Judith *State:* RI *Visitors welcome?* Yes *Hours:* Grounds only *Admission:* FREE *Operated by:* U.S. Coast Guard (District 1) *NR?* Yes *NHL?* No *Year established/built:* 1810 *Latitude:* 41.3610 *Longitude:* -71.4814

POMHAM ROCKS LIGHTHOUSE

Established and built in 1871, the Pomham Rocks Lighthouse was deactivated in 1974 and re-lighted in 2006. *Address:* Pomham Rocks Light *City:* Kent Corner *State:* RI *Visitors welcome?* No *Operated by:* Friends of Pomham Rocks Lighthouse *NR?* Yes *NHL?* No *Year established/built:* 1871 *Latitude:* 41.7778 *Longitude:* -71.3703

POPLAR POINT LIGHTHOUSE

Established and constructed in 1831, the Poplar Point Lighthouse was active until 1882, when the light was moved to a new facility on Gay Rock. The Poplar Point Lighthouse is now a private residence. *Address:* Poplar Point Light *City:* North Kingston *State:* RI *Visitors welcome?* No *Operated by:* Private owner *NR?* Yes *NHL?* No *Year established/built:* 1831 *Latitude:* 41.57084 *Longitude:* -71.43972

PRUDENCE ISLAND LIGHTHOUSE

The Prudence Island Lighthouse was established in 1852, but the current structure was built in 1824 as the Goat Island Lighthouse. That building was dismantled and moved to Prudence Island in 1852. Prudence Island Light is the oldest lighthouse in Rhode Island. *Address:* Prudence Island Light *City:* Prudence Island *State:* RI *Visitors welcome?* Yes *Hours:* Grounds only *Admission:* FREE *Operated by:* Prudence Conservancy *NR?* Yes *NHL?* No *Year established/built:* 1852 *Latitude:* 41.60556 *Longitude:* -71.30306

ROSE ISLAND LIGHTHOUSE

✢ Established and built in 1870, the Rose Island Lighthouse was deactivated in 1971 and re-lighted in 1993. The station accepts visitors and offers overnight stays in the restored keepers quarters. *Address:* Rose Island Light *City:* Newport *State:* RI *Zip:* 02840 *Phone:* 401-847-4242 *Web:* www.roseislandlighthouse.org *Email:* keeper@roseisland.org *Visitors welcome?* Yes *Hours:* April to October: daily, 10 a.m. to 4 p.m. *Admission:* Contact attraction directly *Operated by:* Rose Island Lighthouse Foundation *NR?* Yes *NHL?* No *Year established/built:* 1870 *Latitude:* 41.49556 *Longitude:* -71.34306 **Accommodations for overnight and/or long-term stays available.**

SAKONNET POINT LIGHTHOUSE

Established and built in 1884, the cast-iron Sakonnet Point Lighthouse was shut down in 1955. Relighted in 1997, it is now maintained by a local preservation group. *Address:* Sakonnet Light *City:* Little Compton *State:* RI *Visitors welcome?* No *Operated by:* Friends of Sakonnet Point Lighthouse *NR?* Yes *NHL?* No *Year established/built:* 1884 *Latitude:* 41.4531 *Longitude:* -71.2031

WARWICK LIGHTHOUSE

Established in 1827, the current Warwick Lighthouse was constructed in 1932 and now serves as U.S. Coast Guard housing. The light was automated in 1985. *Address:* Warwick Neck *City:* Warwick *State:* RI *Visitors welcome?* No *Operated by:* U.S. Coast Guard (District 1) *NR?* Yes *NHL?* No *Year established/built:* 1827 *Latitude:* 41.68038 *Longitude:* -71.38228

WATCH HILL LIGHTHOUSE

Established in 1808, the current Watch Hill Lighthouse was built in 1856 and automated in 1986. The grounds and a small museum in the oil house are open to the public. *Address:* Watch Hill Point *City:* Westerly *State:* RI *Visitors welcome?* Yes *Hours:* July to August: Tuesdays and Thursdays, 1 p.m. to 3 p.m. *Admission:* Contact attraction directly *Operated by:* Watch Hill Lighthouse Keepers Association *NR?* Yes *NHL?* No *Year established/built:* 1808 *Latitude:* 41.3037 *Longitude:* -71.8584

SOUTH CAROLINA

BLOODY POINT BAR FRONT RANGE LIGHTHOUSE

Established in 1883, the Bloody Point Bar Front Range Lighthouse and its rear range partner light operated until 1921. The structure is now privately owned. *Address:* Dafuskie Island *City:* Forest Beach *State:* SC *Visitors welcome?* No *Operated by:* Private owner *NR?* No *NHL?* No *Year established/built:* 1883 *Latitude:* 32.1466 *Longitude:* -80.74372

CAPE ROMAIN LIGHTHOUSE

Established in 1827, the Cape Romain Lighthouse is one of the few stations with two towers, the latter built in 1858. The station was shut down in 1947 and later made part of a wildlife refuge. *Address:* Cape Romain National Wildlife Refuge *City:* McClellanville *State:* SC *Phone:* 843-928-3264 *Email:* caperomain@fws.gov *Visitors welcome?* Yes *Hours:* Grounds only *Admission:* FREE *Operated by:* Cape Romain National Wildlife Refuge *NR?* Yes *NHL?* No *Year established/built:* 1827 *Latitude:* 32.9930 *Longitude:* -79.6209

CHARLESTON LIGHTHOUSE

Established and built in 1962, the Charleston Lighthouse on Sullivan's Island was the last major lighthouse built by the federal government. The point of its unique triangle shape points out to sea from Charleston Harbor. *Address:* Charleston Light *City:* Charleston *State:* SC *Visitors welcome?* Yes *Hours:* Grounds only *Admission:* FREE *Operated by:* U.S. Coast Guard (District 7) *NR?* No *NHL?* No *Year established/built:* 1962 *Latitude:* 32.7578 *Longitude:* -79.8431

GEORGETOWN LIGHTHOUSE

Established and built in 1812, the Georgetown Lighthouse was refurbished after damage during the Civil War. Automated in 1986, the lighthouse is now part of a nature preserve. *Address:* Georgetown Light *City:* Georgetown *State:* SC *Visitors welcome?* Yes *Hours:* Grounds only *Admission:* FREE *Operated by:* South Carolina Dept. of Natural Resources *NR?* Yes *NHL?* No *Year established/built:* 1812 *Latitude:* 33.2233 *Longitude:* -79.1850

HAIG POINT REAR RANGE LIGHTHOUSE

Established and built in 1872, the Haig Point Rear Range Lighthouse operated until 1934. It was re-lighted in 1987 as a private aid to navigation as part of the creation of the Daufuskie Island Historic District. *Address:* Daufuskie Island *City:* Hilton Head *State:* SC *Visitors welcome?* Yes *Hours:* Grounds only *Admission:* Contact attraction directly *Operated by:* Private owner *NR?* Yes *NHL?* No *Year established/built:* 1872 *Latitude:* 32.11604 *Longitude:* -80.87122

HARBOUR TOWN LIGHTHOUSE

The Harbour Town Lighthouse was built as a private aid to navigation in 1970. *Address:* 149 Lighthouse Road *City:* Hilton Head *State:* SC *Zip:* 29928 *Phone:* 866-561-8802 *Visitors welcome?* Yes *Hours:* Daily, 10 a.m. to 6 p.m. *Admission:* Contact attraction directly *Operated by:* Private owner *NR?* No *NHL?* No *Year established/built:* 1970 *Latitude:* 32.1396 *Longitude:* -80.8101

HILTON HEAD REAR RANGE LIGHTHOUSE

Established in 1877, the current Hilton Head Rear Range Lighthouse, also called the Leamington Lighthouse, and its companion light were completed in 1880. The lights were decommissioned in 1932 and the front range light dismantled. The rear range light is still an active aid to navigation. *Address:* Hilton Head Rear Range Light *City:* Hilton Head *State:* SC *Phone:* 843-785-1106 *Visitors welcome?* Yes *Hours:* Grounds only *Admission:* Contact attraction directly *Operated by:* Palmetto Dunes Resort *NR?* Yes *NHL?* No *Year established/built:* 1877 *Latitude:* 32.16416 *Longitude:* -80.7400

HUNTING ISLAND LIGHTHOUSE

Established in 1859, the current Hunting Island Lighthouse constructed in 1875 to replaced the original tower destroyed during the Civil War. The light was deactivated in 1933, and the grounds became the most popular state park in South Carolina. *Address:* 2555 Sea Island Parkway *City:* Hunting Island *State:* SC *Zip:* 29920 *Phone:* 843-838-2011 *Email:* huntingisland@scprt.com *Visitors welcome?* Yes *Hours:* Monday through Sunday, 6 a.m. to 6 p.m. (9 p.m. during Daylight Savings Time) *Admission:* $4 adults, $2.50 seniors, $1.50 children six to 15, five and under FREE *Operated by:* South Carolina Dept. of Parks, Recreation and Tourism *NR?* Yes *NHL?* No *Year established/built:* 1859 *Latitude:* 32.3750 *Longitude:* -80.4383

MORRIS ISLAND LIGHTHOUSE

Established in 1673, the current Morris Island Lighthouse was constructed in 1876 to replace a light destroyed by Union troops in the Civil War. Erosion has slowly taken away the shoreline around the lighthouse, leaving the structure standing alone offshore. *Address:* Morris Island Light *City:* Charleston *State:* SC *Visitors welcome?* Yes *Hours:* Grounds only *Admission:* FREE *Operated by:* Save the Light *NR?* Yes *NHL?* No *Year established/built:* 1673 *Latitude:* 32.6953 *Longitude:* -79.8836

VERMONT

BURLINGTON BREAKWATER NORTH LIGHTHOUSE

Established in 1857 after the construction of a stone-crib breakwater, the current Burlington Breakwater North Lighthouse is a replica of the original wooden lighthouse. The replica was opened in 2004. *Address:* Burlington Harbor *City:* Burlington *State:* VT *Visitors welcome?* No *Operated by:* City of Burlington *NR?* No *NHL?* No *Year established/built:* 1857 *Latitude:* 44.42611 *Longitude:* -73.25166

BURLINGTON BREAKWATER SOUTH LIGHTHOUSE

Established in 1857 after the construction of a stone-crib breakwater, the current Burlington Breakwater South Lighthouse is a replica of the original wooden lighthouse. The replica was opened in 2004. *Address:* Burlington Harbor *City:* Burlington *State:* VT *Visitors welcome?* No *Operated by:* City of Burlington *NR?* No *NHL?* No *Year established/built:* 1857 *Latitude:* 44.42611 *Longitude:* -73.25166

COLCHESTER REEF LIGHTHOUSE

Established on a reef off Colchester Point in Lake Champlain, the Colchester Reef Lighthouse served until 1952, when it was purchased by the Shelburne Museum and moved to the museum site as one of several buildings in the museum's collection. *Address:* 5555 Shelburne Rd. *City:* Shelburne *State:* VT *Zip:* 05482 *Phone:* 802-985-3346 *Web:* www.shelburnemuseum.org *Email:* info@shelburnemuseum.org *Visitors welcome?* Yes *Hours:* Contact attraction directly *Admission:* Contact attraction directly *Operated by:* Shelburne Museum *NR?* No *NHL?* No *Year established/built:* 1871 *Latitude:* 44.37684 *Longitude:* -73.22851

ISLE LA MOTTE LIGHTHOUSE

Established in 1829, the current Isle La Motte Lighthouse is a cast-iron tower built in 1881 and decommissioned in 1933. The lighthouse was sold to a private party, although the tower is still an active aid to navigation. *Address:* Isle La Motte Light *City:* Isle La Motte *State:* VT *Visitors welcome?* No *Operated by:* Private owner *NR?* No *NHL?* No *Year established/built:* 1829 *Latitude:* 44.9065 *Longitude:* -73.3435

JUNIPER ISLAND LIGHTHOUSE

Established in 1826, the current Juniper Island Lighthouse was constructed in 1846 of cast-iron. In 1954, a skeletal tower replaced the cast-iron tower, and the lighthouse property was sold into private hands. *Address:* Juniper Island Light *City:* Burlington *State:* VT *Visitors welcome?* No *Operated by:* Private owner *NR?* No *NHL?* No *Year established/built:* 1826 *Latitude:* 44.4500 *Longitude:* -73.2763

WINDMILL POINT LIGHTHOUSE

Established as a private aid to navigation in 1830, the current stone Windmill Point Lighthouse was constructed in 1858. Replaced by a steel skeletal tower on the New York side of Lake Champlain, the Windmill Point Lighthouse was sold into private hands. *Address:* Windmill Point Light *City:* Alburg *State:* VT *Visitors welcome?* No *Operated by:* Private owner *NR?* No *NHL?* No *Year established/built:* 1830 *Latitude:* 44.9818 *Longitude:* -73.3418

VIRGIN ISLANDS

HAMS BLUFF LIGHTHOUSE

The Hams Bluff Lighthouse on St. Croix in the U.S. Virgin Islands is still an active aid to navigation. *Address:* Hams Bluff *City:* St. Croix *State:* VI *Visitors welcome?* Yes *Hours:* Grounds only *Admission:* FREE *Operated by:* U.S. Coast Guard (District 7) *NR?* No *NHL?* No *Year established/built:* 1915 *Latitude:* 17.7708 *Longitude:* -64.8726

VIRGINIA

ASSATEAGUE LIGHTHOUSE

Established in 1833, the current Assateague Lighthouse was constructed in 1967 and automated in 1965. The lighthouse is now within a wildlife refuge and the keepers house is used as ranger quarters. *Address:* Assateague Light *State:* VA *Phone:* 757-336-3696 *Web:* www.assateagueisland.com *Email:* webmaster@assateagueisland.com *Visitors welcome?* Yes *Hours:* Easter through Thanksgiving, Friday to Sunday, 9 a.m. to 3 p.m. *Admission:* $4 adults, $2 children aged two to 12 *Operated by:* Chincoteague Natural History Association *NR?* Yes *NHL?* No *Year established/built:* 1833 *Latitude:* 37.9111 *Longitude:* -75.3558

CAPE CHARLES LIGHTHOUSE

Established in 1828, the current 1895 skeletal tower lighthouse is the third lighthouse to stand on Smith Island. At 191 feet, the lighthouse is the tallest of its type in the U.S., and it is still an active aid to navigation. *Address:* Cape Charles Light *City:* Smith Island *State:* VA *Visitors welcome?* Yes *Hours:* Grounds only *Admission:* Grounds only *Operated by:* U.S. Coast Guard (District 5) *NR?* No *NHL?* No *Year established/built:* 1828 *Latitude:* 37.11981 *Longitude:* -75.90797

JONES POINT LIGHTHOUSE

Established and built in 1856, the Jones Point Lighthouse served until 1926, when the light was moved to a nearby steel skeletal tower. The obsolete structure was deeded to the Mount Vernon chapter of the Daughters of the American Revolution. The lighthouse is located in Jones Point Park. *Address:* Jones Point Light *City:* Alexandria *State:* VA *Visitors welcome?* Yes *Hours:* Grounds only *Admission:* FREE *Operated by:* Daughters of the American Revolution *NR?* Yes *NHL?* No *Year established/built:* 1856 *Latitude:* 38.7904 *Longitude:* -77.0406

NEW CAPE HENRY LIGHTHOUSE

Built in 1881 to replace an older brick tower, the New Cape Henry Lighthouse is constructed of cast-iron and it is still an active aid to navigation. Because the light sits on a military reservation, visiting it is difficult because of tight security. *Address:* Cape Henry Light *City:* Virginia Beach *State:* VA *Visitors welcome?* No *Operated by:* U.S. Coast Guard (District 5) *NR?* Yes *NHL?* Yes *Year established/built:* 1881 *Latitude:* 36.9256 *Longitude:* -76.0083

NEW POINT COMFORT LIGHTHOUSE

Established in 1801, the current New Point Comfort Lighthouse was constructed in 1806, automated in 1930, and deactivated in 1963. The tower was renovated in 1989, although only the grounds are open to the public. *Address:* New Point Comfort Light *City:* Bavon *State:* VA *Visitors welcome?* Yes *Hours:* Grounds only *Admission:* FREE *Operated by:* New

Point Comfort Lighthouse Preservation Task Forc *NR?* Yes *NHL?* No *Year established/built:* 1801 *Latitude:* 37.3006 *Longitude:* -76.2775

NEWPORT NEWS MIDDLE GROUND LIGHTHOUSE

Established in 1871, the current Newport News Middle Ground Lighthouse was constructed in the spark-plug style in 1891. Automated in 1954, it is still an active aid to navigation, although it is now privately owned. *Address:* Newport News Middle Ground Light *City:* Newport News *State:* VA *Visitors welcome?* No *Operated by:* Private owner *NR?* Yes *NHL?* No *Year established/built:* 1871 *Latitude:* 36.9452 *Longitude:* -76.3915

OLD CAPE HENRY LIGHTHOUSE

Established in 1792, the original Cape Henry Lighthouse was deactivated in 1881 and the light moved to a new lighthouse a few hundred feet to the east. The older structure is still standing, though it is on a military reservation and security is tight. *Address:* Old Cape Henry Light *City:* Virginia Beach *State:* VA *Visitors welcome?* No *Operated by:* U.S. Coast Guard (District 5) *NR?* Yes *NHL?* Yes *Year established/built:* 1792 *Latitude:* 36.9256 *Longitude:* -76.0083

OLD POINT COMFORT LIGHTHOUSE

Established in 1774, the current Old Point Comfort Lighthouse was constructed in 1802. The lighthouse sits on one of the most historic military bases in the country, and due to security concerns, access to the lighthouse is limited. *Address:* Old Point Comfort Light *City:* Hampton *State:* VA *Phone:* 757-788-2000 *Visitors welcome?* Yes *Hours:* Contact attraction directly *Admission:* Contact attraction directly *Operated by:* U.S. Coast Guard (District 5) *NR?* Yes *NHL?* No *Year established/built:* 1774 *Latitude:* 37.00178 *Longitude:* -76.30643

SMITH POINT LIGHTHOUSE

Established in 1802 after the Civil War, the current Smith Point Lighthouse, built in 1897, replaced lightships and on-shore structures going back to the early 19th century. The current caisson-style structure is still an active aid to navigation. *Address:* Smith Point Light *City:* Sunnybank *State:* VA *Visitors welcome?* No *Operated by:* Private owner *NR?* Yes *NHL?* No *Year established/built:* 1802 *Latitude:* 37.8800 *Longitude:* -76.1839

THIMBLE SHOAL LIGHTHOUSE

Established in 1870, the current Thimble Shoal Lighthouse was built in 1914 with the spark plug design. Automated in 1963 and still an active aid to navigation, the lighthouse is now privately owned. *Address:* Thimble Shoal Light *City:* Hampton *State:* VA *Visitors welcome?* No *Operated by:* Private owner *NR?* Yes *NHL?* No *Year established/built:* 1870 *Latitude:* 37.0146 *Longitude:* -76.2399

WOLF TRAP LIGHTHOUSE

Established in 1821 with lightships, the current Wolf Trap Lighthouse was constructed in the spark plug style in 1894. Automated in 1973 and still an active aid to navigation, the lighthouse is now privately owned. *Address:* Wolf Trap Light *City:* Mathews *State:* VA *Visitors welcome?* No *Operated by:* Private owner *NR?* Yes *NHL?* No *Year established/built:* 1821 *Latitude:* 37.3904 *Longitude:* -76.1897

Did you spot an error? Email your correction to contact@fyddeye.com.

CHAPTER 2

Great Lakes Lighthouses

Michigan Island (New) Lighthouse, Apostle Islands National Lakeshore, Wisconsin

Lighthouses you can visit today in the states of Illinois, Indiana, Michigan, Minnesota, New York (Lake Erie), Ohio, Pennsylvania (Lake Erie), and Wisconsin.

Use your smart phone QR or bar code reader to visit this Fyddeye web page.

FYDDEYE RECOMMENDS:	
Au Sable Point Lighthouse, Au Sable Point, Michigan	Port Washington Lighthouse, Port Washington, Wisconsin
Fort Gratiot Lighthouse, Port Huron, Michigan	Raspberry Island Lighthouse, Bayfield, Wisconsin
Marblehead Lighthouse, Marblehead, Ohio	Split Rock Lighthouse, Two Harbors, Minnesota
Old Mackinac Point Lighthouse, Mackinaw, Michigan	Whitefish Point Lighthouse, Paradise, Michigan

ILLINOIS

68TH ST. CRIB LIGHTHOUSE

Also called Dunne Crib. *Address:* Yacht Harbor *City:* Chicago *State:* IL *Visitors welcome?* No *Operated by:* Chicago Dept. of Water Management *NR?* No *NHL?* No *Latitude:* 41.77677 *Longitude:* -87.57357

CHICAGO HARBOR LIGHTHOUSE

Established in 1832, the current Chicago Harbor Lighthouse was constructed in 1893. Automated in 1979, the lighthouse is still an active aid to navigation. *Address:* Chicago Harbor Light *City:* Chicago *State:* IL *Visitors welcome?* No *Operated by:* U.S. Coast Guard (District 9) *NR?* Yes *NHL?* No *Year established/built:* 1832 *Latitude:* 41.88945 *Longitude:* -87.59055

CHICAGO HARBOR SOUTHEAST GUIDEWALL LIGHTHOUSE

Address: Navy Pier *City:* Chicago *State:* IL *Visitors welcome?* No *Operated by:* U.S. Coast Guard (District 9) *NR?* No *NHL?* No *Latitude:* 41.8919 *Longitude:* -87.6041

FOUR MILE CRIB LIGHTHOUSE

Address: Navy Pier *City:* Chicago *State:* IL *Visitors welcome?* No *Operated by:* Chicago Dept. of Water Management *NR?* No *NHL?* No *Latitude:* 41.89195 *Longitude:* -87.60413

GROSSE POINT LIGHTHOUSE

Established and built in 1873, the Grosse Point Lighthouse was deactivated in 1935. Now a private aid to navigation, the lighthouse is now operated as a museum. *Address:* 2601 Sheridan Road *City:* Evanston *State:* IL *Zip:* 58449 *Phone:* 847-328-6961 *Web:* www. grossepointlighthouse.net *Email:* lpdnhl@grossepointlighthouse.net *Visitors welcome?* Yes *Hours:* Contact attraction directly *Admission:* $6 adults; $3 children 8 to 12; under 8 FREE *Operated by:* Grosse Point Lighthouse Park District *NR?* No *NHL?* Yes *Year established/ built:* 1873 *Latitude:* 42.06427 *Longitude:* -87.67711

WAUKEGAN HARBOR LIGHTHOUSE

Address: Waukegan Harbor *City:* Waukegan *State:* IL *Visitors welcome?* Yes *Hours:* Grounds only *Admission:* FREE *Operated by:* U.S. Coast Guard (District 9) *NR?* No *NHL?* No *Latitude:* 42.36235 *Longitude:* -87.81114

WILLIAM E. DEVER CRIB LIGHTHOUSE

Address: Milton Lee Olive Park *City:* Chicago *State:* IL *Visitors welcome?* No *Operated by:* Chicago Dept. of Water Management *NR?* No *NHL?* No *Latitude:* 41.89395 *Longitude:* -87.61092

WILSON AVENUE CRIB LIGHTHOUSE

City: Chicago *State:* IL *Visitors welcome?* No *Operated by:* Chicago Dept. of Water Management *NR?* No *NHL?* No *Latitude:* 41.85003 *Longitude:* -87.65006

INDIANA

BUFFINGTON HARBOR BREAKWATER LIGHTHOUSE

The Buffington Harbor Breakwater Lighthouse sits on the end of a private breakwater marking the entrance to Buffington Harbor and historically, the site of large cement plants. Today, the area is in transition from industrial to residential and retail. *Address:* Buffington Harbor *City:* Gary *State:* IN *Visitors welcome?* No *Operated by:* City of Gary *NR?* No *NHL?* No *Year established/built:* 1927 *Latitude:* 41.64393 *Longitude:* -87.41532

CALUMET HARBOR LIGHTHOUSE

First lit in 1853, the Calumet Harbor Lighthouse went through several transitions before its final configuration in 1995. It marks the mouth of the Calumet River, which lies to the west in Illinois, even though the lighthouse is in Indiana. *Address:* Calumet Harbor *State:* IN *Visitors welcome?* No *Operated by:* U.S. Coast Guard (District 9) *NR?* No *NHL?* No *Year established/built:* 1853 *Latitude:* 41.73392 *Longitude:* -87.52393

GARY HARBOR BREAKWATER LIGHTHOUSE

The Gary Harbor Breakwater Light marks the entrance to an artificial harbor built by U.S. Steel in the early 20th century. The light itself was established in 1911. *Address:* Gary Harbor *City:* Gary *State:* IN *Visitors welcome?* No *Operated by:* U.S. Steel *NR?* No *NHL?* No *Year established/built:* 1911 *Latitude:* 41.6311 *Longitude:* -87.32002

INDIANA HARBOR EAST BREAKWATER LIGHTHOUSE

The Indiana Harbor Breakwater Lighthouse was constructed approximately 1930 to mark the entrance to the Indiana Harbor Canal and the heavy industry that lined the canal and the shores of Lake Michigan. *Address:* Indiana Harbor East Breakwater Light *City:* East

Chicago *State:* IN *Visitors welcome?* No *Operated by:* U.S. Coast Guard (District 9) *NR?* No *NHL?* No *Year established/built:* 1930 *Latitude:* 41.68083 *Longitude:* -87.44111

MICHIGAN CITY LIGHTHOUSES

Established in 1837, the Old Michigan City Lighthouse and the Michigan City East Pier-head Lighthouse were constructed in 1858 and 1904 respectively. The Old Michigan City Lighthouse is now a museum, while the pierhead light is still an active aid to navig *Address:* Michigan City East Light *City:* Michigan City *State:* IN *Visitors welcome?* No *Operated by:* U.S. Coast Guard (District 9) *NR?* Yes *NHL?* No *Year established/built:* 1837 *Latitude:* 41.7290 *Longitude:* -86.9117

Au Sable Point Lighthouse, Michigan

MICHIGAN

ALPENA LIGHTHOUSE

Established in 1877, the original wooden tower was destroyed by fire and replaced with a cast-iron skeletal tower in 1914. The light is affectionately known as Sputnik after its resemblance to the first satellite to orbit the earth. *Address:* Alpena Light *City:* Alpena *State:* MI *Visitors welcome?* No *Operated by:* U.S. Coast Guard (District 9) *NR?* Yes *NHL?* No *Year established/built:* 1875 *Latitude:* 45.06042 *Longitude:* -83.4229

AU SABLE POINT LIGHTHOUSE

✤ Established and built in 1874, the Au Sable Point Lighthouse was called Big Sable Lighthouse until 1910. Still a navigation aid, the lighthouse is now part of the Pictured Rocks National Lakeshore, and it is undergoing restoration by the National Park Service. *Address:* Au Sable Point *State:* **MI** *Phone:* 906-387-2607 *Web:* www.nps.gov/piro *Visitors welcome?* Yes *Hours:* Park Ranger-guided tours are available five days a week June, July, August and over the Labor Day weekend. *Admission:* **FREE** *Operated by:* Pictured Rocks National Lakeshore *NR?* Yes *NHL?* No *Year established/built:* 1874 *Latitude:* 46.6722 *Longitude:* -86.1418 **Accommodations for overnight and/or long-term stays available.**

BEAVER ISLAND HARBOR LIGHTHOUSE

The Beaver Island Harbor Lighthouse was established in 1856 and the original tower replaced in 1870. Automated in 1927, the tower is now owned by the local township. *Address:* Beaver Island Harbor Light *City:* Beaver Island *State:* MI *Zip:* 49782 *Visitors welcome?* No *Operated by:* St. James Township *NR?* No *NHL?* No *Year established/built:* 1856 *Latitude:* 45.74278 *Longitude:* -85.50861

Lighthouses of Michigan Tour Itinerary

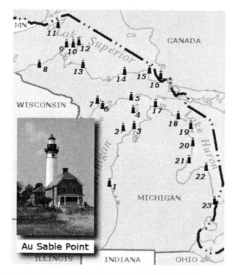

Au Sable Point

1. Big Sable Point (Ludington)
2. South Manitou Island
3. Grand Traverse (Northport)
4. Beaver Island
5. Seul Choix (Gulliver)
6. Peninsula Point (Rapid River)
7. Sand Point (Escanaba)
8. Ontonagon County (Ontonagon)
9. Sand Hill (Ahmeek)
10. Eagle Harbor (Eagle Harbor)
11. Rock Harbor (Isle Royale)
12. Copper Harbor (Copper Harbor)
13. Big Bay Point (Big Bay)
14. Au Sable Point (Grand Marais)
15. Whitefish Point (Paradise)
16. Point Iroquois (Brimley)
17. Old Mackinac Point (Mackinaw City)
18. Forty Mile Point (Rogers City)
19. New/Old Presque Isle (Presque Isle)
20. Sturgeon Point (Harrisville)
21. Tawas Point (East Tawas)
22. Pointe Aux Barques (Port Hope)
23. Fort Gratiot (Port Huron)

All the Great Lakes states are steeped in lighthouse history and lore, but Michigan features the most lighthouses of any state: 115. Begin a tour at Big Sable Point on Lake Michigan and follow U.S. Highway 31 north to Interstate 75. Cross the Mackinaw Bridge and head west on U.S. Highway 2 to Ontonagon. Backtrack to U.S. Highway 41 to Copper Harbor. Backtrack again on U.S. 41 and U.S. 2 and head south on I-75 across the Mackinaw Bridge. Find U.S. Highway 23 and head east, then south along with west shore of Lake Huron to Port Huron, almost the furthest point east of the Wolverine State.

BEAVER ISLAND LIGHTHOUSE

Established in 1851, the Beaver Island Lighthouse, also known as Beaver Head Lighthouse, was lit in 1858 and operated until 1962. It is now the site of an educational facility run by a local public school district. *Address:* Beaver Island Head Light *City:* Beaver Island *State:* MI *Phone:* 231-547-3200 *Visitors welcome?* Yes *Hours:* Contact attraction directly *Admission:* Contact attraction directly *Operated by:* Beaver Island Lighthouse School *NR?* Yes *NHL?* No *Year established/built:* 1851 *Latitude:* 45.57639 *Longitude:* -85.5725

Big Bay Point Lighthouse, Big Bay, Michigan

BIG BAY POINT LIGHTHOUSE

✦ Established and constructed in 1896, the Big Point Point Lighthouse was operational until 1961. In 1990, the facility was re-activated and is now operated as a bed and breakfast. *Address:* 3 Lighthouse Road *City:* Big Bay *State:* MI *Zip:* 49808 *Phone:* 906-345-9957 *Web:* www.bigbaylighthouse.com *Email:* keepers@BigBayLighthouse.com *Visitors welcome?* Yes *Hours:* Contact attraction directly *Admission:* Contact attraction directly *Operated by:* Big Bay Point Lighthouse Bed & Breakfast *NR?* Yes *NHL?* No *Year established/built:* 1896 *Latitude:* 46.8320 *Longitude:* -87.6851 **Accommodations for overnight and/or long-term stays available.**

BIG SABLE POINT LIGHTHOUSE

✦ Completed in 1867, Big Sable Point Lighthouse was encased in steel in 1902 after the brick tower began to deteriorate. The station was automated in 1968. Some tours are available in the summer. *Address:* Big Sable Point Light *City:* Ludington *State:* **MI** *Phone:* 231-845-7343 *Web:* www.splka.org *Email:* bsplka@t-one.net *Visitors welcome?* Yes *Hours:* Grounds only *Admission:* **FREE** *Operated by:* Sable Point Lightkeepers Association *NR?* Yes *NHL?* No *Year established/built:* 1867 *Latitude:* 44.05772 *Longitude:* -86.51444 **Accommodations for overnight and/or long-term stays available.**

BOIS BLANC ISLAND LIGHTHOUSE

Established in 1829, the current Bois Blanc Island Lighthouse was constructed in 1867 and operated until 1924. It is now privately owned. *Address:* Bois Blanc Island Light *City:* Bois Blanc *State:* **MI** *Visitors welcome?* No *Operated by:* Private owner *NR?* No *NHL?* No *Year established/built:* 1829 *Latitude:* 45.75086 *Longitude:* -84.45942

CEDAR RIVER LIGHTHOUSE

The tower no longer exists, but the keeper's dwelling still stands, now used as a private residence. *Address:* Big Cedar River *City:* Cedar River *State:* **MI** *Visitors welcome?* No *Operated by:* Private owner *NR?* No *NHL?* No *Latitude:* 45.41109 *Longitude:* -87.35456

CHARITY ISLAND LIGHTHOUSE

Established and built in 1857, the Charity Island Lighthouse is now owned by a private party. *Address:* Charity Island Light *State:* **MI** *Visitors welcome?* No *Operated by:* Private owner *NR?* No *NHL?* No *Year established/built:* 1857 *Latitude:* 44.03139 *Longitude:* -83.43556

CHARLEVOIX SOUTH PIER LIGHTHOUSE

Originally a wooden structure built in 1885, the current steel tower Charlevoix South Pierhead Lighthouse was constructed in 1948. It is still an active aid to navigation. *Address:* Charlevoix South Pier Light Station *City:* Charlevoix *State:* **MI** *Visitors welcome?* Yes *Hours:* Grounds only *Admission:* **FREE** *Operated by:* U.S. Coast Guard (District 9) *NR?* Yes *NHL?* No *Year established/built:* 1885 *Latitude:* 45.32278 *Longitude:* -85.26972

CHEBOYGAN CRIB LIGHTHOUSE

Established in 1852 and originally built on a crib (artificial island) in the Cheboygan River, the Cheboygan Crib Lighthouse is now relocated to the mouth of the Cheboygan River. It is no longer an active aid to navigation. *Address:* Cheboygan Crib Light *City:* Cheboygan *State:* **MI** *Visitors welcome?* Yes *Hours:* Grounds only *Admission:* **FREE** *Operated by:* City of Cheboygan *NR?* No *NHL?* No *Year established/built:* 1852 *Latitude:* 45.6568 *Longitude:* -84.4650

CHEBOYGAN RIVER FRONT RANGE LIGHTHOUSE

✢ The Cheboygan River Front Range Lighthouse was constructed in 1880, and it is still an active aid to navigation. The lighthouse is owned and operated by the Great Lakes Lighthouse Keepers Association. *Address:* Cheboygan River, Lake Huron *City:* Cheboygan *State:*

MI *Phone:* 231-436-5580 *Web:* www.gllka.com *Email:* info@gllka.com *Visitors welcome?* Yes *Hours:* Saturdays, Sundays, and holidays from Memorial Day through the second weekend of October *Admission:* Contact attraction directly *Operated by:* Great Lakes Lighthouse Keepers Association *NR?* No *NHL?* No *Year established/built:* 1880 *Latitude:* 45.6470 *Longitude:* -84.4745 **Accommodations for overnight and/or long-term stays available.**

CHRISTMAS RANGE LIGHTHOUSE
The Christmas Range Lighthouses, also known as the End of the Road Lighthouses, mark the channel between Trout Bay and South Bay near Munising. *Address:* State Highway 28 *City:* Christmas *State:* MI *Visitors welcome?* Yes *Hours:* Grounds only *Admission:* FREE *Operated by:* Hiawatha National Forest *NR?* No *NHL?* No *Latitude:* 46.4369 *Longitude:* -86.7015

COPPER HARBOR LIGHTHOUSE
Established in 1849, the current tower of the Copper River Lighthouse was constructed in 1866. The light was automated in 1919 and deactivated in 1933. The site is now owned by the state of Michigan and managed as an historic site. *Address:* Copper Harbor Light *City:* Copper Harbor *State:* MI *Phone:* 906-289-4966 *Visitors welcome?* Yes *Hours:* Contact attraction directly *Admission:* Contact attraction directly *Operated by:* Michigan Historical Museum System *NR?* No *NHL?* No *Year established/built:* 1849 *Latitude:* 47.4743 *Longitude:* -87.86014

COPPER HARBOR RANGE LIGHTHOUSES
Established in 1849, the current tower of the Copper River Lighthouse was constructed in 1866. The light was automated in 1919 and deactivated in 1933. The site is now owned by the state of Michigan and managed as an historic site. *Address:* Copper Harbor Front Range Light *City:* Copper Harbor *State:* MI *Phone:* 906-289-4966 *Visitors welcome?* Yes *Hours:* Contact attraction directly *Admission:* Contact attraction directly *Operated by:* Michigan Historical Museum System *NR?* No *NHL?* No *Year established/built:* 1849 *Latitude:* 47.48111 *Longitude:* -87.86667

CRISP POINT LIGHTHOUSE
✦ Established in built in 1904, the Crisp Point Lighthouse was deactivated in 1992. The station is maintained by a local not-for-profit. *Address:* Crisp Point Light *State:* MI *Phone:* 906-492-3206 *Web:* www.crisppointlighthouse.org *Visitors welcome?* Yes *Hours:* Daily, mid-June to September, noon to 5 p.m. *Admission:* Contact attraction directly *Operated by:* Crisp Point Light Historical Society *NR?* No *NHL?* No *Year established/built:* 1904 *Latitude:* 46.75288 *Longitude:* -85.25733 **Accommodations for overnight and/or long-term stays available.**

DETOUR REEF LIGHTHOUSE
✦ The DeTour Reef Lighthouse was established in 1847, and the existing tower was constructed in 1931. The light is located one mile offshore in the St. Mary's River, the connection between Lakes Huron and Superior. The light was automated in 1974, and

the structure is now operated by a not-for-profit, which offers tours and overnight stays. *State:* **MI** *Phone:* 906-493-6609 *Email:* drlps@drlps.com *Visitors welcome?* Yes *Hours:* By appointment *Admission:* Contact attraction directly *Operated by:* DeTour Reef Light Preservation Society *NR?* Yes *NHL?* No *Year established/built:* 1847 *Latitude:* 45.9489 *Longitude:* -83.9031 **Accommodations for overnight and/or long-term stays available.**

DETROIT RIVER LIGHTHOUSE

Established in 1875, the current Detroit River Lighthouse, also called the Bar Point Shoal Lighthouse, was built in 1885 and automated in 1979. *Address:* Detroit River *City:* Detroit *State:* **MI** *Visitors welcome?* No *Operated by:* U.S. Coast Guard (District 9) *NR?* Yes *NHL?* No *Year established/built:* 1875 *Latitude:* 42.35246 *Longitude:* -82.88361

EAGLE HARBOR LIGHTHOUSE

Established in 1851, the current Eagle Harbor Lighthouse was constructed in 1871. Automated in 1980, the light is still an active aid to navigation. The lighthouse is now a museum operated by a local historical society. *Address:* Eagle Harbor Light *City:* Eagle Harbor *State:* **MI** *Visitors welcome?* Yes *Hours:* Mid-June to early October *Admission:* $4 adults, children **FREE** *Operated by:* Keweenaw County Historical Society *NR?* Yes *NHL?* No *Year established/built:* 1851 *Latitude:* 47.45956 *Longitude:* -88.15903

EAGLE HARBOR RANGE LIGHTHOUSE

Address: Highway 26 *City:* Eagle Harbor *State:* **MI** *Visitors welcome?* No *Operated by:* Private owner *NR?* No *NHL?* No *Latitude:* 47.45824 *Longitude:* -88.16232

EAGLE RIVER LIGHTHOUSE

Established in 1854, the current Eagle River Lighthouse was built in 1974 and deactivated in 1908. Located on West Main Street in Eagle River, the structure is now privately owned. *Address:* Eagle River Light *City:* Eagle River *State:* **MI** *Visitors welcome?* No *Operated by:* Private owner *NR?* Yes *NHL?* No *Year established/built:* 1854 *Latitude:* 47.4137 *Longitude:* -88.29828

FORT GRATIOT LIGHTHOUSE

The oldest light station in Michigan, the current tower was constructed in 1829 and extended in the 1860s. The lighthouse is now operated by the Port Huron Museum. *Address:* Fort Gratiot Light *City:* Port Huron *State:* **MI** *Zip:* 48060 *Phone:* 810-455-0214 *Web:* www.phmuseum.org *Visitors welcome?* Yes *Hours:* May to October, Friday, Saturday, Sunday, Monday, 11 a.m. to 5 p.m. *Admission:* Contact attraction directly *Operated by:* Port Huron Museum *NR?* No *NHL?* No *Year established/built:* 1814 *Latitude:* 43.00611 *Longitude:* -82.42223

FORTY MILE POINT LIGHTHOUSE

✦ The Forty Mile Point Lighthouse was established and built in 1897 and automated in 1969. The site is now a museum. *Address:* Forty Mile Point Light *City:* Rogers City *State:*

MI *Web:* www.40milepointlighthouse.org *Email:* webmaster@40milepointlighthouse.org *Visitors welcome?* Yes *Hours:* Memorial Day to mid-October; Saturdays and Sundays, noon to 4 p.m. *Admission:* Contact attraction directly *Operated by:* 40 Mile Point Lighthouse Society *NR?* Yes *NHL?* No *Year established/built:* 1897 *Latitude:* 45.48667 *Longitude:* -83.91333 **Accommodations for overnight and/or long-term stays available.**

FOURTEEN FOOT SHOAL LIGHTHOUSE

Established and constructed in 1930, the Fourteen Foot Shoal Lighthouse is still an active aid to navigation. *Address:* Fourteen Foot Shoal Light *City:* Cheboygan *State:* MI *Visitors welcome?* No *Operated by:* U.S. Coast Guard (District 9) *NR?* Yes *NHL?* No *Year established/built:* 1930 *Latitude:* 45.6798 *Longitude:* -84.4350

FOURTEEN MILE POINT LIGHTHOUSE

Established and constructed in 1894, the Fourteen Mile Point Lighthouse was deactivated in 1934. *Address:* Fourteen Mile Point *City:* Ontonagon *State:* MI *Visitors welcome?* No *Operated by:* Private owner *NR?* No *NHL?* No *Year established/built:* 1894 *Latitude:* 46.9916 *Longitude:* -89.1168

FRANKFORT NORTH BREAKWATER LIGHTHOUSE

Established in 1873, the existing cast-iron Frankfort North Breakwater Lighthouse has operated since 1932. *Address:* Frankfort North Breakwater Light *City:* Frankfort *State:* MI *Visitors welcome?* Yes *Hours:* Grounds only *Admission:* FREE *Operated by:* U.S. Coast Guard (District 9) *NR?* Yes *NHL?* No *Year established/built:* 1873 *Latitude:* 44.6306 *Longitude:* -86.2522

FRYING PAN ISLAND

Formerly located on Frying Pan Island in the St. Mary's River, the Frying Pan Island lighthouse is now on the grounds of the Sault Ste. Marie Coast Guard Station. *Address:* 337 Water Street *City:* Sault Ste. Marie *State:* MI *Visitors welcome?* Yes *Hours:* Grounds only *Admission:* FREE *Operated by:* U.S. Coast Guard (District 9) *NR?* No *NHL?* No *Latitude:* 46.49899 *Longitude:* -84.33835

GRAND HAVEN LIGHTHOUSE

Established in 1839, the Grand Haven Lighthouse is actually two lights placed on a pier extending into Lake Michigan. The current inner and outer pier lights were constructed in 1905 and automated in 1969. *Address:* Grand Haven Light *City:* Grand Haven *State:* MI *Visitors welcome?* Yes *Hours:* Grounds only *Admission:* FREE *Operated by:* U.S. Coast Guard (District 9) *NR?* No *NHL?* No *Year established/built:* 1839 *Latitude:* 43.0570 *Longitude:* -86.2539

GRAND ISLAND EAST CHANNEL

The wood-frame Grand Island East Channel lighthouse was established and built in 1870. It was deactivated in 1913. Recent work on the lighthouse was supported by the East Channel Lights Rescue Project. *Address:* Grand Island East Channel Light *City:* Munising

State: **MI** *Visitors welcome?* No *Operated by:* Private owner *NR?* Yes *NHL?* No *Year established/built:* 1870 *Latitude:* 46.45017 *Longitude:* -86.62241

GRAND ISLAND NORTH LIGHTHOUSE
Established in 1854, the current Grand Island North Lighthouse, also called the Old North Lighthouse, was constructed in 1867 near the original site, which was high on a cliff. Automated in 1961, the property was sold to a private party in 1972. *Address:* Grand Island *City:* Munising *State:* **MI** *Visitors welcome?* No *Operated by:* Private owner *NR?* Yes *NHL?* No *Year established/built:* 1854 *Latitude:* 46.5255 *Longitude:* -86.6640

GRAND MARAIS RANGE LIGHTHOUSES
Established and built in 1908, the Grand Marais Range Lighthouses are still active aids to navigation. *Address:* Coast Guard Point *City:* Grand Marais *State:* **MI** *Zip:* 49839 *Visitors welcome?* Yes *Hours:* Grounds only *Admission:* **FREE** *Operated by:* U.S. Coast Guard (District 9) *NR?* No *NHL?* No *Year established/built:* 1908 *Latitude:* 46.6708 *Longitude:* -85.9852

GRAND TRAVERSE LIGHTHOUSE
✦ Established by the government in 1852, the current Grand Traverse Lighthouse was built in 1858. The station was automated in 1972, and then opened as a museum in 1986 inside Leelanau State Park. *Address:* Grand Traverse Light *State:* **MI** *Phone:* 231-386-7195 *Web:* www.grandtraverselighthouse.com *Email:* gtlthse@triton.net *Visitors welcome?* Yes *Hours:* Daily: May, noon to 4 p.m.; June to Labor Day, 10 a.m. to 4 p.m.; Labor Day to 10/31, noon to 4 p.m. *Admission:* $4 adults, $2 children six to 12, under six FREE *Operated by:* Grand Traverse Lighthouse *NR?* Yes *NHL?* No *Year established/built:* 1852 *Latitude:* 45.2100 *Longitude:* -85.5500 **Accommodations for overnight and/or long-term stays available.**

GRANITE ISLAND LIGHTHOUSE
Established and constructed in 1868, the Granite Island Lighthouse was automated in 1939. The lighthouse, now restored, is in private hands. *Address:* Granite Island *State:* **MI** *Web:* www.graniteisland.com *Email:* sholman@graniteisland.com *Visitors welcome?* No *Operated by:* Private owner *NR?* Yes *NHL?* No *Year established/built:* 1868 *Latitude:* 46.72076 *Longitude:* -87.41153

GRAVELLY SHOAL LIGHTHOUSE
Address: Gravelly Shoal Light *State:* **MI** *Visitors welcome?* No *Operated by:* U.S. Coast Guard (District 9) *NR?* No *NHL?* No *Latitude:* 44.01833 *Longitude:* -83.53722

GRAYS REEF LIGHTHOUSE
The U.S. Lighthouse Service established the Grays Reef Lighthouse in 1891, and rebuilt the tower in 1936. The art-deco structure was automated in 1976. *Address:* Grays Reef *State:* **MI** *Visitors welcome?* No *Operated by:* U.S. Coast Guard (District 9) *NR?* Yes *NHL?* No *Year established/built:* 1891 *Latitude:* 45.77417 *Longitude:* -85.17535

GROSSE ILE NORTH CHANNEL RANGE LIGHTHOUSE
Established in 1894, the current Grosse Ile North Channel Range Front Lighthouse was constructed in 1906 and deactivated in 1963. *Address:* Grosse Ile Island *City:* Grosse Ile *State:* MI *Visitors welcome?* Yes *Hours:* Contact attraction directly *Admission:* Contact attraction directly *Operated by:* Grosse Ile Historical Society *NR?* Yes *NHL?* No *Year established/built:* 1894 *Latitude:* 42.12532 *Longitude:* -83.15826

GULL ROCK LIGHTHOUSE
Established and built in 1867, the light was later automated and the structures turned over to the Michigan Lighthouse Conservancy and the Gull Rock Lighthouse Keepers, which is working to restore the buildings. *Address:* Gull Rock Light *City:* Grant *State:* MI *Visitors welcome?* No *Operated by:* Gull Rock Lighthouse Keepers *NR?* Yes *NHL?* No *Year established/built:* 1867 *Latitude:* 47.4172 *Longitude:* -87.6636

HARBOR BEACH LIGHTHOUSE
Also known as Sand Beach Lighthouse, Harbor Beach Lighthouse was established in 1858, and the current cast-iron structure was completed in 1885. The tower was automated in 1968, and a local not-for-profit is working to restore the building and open it for *Address:* Harbor Beach Light *City:* Harbor Beach *State:* MI *Visitors welcome?* No *Operated by:* Harbor Beach Lighthouse Preservation Society *NR?* Yes *NHL?* No *Year established/built:* 1858 *Latitude:* 43.8333 *Longitude:* -82.6167

HARSENS ISLAND REAR RANGE LIGHTHOUSE
Address: Harsens Island, St. Clair River *City:* Harsens Island *State:* MI *Visitors welcome?* No *Operated by:* Private owner *NR?* No *NHL?* No *Latitude:* 44.31485 *Longitude:* -85.60236

HOLLAND HARBOR LIGHTHOUSE
Established in 1872, the current 1936 Holland Harbor Lighthouse was constructed on a pier that extends into Lake Michigan. Automated in 1970, the lighthouse is now owned by the Holland Harbor Lighthouse Historical Commission. *Address:* Holland Harbor Light *City:* Macatawa *State:* MI *Visitors welcome?* Yes *Hours:* Grounds only *Admission:* FREE *Operated by:* Private owner *NR?* Yes *NHL?* No *Year established/built:* 1872 *Latitude:* 42.77269 *Longitude:* -86.21242

HURON ISLAND LIGHTHOUSE
Established in 1868, the Huron Island Lighthouse was first lit in 1871 and has been in continuous operation since, although it was automated in 1972. It is now located in a wildlife refuge in Lake Superior. *Address:* Lighthouse Island *State:* MI *Visitors welcome?* Yes *Hours:* Grounds only *Admission:* FREE *Operated by:* Huron National Wildlife Refuge *NR?* Yes *NHL?* No *Year established/built:* 1868 *Latitude:* 46.96242 *Longitude:* -87.99957

ISLE ROYALE LIGHTHOUSE

Established and built in 1875, the Isle Royale Lighthouse, formerly known as the Menagerie Island Lighthouse, was automated in 1913. It is now located within Isle Royale National Park. *Address:* Isle Royale Light *City:* Houghton *State:* MI *Visitors welcome?* Yes *Hours:* Grounds only *Admission:* FREE *Operated by:* U.S. Coast Guard (District 9) *NR?* Yes *NHL?* No *Year established/built:* 1875 *Latitude:* 47.9479 *Longitude:* -88.7612

JACOBSVILLE LIGHTHOUSE

✦ Established in 1856, the current Jacobsville Lighthouse, also called the Portage River Lighthouse, was constructed in 1870. The station was deactivated in 1900 and is now operated as a bed and breakfast. *Address:* 38741 Jacobs St. *City:* Lake Linden *State:* MI *Phone:* 906-523-4137 *Web:* www.jacobsvillelighthouse.com *Email:* mditty23@netzero.com *Visitors welcome?* Yes *Hours:* Open year round *Admission:* Contact attraction directly *Operated by:* Jacobsville Lighthouse Inn *NR?* No *NHL?* No *Year established/built:* 1856 *Latitude:* 46.97953 *Longitude:* -88.4140 **Accommodations for overnight and/or long-term stays available.**

KEWEENAW WATERWAY LOWER ENTRANCE LIGHTHOUSE

Established in 1868, the current Keweenaw Waterway Lighthouse was constructed in 1920 and automated in 1973. The lighthouse is still an active aid to navigation. *Address:* Portage Lake *City:* Jacobsville *State:* MI *Visitors welcome?* No *Operated by:* U.S. Coast Guard (District 9) *NR?* No *NHL?* No *Year established/built:* 1868 *Latitude:* 46.98076 *Longitude:* -88.41013

KEWEENAW WATERWAY UPPER ENTRANCE LIGHTHOUSE

Address: Keweenaw Waterway *City:* Houghton *State:* MI *Visitors welcome?* No *Operated by:* U.S. Coast Guard (District 9) *NR?* No *NHL?* No *Latitude:* 47.1136 *Longitude:* -88.52165

LAKE ST. CLAIR LIGHTHOUSE

Address: Lake St. Clair *City:* St. Clair Shores *State:* MI *Visitors welcome?* No *Operated by:* U.S. Coast Guard (District 9) *NR?* No *NHL?* No *Latitude:* 42.49741 *Longitude:* -82.89636

LANSING SHOAL LIGHTHOUSE

Established in 1900, the current structure replaced a lightship in 1928. The lighthouse was automated in 1976. *Address:* Beaver Island *State:* MI *Visitors welcome?* No *Operated by:* U.S. Coast Guard (District 9) *NR?* Yes *NHL?* No *Year established/built:* 1900 *Latitude:* 45.7447 *Longitude:* -85.5213

LITTLE SABLE POINT LIGHTHOUSE

✦ Established in 1874, the tower was once white-washed, then sandblasted clean after it was automated in 1955. *Address:* Little Sable Point Light *State:* MI *Phone:* 231-845-7343 *Web:* www.splka.org *Email:* bsplka@t-one.net *Visitors welcome?* Yes *Hours:* Grounds only *Admission:* FREE *Operated by:* Sable Point Lightkeepers Association *NR?* Yes *NHL?* No

Year established/built: 1874 *Latitude:* 43.65167 *Longitude:* -86.53889 **Accommodations for overnight and/or long-term stays available.**

LITTLE TRAVERSE LIGHTHOUSE

The Little Traverse Lighthouse is located in a gated community. *Address:* Little Traverse Light *City:* Harbor Springs *State:* **MI** *Visitors welcome?* No *Operated by:* Private owner *NR?* No *NHL?* No *Latitude:* 45.41889 *Longitude:* -84.97833

LUDINGTON NORTH BREAKWATER LIGHTHOUSE

✦ Built of steel in 1924 to resemble the prow of a ship, the North Ludington Breakwater Lighthouse was established in 1871. The structure was renovated by the U.S. Coast Guard in 1993. *Address:* Ludington Light *City:* Ludington *State:* **MI** *Phone:* 231-845-7343 *Web:* www.splka.org *Email:* bsplka@t-one.net *Visitors welcome?* Yes *Hours:* Grounds only *Admission:* **FREE** *Operated by:* Sable Point Lightkeepers Association *NR?* Yes *NHL?* No *Year established/built:* 1924 *Latitude:* 43.9536 *Longitude:* -86.4694 **Accommodations for overnight and/or long-term stays available.**

MANISTEE LIGHTHOUSE

Established in 1875, the current Manistee North Pierhead Lighthouse was built in 1927 and automated the same year. The lighthouse is located on the end of a pier that marks the entrance to the Manistee River. *Address:* Manistee Pierhead Lights *City:* Manistee *State:* **MI** *Visitors welcome?* Yes *Hours:* Grounds only *Admission:* **FREE** *Operated by:* U.S. Coast Guard (District 9) *NR?* Yes *NHL?* No *Year established/built:* 1875 *Latitude:* 44.2517 *Longitude:* -86.3464

Manistique East Breakwater Lighthouse, Manistique, Michigan

MANISTIQUE EAST BREAKWATER LIGHTHOUSE

Located on the end of a breakwater at the mouth of the Manistique River, the concrete Manistique Breakwater East Breakwater Lighthouse was constructed in 1915 and automated in 1969. *Address:* Manistique East Breakwater Light *City:* Manistique *State:* MI *Visitors welcome?* Yes *Hours:* Grounds only *Admission:* FREE *Operated by:* U.S. Coast Guard (District 9) *NR?* Yes *NHL?* No *Year established/built:* 1913 *Latitude:* 45.9446 *Longitude:* -86.2472

MANITOU ISLAND LIGHTHOUSE

Established in 1850, the current skeletal tower structure was built in 1861. The light was automated in 1978 and is now owned by a local land conservancy. *Address:* Manitou Island Light *City:* Hancock *State:* MI *Phone:* 906-482-0820 *Email:* evanmcdonald@keweenaw-landtrust.org *Visitors welcome?* Yes *Hours:* Grounds only *Admission:* Contact attraction directly *Operated by:* Keweenaw Land Trust *NR?* Yes *NHL?* No *Year established/built:* 1850 *Latitude:* 45.0072 *Longitude:* -86.0939

MARQUETTE BREAKWATER LIGHTHOUSE

City: Marquette *State:* MI *Visitors welcome?* Yes *Hours:* Grounds only *Admission:* FREE *Operated by:* U.S. Coast Guard (District 9) *NR?* No *NHL?* No *Latitude:* 46.5336 *Longitude:* -87.3753

MARQUETTE HARBOR LIGHTHOUSE

Established in 1853, the current Marquette Harbor Lighthouse was constructed in 1866 with a second story added in 1909. Still an active aid to navigation, the lighthouse is now managed by the Marquette Maritime Museum. *Address:* Marquette Harbor Light *City:* Marquette *State:* MI *Zip:* 49855 *Phone:* 906-226-2006 *Web:* mqtmaritimemuseum.com *Email:* mqtmaritimemuseum@yahoo.com *Visitors welcome?* Yes *Hours:* Contact attraction directly *Admission:* Contact attraction directly *Operated by:* Marquette Maritime Museum *NR?* Yes *NHL?* No *Year established/built:* 1853 *Latitude:* 46.5468 *Longitude:* -87.3763

MARTIN REEF LIGHTHOUSE

The Martin Reef Lighthouse was established and built in 1927 and it is still an active aid to navigation. *City:* Port Dolomite *State:* MI *Visitors welcome?* No *Operated by:* U.S. Coast Guard (District 9) *NR?* Yes *NHL?* No *Year established/built:* 1927 *Latitude:* 45.9847 *Longitude:* -84.2750

MCGULPIN POINT LIGHTHOUSE

Established in 1869, the McGulpins Point Lighthouse was deactivated in 1906 after construction of the nearby Mackinac Point Lighthouse in 1892. *Address:* McGulpin Point Light *City:* Mackinaw City *State:* MI *Visitors welcome?* No *Operated by:* Private owner *NR?* No *NHL?* No *Year established/built:* 1869 *Latitude:* 45.7869 *Longitude:* -84.7722

MENDOTA LIGHTHOUSE

Established in 1870, the Mendota Lighthouse, also known as the Bete Grise Lighthouse, marks the Mendota Ship Channel from Bete Grise Bay to Lac La Belle. The current tower was constructed in 1895 and the light was deactivated in 1960. *City:* Lac La Belle *State:* MI *Visitors welcome?* No *Operated by:* Private owner *NR?* Yes *NHL?* No *Year established/built:* 1870 *Latitude:* 47.37455 *Longitude:* -87.96294

MENOMINEE NORTH PIER LIGHTHOUSE

Established in 1877, the current Menominee North Pier Lighthouse was constructed in 1927 and automated in 1972. *Address:* Menominee Pier Light *City:* Menominee *State:* MI *Visitors welcome?* Yes *Hours:* Grounds only *Admission:* FREE *Operated by:* U.S. Coast Guard (District 9) *NR?* No *NHL?* No *Year established/built:* 1877 *Latitude:* 45.1000 *Longitude:* -87.5833

MIDDLE ISLAND LIGHTHOUSE

✦ Established and built in 1905, the Middle Island Lighthouse is still an operational aid to navigation. The tower is operated by the Friends of Middle Island Lighthouse, while the keeper's house is owned and operated by the Middle Island Lightkeepers Association. *Address:* Middle Island *City:* Alpena *State:* MI *Visitors welcome?* Yes *Hours:* Contact attraction directly *Admission:* Contact attraction directly *Operated by:* Friends of Middle Island Lighthouse *NR?* Yes *NHL?* No *Year established/built:* 1905 *Latitude:* 45.1925 *Longitude:* -83.3272 **Accommodations for overnight and/or long-term stays available.**

MIDDLE NEEBISH RANGE LIGHTHOUSE

Also called the Lower Nicolet Range Lighthouse, the Middle Neebish Lighthouse marks the entrance to the Middle Neebish Channel near Richards Landing. *Address:* Neebish Island *State:* MI *Visitors welcome?* No *Operated by:* U.S. Coast Guard (District 9) *NR?* No *NHL?* No *Latitude:* 46.3185 *Longitude:* -84.1707

MINNEAPOLIS SHOAL LIGHTHOUSE

Built in 1935, the concrete tower of Minneapolis Shoal Lighthouse was automated in 1979. *Address:* Minneapolis Shoal *City:* Delta *State:* MI *Visitors welcome?* No *Operated by:* U.S. Coast Guard (District 9) *NR?* Yes *NHL?* No *Year established/built:* 1935 *Latitude:* 45.5800 *Longitude:* -86.9987

MUNISING RANGE LIGHTHOUSES

Established in 1908, the Munising Range Lighthouses front range facility is now offices for the Pictured Rocks National Lakeshore. The smaller rear range light is about two blocks of the front range light. *Address:* 604 W. Munising Ave. *City:* Munising *State:* MI *Zip:* 49822 *Phone:* 906-387-2607 *Visitors welcome?* Yes *Hours:* Grounds only *Admission:* FREE *Operated by:* Pictured Rocks National Lakeshore *NR?* No *NHL?* No *Year established/built:* 1908 *Latitude* 46.414963 *Longitude* - 86.661835

MUSKEGON SOUTH BREAKWATER LIGHTHOUSE

Established in 1851, the current tower of the Muskegon South Breakwater Lighthouse was built in 1903. The tower is one of three lights that mark the channel from Lake Michigan to Lake Muskegon. *Address:* Muskegon Breakwater Light *City:* Muskegon *State:* MI *Visitors welcome?* Yes *Hours:* Grounds only *Admission:* FREE *Operated by:* U.S. Coast Guard (District 9) *NR?* Yes *NHL?* No *Year established/built:* 1851 *Latitude:* 43.2241 *Longitude:* -86.3471

NORTH MANITOU SHOAL LIGHTHOUSE

Constructed in 1935 to replace a series of lightships at its location, the North Manitou Shoal Lighthouse was automated in 1980. *Address:* Manitou Island *State:* MI *Visitors welcome?* No *Operated by:* U.S. Coast Guard (District 9) *NR?* Yes *NHL?* No *Year established/built:* 1935 *Latitude:* 47.40941 *Longitude:* -87.60587

OLD MACKINAC POINT LIGHTHOUSE

The castle-like structure, whose design is unique in the Great Lakes, has been restored to its 1910 appearance. *Address:* 526 North Huron Avenue *City:* Mackinaw City *State:* MI *Zip:* 49701 *Phone:* 231-436-4100 *Web:* www.mackinacparks.com *Email:* cottonl@ michigan.gov *Visitors welcome?* Yes *Hours:* Daily, contact attraction directly for specifics *Admission:* $6 adults; $3.50 youths five to 17; children four and under FREE *Operated by:* Mackinac State Historic Parks *NR?* Yes *NHL?* No *Year established/built:* 1890 *Latitude:* 45.7780 *Longitude:* -84.7264

OLD MISSION POINT LIGHTHOUSE

✦ Established and built in 1870, the Old Mission Point Lighthouse is no longer an active aid to navigation. Visitors are permitted to stay overnight with advance reservations. *Address:* Mission Point Light *State:* MI *Phone:* 231-223-7322 *Visitors welcome?* Yes *Hours:* Contact attraction directly *Admission:* Contact attraction directly *Operated by:* Peninsula Township *NR?* Yes *NHL?* No *Year established/built:* 1870 *Latitude:* 44.9913 *Longitude:* -85.4795 **Accommodations for overnight and/or long-term stays available.**

ONTONAGON LIGHTHOUSE

Established in 1852, the Ontonagon Lighthouse was active until 1964. It is now operated as an historic site by a local historical society. *Address:* 422 River Street *City:* Ontonagen *State:* MI *Zip:* 49953 *Phone:* 906-884-6165 *Visitors welcome?* Yes *Hours:* By appointment *Admission:* Contact attraction directly *Operated by:* Ontonagon County Historical Society *NR?* Yes *NHL?* No *Year established/built:* 1852 *Latitude:* 46.87186 *Longitude:* -89.31593

ONTONAGON PIERHEAD LIGHTHOUSE

Established in 1852, the Ontonagen Pierhead Lighthouse marks the entrance to the Ontonagon River. *Address:* Ontonagon River *City:* Ontonagen *State:* MI *Zip:* 49953 *Visitors welcome?* No *Operated by:* U.S. Coast Guard (District 9) *NR?* No *NHL?* No *Year established/built:* 1852 *Latitude:* 46.87598 *Longitude:* -89.32606

PASSAGE ISLAND LIGHTHOUSE

Established and constructed in 1882, the Passage Island Lighthouse was automated in 1978. The site is now part of Isle Royale National Park. *Address:* Passage Island *State:* MI *Visitors welcome?* Yes *Hours:* Grounds only *Admission:* FREE *Operated by:* U.S. Coast Guard (District 9) *NR?* Yes *NHL?* No *Year established/built:* 1885 *Latitude:* 48.23348 *Longitude:* -88.3509

PECHE ISLAND LIGHTHOUSE

Originally standing in Lake St. Clair, the Peche Island Lighthouse, also called the Peche Island Rear Range Light, is now in Marine City along the St. Clair riverfront. *Address:* Peche Island Light *City:* Marine City *State:* MI *Visitors welcome?* Yes *Hours:* Grounds only *Admission:* FREE *Operated by:* City of Marine City *NR?* No *NHL?* No *Year established/built:* 1908 *Latitude:* 42.71948 *Longitude:* -82.49213

PENINSULA POINT LIGHTHOUSE

Constructed in 1865, the Peninsula Point Lighthouse operated until 1936. It is now part of the Hiawatha National Forest. *Address:* Peninsula Point Light *State:* MI *Phone:* 906-786-4062 *Visitors welcome?* Yes *Hours:* Grounds only *Admission:* FREE *Operated by:* Hiawatha National Forest *NR?* Yes *NHL?* No *Year established/built:* 1865 *Latitude:* 45.6682 *Longitude:* -86.9666

PENTWATER/PORTAGE LAKE PIERHEAD LIGHTHOUSE

A pair of lights marks the entrance to a short channel leading to Pentwater Lake. *City:* Pentwater *State:* MI *Visitors welcome?* Yes *Hours:* Grounds only *Admission:* FREE *Operated by:* U.S. Coast Guard (District 9) *NR?* No *NHL?* No *Latitude:* 43.78225 *Longitude:* -86.44386

PETOSKEY PIERHEAD LIGHTHOUSE

The Petoskey Pierhead Light marks the breakwater at Petoskey, Mich. *City:* Petoskey *State:* MI *Visitors welcome?* Yes *Hours:* Grounds only *Admission:* FREE *Operated by:* U.S. Coast Guard (District 9) *NR?* No *NHL?* No *Latitude:* 45.3802 *Longitude:* -84.9617

PIPE ISLAND LIGHTHOUSE

Address: Pipe Island *State:* MI *Visitors welcome?* No *Operated by:* Private owner *NR?* No *NHL?* No *Latitude:* 46.01724 *Longitude:* -83.8989

POE REEF LIGHTHOUSE

Established in 1893, the current Poe Reef Lighthouse was constructed in 1929 on a site formerly marked by lightships. The lighthouse was automated in 1974. *Address:* Poe Reef Light *State:* MI *Visitors welcome?* No *Operated by:* U.S. Coast Guard (District 9) *NR?* Yes *NHL?* No *Year established/built:* 1893 *Latitude:* 45.6870 *Longitude:* -84.44367

POINT BETSIE LIGHTHOUSE

✛ Established and built in 1858, the Point Betsie Lighthouse is still operational, though it was automated in 1983. The lighthouse is operated as a museum by a local not-for-profit organization. *Address:* Point Betsie Light *City:* Frankfort *State:* MI *Zip:* 49034 *Phone:* 231-352-4915 *Email:* info@pointbetsie.org *Visitors welcome?* Yes *Hours:* Contact attraction directly *Admission:* $2 adults, $1 children under 12 *Operated by:* Friends of Point Betsie Lighthouse *NR?* Yes *NHL?* No *Year established/built:* 1858 *Latitude:* 44.6913 *Longitude:* -86.2552 **Accommodations for overnight and/or long-term stays available.**

POINT IROQUOIS LIGHTHOUSE

Established in 1855, the current tower of the Point Iroqouis Lighthouse was built in 1871 and operated until 1971. The site is now within the Hiawatha National Forest. *Address:* 12942 West Lakeshore Drive *City:* Brimley *State:* MI *Phone:* 906-786-4062 *Visitors welcome?* Yes *Hours:* Grounds only *Admission:* FREE *Operated by:* Hiawatha National Forest *NR?* Yes *NHL?* No *Year established/built:* 1855 *Latitude:* 46.48163 *Longitude:* -84.62832

POINT SANILAC LIGHTHOUSE

Established and built in 1866, the Port Sanilac Lighthouse is still an operational aid to navigation. *Address:* Cherry Street and South Lake Street *City:* Port Sanilac *State:* MI *Visitors welcome?* No *Operated by:* Private owner *NR?* No *NHL?* No *Year established/built:* 1866 *Latitude:* 43.4287 *Longitude:* -82.5405

POINTE AUX BARQUES LIGHTHOUSE

Established in 1848, the current Pointe aux Barques Lighthouse was built in 1857 and automated in 1958. The facility is now a public park and museum, and it is operated by a local not-for-profit organization. *Address:* Pointe aux Barques Light *City:* Port Hope *State:* MI *Email:* info@pointeauxbarqueslighthouse.org *Visitors welcome?* Yes *Hours:* Daily, Memorial Day weekend to Oct. 1 *Admission:* Contact attraction directly *Operated by:* Point aux Barques Lighthouse Society *NR?* Yes *NHL?* No *Year established/built:* 1848 *Latitude:* 44.02334 *Longitude:* -82.79334

PORT AUSTIN REEF LIGHTHOUSE

Established in 1878, the current Port Austin Reef Lighthouse was constructed the same year. The lighthouse is still an active aid to navigation. *Address:* Port Austin Light *City:* Port Austin *State:* MI *Visitors welcome?* No *Operated by:* U.S. Coast Guard (District 9) *NR?* No *NHL?* No *Year established/built:* 1878 *Latitude:* 44.08333 *Longitude:* -82.98333

POVERTY ISLAND LIGHTHOUSE

Established and built in 1874, the Poverty Island Lighthouse operated until 1976. It was reactivated in 1982 with an automated aid to navigation. *Address:* Poverty Island *State:* MI *Visitors welcome?* No *Operated by:* U.S. Coast Guard (District 9) *NR?* Yes *NHL?* No *Year established/built:* 1874 *Latitude:* 45.52749 *Longitude:* -86.66457

PRESQUE ISLE (NEW) LIGHTHOUSE

The Presque Isle (New) Lighthouse was established in 1840, with the newer of the peninsula's two lighthouses constructed in 1871. The station is now operated by a not-for-profit organization. *Address:* 4500 E. Grand Lake Road *City:* Presque Isle *State:* MI *Web:* www.keepershouse.org *Email:* neilsbungalow@yahoo.com *Visitors welcome?* Yes *Hours:* Contact attraction directly *Admission:* Contact attraction directly *Operated by:* Presque Isle Township Museum Society *NR?* Yes *NHL?* No *Year established/built:* 1840 *Latitude:* 45.35445 *Longitude:* -83.49021

PRESQUE ISLE (OLD) LIGHTHOUSE

The Presque Isle (Old) Lighthouse was established and built in 1840. It was deactivated in 1870 and a replacement built in 1871 a short distance north. The station is now operated by a not-for-profit organization. *Address:* 4500 E. Grand Lake Road *City:* Presque Isle *State:* MI *Web:* www.keepershouse.org *Email:* neilsbungalow@yahoo.com *Visitors welcome?* Yes *Hours:* Contact attraction directly *Admission:* Contact attraction directly *Operated by:* Presque Isle Township Museum Society *NR?* Yes *NHL?* No *Year established/built:* 1840 *Latitude:* 45.35445 *Longitude:* -83.49021

PRESQUE ISLE HARBOR BREAKWATER LIGHTHOUSE

Address: Presque Isle Harbor *City:* Marquette *State:* MI *Visitors welcome?* Yes *Hours:* Grounds only *Admission:* FREE *Operated by:* U.S. Coast Guard (District 9) *NR?* No *NHL?* No *Latitude:* 46.57397 *Longitude:* -87.37495

PRESQUE ISLE RANGE LIGHTHOUSES

The Presque Isle Front Range Lighthouse was restored by a private party and is now located in Presque Isle Range Light Park. The rear range light is at its original location off Grand Lake Road. *Address:* E. Grand Lake Road *City:* Presque Isle *State:* MI *Visitors welcome?* Yes *Hours:* Grounds only *Admission:* FREE *Operated by:* Private owner *NR?* No *NHL?* No *Latitude:* 45.2832 *Longitude:* -83.4619

ROCK HARBOR LIGHTHOUSE

Established in 1858, the Rock Harbor Lighthouse was deactivated in 1879 by the Lighthouse Service. The structure is now part of the Isle Royale National Park, and it is accessible only by boat. *Address:* Rock Harbor *City:* Isle Royale *State:* MI *Visitors welcome?* Yes *Hours:* Grounds only *Admission:* FREE *Operated by:* Isle Royale National Park *NR?* No *NHL?* No *Year established/built:* 1858 *Latitude:* 47.99587 *Longitude:* -88.90929

ROCK OF AGES LIGHTHOUSE

The Rock of Ages Lighthouse was established on an exposed rock in Lake Superior in 1908. It was automated in 1978 and its original Fresnel lens is now on display at Windigo Information Station at Indigo National Park. *Address:* Rock of Ages Light *State:* MI

Visitors welcome? No *Operated by:* U.S. Coast Guard (District 9) *NR?* Yes *NHL?* No *Year established/built:* 1908 *Latitude:* 47.86639 *Longitude:* -89.31458

ROUND ISLAND LIGHTHOUSE

Established and built in 1892, the Round Island Lighthouse is no longer operational, and it is now a private residence. *Address:* Round Island *City:* DeTour *State:* MI *Visitors welcome?* No *Operated by:* Private owner *NR?* Yes *NHL?* No *Year established/built:* 1892 *Latitude:* 45.9953 *Longitude:* -84.01463

ROUND ISLAND LIGHTHOUSE

Established and built in 1895, the Round Island Lighthouse operated until 1947, and it was relit in 1996. *Address:* Round Island Light *City:* Mackinac Island *State:* MI *Visitors welcome?* Yes *Hours:* Grounds only *Admission:* FREE *Operated by:* U.S. Coast Guard (District 9) *NR?* No *NHL?* No *Year established/built:* 1895 *Latitude:* 45.83717 *Longitude:* -84.61659

ROUND ISLAND PASSAGE LIGHTHOUSE

One of the newer lighthouses in the nation's inventory, Round Island Passage lighthouse was established and *constructed* in 1948 and automated in 1973. *Address:* Mackinac Island *City:* Mackinac Island *State:* MI *Visitors welcome?* No *Operated by:* U.S. Coast Guard (District 9) *NR?* No *NHL?* No *Year established/built:* 1948 *Latitude:* 45.84918 *Longitude:* -84.61894

SAGINAW RIVER REAR RANGE LIGHTHOUSE

Established and constructed in 1876, the Saginaw River Rear Range Lighthouse and its companion front range light replaced an earlier light station built in 1841. The deactivated range lighthouses are now owned by the Dow Chemical Company. *Address:* Saginaw River Rear Range Light *City:* Bay City *State:* MI *Visitors welcome?* No *Operated by:* Saginaw River Marine Historical Society *NR?* Yes *NHL?* No *Year established/built:* 1876 *Latitude:* 43.6355 *Longitude:* -83.85056

SAND HILLS LIGHTHOUSE

✛ Established and built in 1919, the yellow brick Sand Hills Lighthouse was deactivated in 1954. It is now operated as a bed and breakfast. *Address:* Sand Hills Light *State:* MI *Zip:* 49901 *Phone:* 906-337-1744 *Web:* www.sandhillslighthouseinn.com *Visitors welcome?* Yes *Hours:* Contact attraction directly *Admission:* Contact attraction directly *Operated by:* Sand Hills Lighthouse Inn *NR?* Yes *NHL?* No *Year established/built:* 1919 *Latitude:* 47.39195 *Longitude:* -88.37042 **Accommodations for overnight and/or long-term stays available.**

SAND POINT (BARAGA) LIGHTHOUSE

Established in 1878, the Sand Point Lighthouse, also known as the Baraga Lighthouse, was constructed the same year. The light is now deactivated. *Address:* Sand Point *City:* Baraga *State:* MI *Visitors welcome?* Yes *Hours:* Grounds only *Admission:* FREE *Operated by:*

Keeweenaw Bay Indian Community *NR?* Yes *NHL?* No *Year established/built:* 1878 *Latitude:* 46.7816 *Longitude:* -88.47096

SAND POINT (ESCANABA) LIGHTHOUSE

Established and built in 1867, the Sand Point (Escanaba) Lighthouse was deactivated in 1939. It is now operated as a museum. *Address:* Sand Point *City:* Escanaba *State:* MI *Phone:* 906-789-6790 *Web:* www.deltahistorical.org/lighthouse.htm *Email:* deltacountyhistsoc@ sbcglobal.net *Visitors welcome?* Yes *Hours:* June, July, and August: 9 a.m. to 5 p.m.; September: 1 p.m. to 5 p.m. *Admission:* Contact attraction directly *Operated by:* Delta County Historical Society *NR?* Yes *NHL?* No *Year established/built:* 1867 *Latitude:* 45.74358 *Longitude:* -87.04153

SEUL CHOIX POINTE LIGHTHOUSE

Established in 1892, the Seul Choix Pointe Lighthouse was constructed three years later. The light is still an active aid to navigation, and the facility is operated as a museum by a local historical society. *Address:* Seul Choix Point *City:* Gulliver *State:* MI *Phone:* 906-283-3183 *Web:* www.greatlakelighthouse.com *Email:* seulchoix@reiters.net *Visitors welcome?* Yes *Hours:* Daily, Memorial Day to mid-October, 10 a.m to 6 p.m. *Admission:* Contact attraction directly *Operated by:* Gulliver Historical Society *NR?* Yes *NHL?* No *Year established/built:* 1892 *Latitude:* 45.92165 *Longitude:* -85.91094

SKILLAGALEE ISLAND LIGHTHOUSE

Established in 1850, the Skillagelee Lighthouse, also known as the Ile Aux Galets Lighthouse, was constructed in 1888. *Address:* Skillagallee Island Light Station *State:* MI *Visitors welcome?* No *Operated by:* U.S. Coast Guard (District 9) *NR?* No *NHL?* No *Year established/built:* 1850 *Latitude:* 45.6764 *Longitude:* -85.17313

SOUTH FOX ISLAND LIGHTHOUSES

Established in 1867, two lighthouses sit on the southern tip of South Fox Island, one a brick structure, the other a skeletal metal tower. The lights were deactivated in 1934. *Address:* South Fox Island *State:* MI *Visitors welcome?* Yes *Hours:* Grounds only *Admission:* FREE *Operated by:* Michigan Dept. of Natural Resources *NR?* No *NHL?* No *Year established/built:* 1867 *Latitude:* 45.39916 *Longitude:* -85.83008

SOUTH HAVEN SOUTH PIER LIGHTHOUSE

Established in 1872, the current South Haven Lighthouse was constructed on the end of a pier in 1903. *Address:* South Haven Light *City:* South Haven *State:* MI *Visitors welcome?* No *Operated by:* U.S. Coast Guard (District 9) *NR?* No *NHL?* No *Year established/built:* 1872 *Latitude:* 42.40222 *Longitude:* -86.28445

SOUTH MANITOU ISLAND LIGHTHOUSE

Established in 1839, the current lighthouse tower was constructed in 1872. The lighthouse was discontinued in 1958 and incorporated in the Sleeping Bear Dunes National

Lakeshore. *Address:* South Manitou Island Light *State:* MI *Phone:* 231-326-5134 *Visitors welcome?* Yes *Hours:* Grounds only *Admission:* FREE *Operated by:* Sleeping Bear Dunes National Lakeshore *NR?* Yes *NHL?* No *Year established/built:* 1839 *Latitude:* 45.0072 *Longitude:* -86.0939

SPECTACLE REEF LIGHTHOUSE

Established and built in 1867, the Spectacle Reef Lighthouse is described as the best specimen of monolithic stone masonry in the U.S. Still an active aid to navigation, the light was automated in 1972. *Address:* Spectacle Reef Light *State:* MI *Visitors welcome?* No *Operated by:* U.S. Coast Guard (District 9) *NR?* Yes *NHL?* No *Year established/built:* 1870 *Latitude:* 45.7732 *Longitude:* -84.1367

SQUAW ISLAND LIGHTHOUSE

Established and constructed in 1892, the Squaw Island Lighthouse is no longer operational and is now a private residence. *Address:* Squaw Island *State:* MI *Visitors welcome?* No *Operated by:* Private owner *NR?* No *NHL?* No *Year established/built:* 1892 *Latitude:* 46.03946 *Longitude:* -83.90418

ST. CLAIR FLATS OLD CHANNEL RANGE LIGHTHOUSE

Established in 1859, the two range lights were automated in 1970 and transferred to a not-for-profit, which is attempting to restore them. *City:* St. Clair Flats *State:* MI *Visitors welcome?* Yes *Hours:* By appointment *Admission:* Contact attraction directly *Operated by:* Save Our South Channel Lights *NR?* Yes *NHL?* No *Year established/built:* 1859 *Latitude:* 42.5959 *Longitude:* -82.6327

ST. HELENA ISLAND LIGHTHOUSE

✦ Established and built in 1873, the St. Helena Lighthouse was automated in 1922. It is now owned and operated by the Great Lakes Lighthouse Keepers Association as an educational facility. Visitors are welcome to visit the lighthouse at any time by boat or snowmobile (in the winter), but the lighthouse is open only when a volunteer is in residence, usually from mid-June through mid-August. GLLKA also offers boat trips to the island several times a year for a fee. *City:* St. Ignace *State:* MI *Phone:* 231-436-5580 *Email:* info@gllka.com *Visitors welcome?* Yes *Hours:* By appointment *Admission:* Contact attraction directly *Operated by:* Great Lakes Lighthouse Keepers Association *NR?* Yes *NHL?* No *Year established/built:* 1873 *Latitude:* 45.8583 *Longitude:* -84.8708 **Accommodations for overnight and/or long-term stays available.**

ST. JOSEPH NORTH PIER LIGHTS

Established in 1832, the St. Joseph North Pier Lighthouses are today a pair of range rights built in 1906 and 1907. They are still active aids to navigation. *Address:* St. Joseph River *City:* St. Joseph *State:* MI *Visitors welcome?* Yes *Hours:* Grounds only *Admission:* FREE *Operated by:* U.S. Coast Guard (District 9) *NR?* No *NHL?* No *Year established/built:* 1832 *Latitude:* 42.1158 *Longitude:* -86.49365

ST. MARTIN ISLAND LIGHTHOUSE

Constructed in 1905 with a unique hexagonal shape, the St. Martin Island Lighthouse has since been deactivated and is now owned by a Native American tribe. *Address:* St. Martin Island *State:* MI *Visitors welcome?* No *Operated by:* Little Traverse Bay Band of Odawa Indians *NR?* Yes *NHL?* No *Year established/built:* 1905 *Latitude:* 45.5042 *Longitude:* -86.7590

STANNARD ROCK LIGHTHOUSE

Stannard Rock Lighthouse was constructed in 1882, 34 years after it was discovered by a ship that wrecked on it. The station was automated by the U.S. Coast Guard after a gas explosion killed one Coast Guardsman and hurt two others. The lighthouse is still an active aid to navigation. *Address:* Stannard Rock Light *State:* MI *Zip:* 49855 *Phone:* 906-226-2006 *Web:* mqtmaritimemuseum.com *Email:* mqtmaritimemuseum@yahoo.com *Visitors welcome?* No *Operated by:* Marquette Maritime Museum *NR?* Yes *NHL?* No *Year established/built:* 1882 *Latitude:* 47.18351 *Longitude:* -87.22511

STURGEON POINT LIGHTHOUSE

Established and constructed in 1869, the Sturgeon Point Lighthouse is still an active aid to navigation and is now operated by a local historical society. *Address:* Sturgeon Point Light *City:* Harrisville *State:* MI *Phone:* 989-724-6297 *Web:* theenchantedforest.com/AlconaHistoricalSociety/ *Visitors welcome?* Yes *Hours:* Memorial Day through September, Monday to Thursday, 12 p.m. to 3 p.m., Saturday and Sunday, 11 a.m. to 4 p.m.; Tower open 12 p.m to 3 p.m. Friday, Saturday and Sunday *Admission:* Contact attraction directly *Operated by:* Alcona Historical Society *NR?* Yes *NHL?* No *Year established/built:* 1869 *Latitude:* 44.7127 *Longitude:* -83.27272

TAWAS POINT LIGHTHOUSE

✦ Established in 1853, the current Tawas Point Lighthouse was constructed in 1876. Tawas Point has been called the Cape Cod of the West, and the tower was an important part of the development of transportation on Lake Huron. *Address:* Tawas Point Light *City:* East Tawas *State:* MI *Zip:* 48730 *Phone:* 989 362 5041 *Visitors welcome?* Yes *Hours:* Grounds only, tower in season *Admission:* FREE *Operated by:* Michigan Dept. of Natural Resources *NR?* Yes *NHL?* No *Year established/built:* 1853 *Latitude:* 44.2540 *Longitude:* -83.4490 **Accommodations for overnight and/or long-term stays available.**

THUNDER BAY ISLAND LIGHTHOUSE

Established and built in 1832, the Thunder Bay Island Lighthouse was automated in 1980. In 1997, a local not-for-profit leased the property from the U.S. Coast Guard, and it is now in the process of restoring the structures. *Address:* Thunder Bay Island *City:* Alpena *State:* MI *Visitors welcome?* Yes *Hours:* By appointment *Admission:* Contact attraction directly *Operated by:* Thunder Bay Island Lighthouse Preservation Society *NR?* Yes *NHL?* No *Year established/built:* 1832 *Latitude:* 45.0417 *Longitude:* -83.2000

WAUGOSHANCE LIGHTHOUSE

Established in 1832, the current tower was built in 1851. The lighthouse is no longer operational, though a local historical society is working to restore it. *Address:* Waugoshance Light *City:* Mackinaw City *State:* MI *Web:* www.waugoshance.org *Email:* info@ waugoshance.org *Visitors welcome?* No *Operated by:* Waugoshance Lighthouse Preservation Society *NR?* Yes *NHL?* No *Year established/built:* 1832 *Latitude:* 45.7862 *Longitude:* -85.0912

WHITE RIVER LIGHTHOUSE

Established and built in 1875, the White River Lighthouse was automated in 1945 and deactivated in 1960. It is now managed by a not-for-profit as a museum. *Address:* 6199 Murray Road *City:* Whitehall *State:* MI *Zip:* 49461 *Phone:* 231-894-8265 *Web:* www.whiteriverlightstation.org *Visitors welcome?* Yes *Hours:* Grounds only, tower in season *Admission:* Contact attraction directly *Operated by:* White River Light Station Museum *NR?* No *NHL?* No *Year established/built:* 1875 *Latitude:* 43.3728 *Longitude:* -86.4226

WHITE SHOAL LIGHTHOUSE

Established in 1891, the current White Shoal Lighthouse tower was first lit in 1910. The light is still an active aid to navigation. *Address:* White Shoal Light *State:* MI *Visitors welcome?* No *Operated by:* U.S. Coast Guard (District 9) *NR?* Yes *NHL?* No *Year established/built:* 1891 *Latitude:* 45.8417 *Longitude:* -85.1349

Whitefish Point Lighthouse, Paradise, Michigan

WHITEFISH POINT LIGHTHOUSE

✦ Established in 1848, the current skeletal metal tower was constructed in 1861. The lighthouse was automated in 1870 and operations turned over to the Great Lakes Shipwreck Historical Society, which invites guests for overnight stays in the keepers quarters. *Address:* Whitefish Point Light *City:* Paradise *State:* **MI** *Zip:* 49768 *Phone:* 888-492-3747 *Web:* www.shipwreckmuseum.com *Visitors welcome?* Yes *Hours:* Contact attraction directly *Admission:* Contact attraction directly *Operated by:* Great Lakes Shipwreck Historical Society *NR?* Yes *NHL?* No *Year established/built:* 1848 *Latitude:* 46.7706 *Longitude:* -84.9567 **Accommodations for overnight and/or long-term stays available.**

WINDMILL POINT LIGHTHOUSE

The Windmill Point Lighthouse marks the entrance to the Detroit River from Lake St. Clair. *Address:* Windmill Point *City:* Detroit *State:* **MI** *Visitors welcome?* Yes *Hours:* Grounds only *Admission:* **FREE** *Operated by:* U.S. Coast Guard (District 9) *NR?* No *NHL?* No *Latitude:* 42.35782 *Longitude:* -82.92992

MINNESOTA

DULUTH HARBOR NORTH BREAKWATER LIGHTHOUSE

Established in 1908, the cast-iron tower of the Duluth Harbor North Breakwater Lighthouse was finished in 1910. The light remains an active aid to navigation. *Address:* Duluth Harbor *City:* Duluth *State:* **MN** *Visitors welcome?* Yes *Hours:* Grounds only *Admission:* **FREE** *Operated by:* U.S. Coast Guard (District 9) *NR?* No *NHL?* No *Year established/built:* 1908 *Latitude:* 46.72189 *Longitude:* -92.04332

DULUTH HARBOR SOUTH BREAKWATER INNER LIGHTHOUSE

Established in 1889, the current skeletal tower of the Duluth Harbor South Breakwater Inner Lighthouse was completed in 1901. The light is still an active aid to navigation. *Address:* South Lake Avenue *City:* Duluth *State:* **MN** *Visitors welcome?* Yes *Hours:* Grounds only *Admission:* **FREE** *Operated by:* U.S. Coast Guard (District 9) *NR?* No *NHL?* No *Year established/built:* 1889 *Latitude:* 46.77785 *Longitude:* -92.09238

DULUTH HARBOR SOUTH BREAKWATER OUTER LIGHTHOUSE

Established in 1874 on a new breakwater for the port of Duluth, the Duluth Harbor South Breakwater Outer Lighthouse guides mariners through some of the thickest and most persistent fogs in the world. The current tower was completed in 1901. *Address:* South Lake Avenue *City:* Duluth *State:* **MN** *Visitors welcome?* Yes *Hours:* Grounds only *Admission:* **FREE**

Operated by: U.S. Coast Guard (District 9) *NR?* No *NHL?* No *Year established/built:* 1874 *Latitude:* 46.7775 *Longitude:* -92.0917

GRAND MARAIS LIGHTHOUSE

Established in 1885, the Grand Marais Lighthouse marks the entrance to the small Grand Marais harbor on the north shore of Lake Superior. *Address:* Grand Marais Harbor *City:* Grand Marais *State:* MN *Visitors welcome?* Yes *Hours:* Grounds only *Admission:* **FREE** *Operated by:* U.S. Coast Guard (District 9) *NR?* No *NHL?* No *Year established/built:* 1885 *Latitude:* 47.75045 *Longitude:* -90.33427

MINNESOTA POINT LIGHTHOUSE

Established in 1858, the Minnesota Point Lighthouse was abandoned in 1885. Only a portion of the tower remains. *Address:* Minnesota Point *City:* Duluth *State:* MN *Visitors welcome?* Yes *Hours:* Grounds only *Admission:* **FREE** *Operated by:* U.S. Army Corps of Engineers (Duluth) *NR?* No *NHL?* No *Year established/built:* 1858 *Latitude:* 46.73071 *Longitude:* -92.05222

SPLIT ROCK LIGHTHOUSE

Completed by the U.S. Lighthouse Service in 1910, Split Rock Lighthouse was soon one of Minnesota's best known landmarks. Restored to its 1920s appearance, the lighthouse offers a glimpse of lighthouse life in this remote and spectacular setting. *Address:* 3713 Split Rock Lighthouse Rd *City:* Two Harbors *State:* MN *Zip:* 55616 *Phone:* 218-226-6372 *Web:* www.mnhs.org/places/sites/srl/ *Email:* splitrock@mnhs.org *Visitors welcome?* Yes *Hours:* Daily, May 15 to October 15, 10 a.m. to 6 p.m.; Thursdays to Mondays, 11 a.m. to 4 p.m. (Visitor Center only) *Admission:* Contact attraction directly *Operated by:* Minnesota Historical Society *NR?* Yes *NHL?* Yes *Year established/built:* 1910 *Latitude:* 47.02271 *Longitude:* -91.67073

TWO HARBORS BREAKWATER LIGHTHOUSE

City: Two Harbors *State:* MN *Visitors welcome?* Yes *Hours:* Grounds only *Admission:* **FREE** *Operated by:* U.S. Coast Guard (District 9) *NR?* No *NHL?* No *Latitude:* 47.01058 *Longitude:* -91.66958

TWO HARBORS LIGHTHOUSE

✛ Constructed in 1892, the Two Harbors Lighthouse is now operated as a bed and breakfast by the Lake County Historical Society. The light is still an active aid to navigation. *Address:* Two Harbors Light *City:* Two Harbors *State:* MN *Zip:* 55616 *Phone:* 218-834-4814 *Web:* www.lighthousebb.org *Email:* lakehist@lakenet.com *Visitors welcome?* Yes *Hours:* Contact attraction directly *Admission:* Contact attraction directly *Operated by:* Lighthouse Bed & Breakfast *NR?* Yes *NHL?* No *Year established/built:* 1892 *Latitude:* 47.01402 *Longitude:* -91.66355 **Accommodations for overnight and/or long-term stays available.**

NEW YORK

BARCELONA LIGHTHOUSE
Also called the Portland Harbor Lighthouse, the Barcelona Lighthouse was built in 1829 to serve cargo and passenger vessels traveling between Erie, Penn. and Buffalo. The tower was constructed of fieldstone around a wooden framework. *Address:* State Highway 5 *City:* Barcelona *State:* NY *Visitors welcome?* No *Operated by:* Private owner *NR?* Yes *NHL?* No *Year established/built:* 1829 *Latitude:* 42.3408 *Longitude:* -79.5950

BRADDOCK POINT LIGHTHOUSE
✦ Established and built in 1896, the Braddock Point Lighthouse was deactivated in 1954 and is now a private residence. *Address:* Braddock Point Light *City:* Davison Beach *State:* NY *Visitors welcome?* No *Operated by:* Private owner *NR?* No *NHL?* No *Year established/built:* 1896 *Latitude:* 43.3411 *Longitude:* -77.7625 **Accommodations for overnight and/or long-term stays available.**

BUFFALO INTAKE CRIB LIGHTHOUSE
Mariners in Lake Erie needed better markers of the treacherous shoals and reefs near Buffalo. Engineers determined that the area around Horseshoe Reef was a good location, but it was on the Canadian side of the international border. After years of diplomacy, the lighthouse was located at its current location. *Address:* Buffalo Harbor *City:* Buffalo *State:* NY *Visitors welcome?* No *Operated by:* City of Buffalo *NR?* No *NHL?* No *Year established/built:* 1856 *Latitude:* 42.8967 *Longitude:* -78.8937

BUFFALO MAIN LIGHTHOUSE
Established in 1818, the current Buffalo Lighthouse was constructed in 1833 and deactivated in 1914. It is now managed by a local not-for-profit organization. *Address:* Buffalo Harbor *City:* Buffalo *State:* NY *Visitors welcome?* No *Operated by:* U.S. Coast Guard (District 9) *NR?* Yes *NHL?* No *Year established/built:* 1818 *Latitude:* 42.89671 *Longitude:* -78.89367

BUFFALO SOUTH ENTRANCE NORTH SIDE LIGHTHOUSE
The Buffalo South Entrance North Side lighthouse and its companion South Side lighthouse were constructed in 1903, and they guided grain and lumber ships into the bustling Buffalo harbor. The North Side Lighthouse was decommissioned in 1988. *Address:* Point Gratiot *City:* Dunkirk *State:* NY *Zip:* 14048 *Phone:* 716-366-5050 *Email:* LST551@juno.com *Visitors welcome?* Yes *Hours:* Contact attraction directly *Admission:* Contact attraction directly *Operated by:* Dunkirk Lighthouse & Veterans Park Museum *NR?* No *NHL?* No *Year established/built:* 1903 *Latitude:* 42.4937 *Longitude:* -79.3542

BUFFALO SOUTH ENTRANCE SOUTH SIDE LIGHTHOUSE
Completed in 1903, the Buffalo South Entrance South Side Lighthouse guards the shoreline near the Lackawanna Steel Plant, one of the largest and most historic steel facilities in

the country. The U.S. Coast Guard deactivated the lighthouse in 1935. *City:* Buffalo *State:* NY *Visitors welcome?* Yes *Hours:* By appointment *Admission:* Grounds open, tower closed *Operated by:* U.S. Coast Guard (District 9) *NR?* No *NHL?* No *Year established/built:* 1903 *Latitude:* 42.8864 *Longitude:* -78.8784

CAPE VINCENT BREAKWATER LIGHTHOUSE

Built in 1907 to replace a pair of post lights, the Cape Vincent Breakwater Lighthouse was constructed on the end of a breakwater that the keeper could reach by holding on to a lifeline during stormy periods. *Address:* Market Street *City:* Cape Vincent *State:* NY *Visitors welcome?* Yes *Hours:* Daily *Admission:* FREE *Operated by:* Village of Cape Vincent *NR?* No *NHL?* No *Year established/built:* 1907 *Latitude:* 44.1244 *Longitude:* -76.3355

CROSSOVER ISLAND LIGHTHOUSE

Established in 1842, the current Crossover Island Lighthouse was built in 1882 and deactivated in 1941. *Address:* Crossover Island *City:* Oak Point *State:* NY *Visitors welcome?* No *Operated by:* Private owner *NR?* No *NHL?* No *Year established/built:* 1848 *Latitude:* 44.4961 *Longitude:* -75.7781

EAST CHARITY SHOAL LIGHTHOUSE

Established in 1929, the East Charity Shoal Lighthouse structure was built in 1877, and originally served as the Vermillion Lighthouse. The East Charity station is still an active aid to navigation. *Address:* East Charity Shoal Light *City:* Cape Vincent *State:* NY *Visitors welcome?* No *Operated by:* U.S. Coast Guard (District 9) *NR?* No *NHL?* No *Year established/built:* 1929 *Latitude:* 44.0481 *Longitude:* -76.4758

FORT NIAGARA LIGHTHOUSE

Established in 1782, the current Fort Niagara Lighthouse was built in 1872 and deactivated in 1993. It is now part of Fort Niagara National Historic Landmark. *Address:* Fort Niagara Light *City:* Youngstown *State:* NY *Phone:* 716-745-7611 *Visitors welcome?* Yes *Hours:* Daily, 9 a.m. to 5 p.m. *Admission:* $10 adults; $6 children 6 to 12; Under six, FREE *Operated by:* Old Fort Niagara Association *NR?* Yes *NHL?* No *Year established/built:* 1782 *Latitude:* 43.2617 *Longitude:* -79.0633

GALLOO ISLAND LIGHTHOUSE

Established in 1820, the current Galloo Island Lighthouse was constructed in 1867 and automated in 1963. It is no longer an active aid to navigation. *Address:* Galloo Island Light *City:* Galloo Island *State:* NY *Visitors welcome?* No *Operated by:* Private owner *NR?* Yes *NHL?* No *Year established/built:* 1820 *Latitude:* 43.8883 *Longitude:* -76.4450

GRAND ISLAND FRONT RANGE LIGHTHOUSE

First used by the Seneca tribe for hunting and fishing, Grand Island became a getaway for the wealthy in the late 19th century. *Address:* 503 East River Road *City:* Grand Island

State: NY *Zip:* 14072 *Phone:* 716-773-7629 *Email:* jim@buffalolaunchclub.com *Visitors welcome?* Yes *Hours:* By appointment *Admission:* FREE with permission *Operated by:* Buffalo Launch Club *NR?* No *NHL?* No *Year established/built:* 1917 *Latitude:* 42.9756 *Longitude:* -78.9466

HORSE ISLAND LIGHTHOUSE

Established in 1831, the current Horse Island Lighthouse, also called the Sacketts Harbor Lighthouse, was constructed in 1870 and deactivated in 1957. It is now privately owned. *Address:* Horse Island Light *City:* Sackets Harbor *State:* NY *Visitors welcome?* No *Operated by:* Private owner *NR?* No *NHL?* No *Year established/built:* 1831 *Latitude:* 43.9431 *Longitude:* -76.1444

HORSESHOE REEF LIGHTHOUSE

Growing commerce in the eastern end of Lake Erie led to needs for a more extensive set of navigation aids, including a lighthouse on Horseshoe Reef, built in 1856. Horseshoe Reef was abandoned in 1930 and is now in ruins. *Address:* Lake Erie *City:* Buffalo *State:* NY *Visitors welcome?* No *Operated by:* U.S. Coast Guard (District 9) *NR?* No *NHL?* No *Year established/built:* 1856 *Latitude:* 42.0669 *Longitude:* -81.3399

OAK ORCHARD HARBOR LIGHTHOUSE

The Oak Orchard Harbor Lighthouse, sometimes called the Point Breeze Lighthouse, is a replica of an 1871 lighthouse that stood on a pier in the Oak Orchard River. The replica is next to the river in Point Breeze. *City:* Point Breeze *State:* NY *Phone:* 585-752-0647 *Web:* www.oakorchardlighthouse.com *Email:* OOOTL@aol.com *Visitors welcome?* Yes *Operated by:* Oak Orchard Lighthouse Museum *NR?* No *NHL?* No *Year established/built:* 2010 *Latitude:* 43.3701 *Longitude:* -78.1903

OGDENSBURG HARBOR LIGHTHOUSE

Established and built in 1834, the Ogdensburg Harbor Lighthouse is no longer an active aid to navigation and privately owned. *Address:* Ogdensburg Harbor Light *City:* Ogdensburg *State:* NY *Visitors welcome?* No *Operated by:* Private owner *NR?* No *NHL?* No *Year established/built:* 1834 *Latitude:* 44.6978 *Longitude:* -75.5033

OLCOTT LIGHTHOUSE

The Olcott Lighthouse is a 2003 replica of an historic lighthouse that guided ships into Olcott Harbor starting in 1873. *Address:* Lockport-Olcott Road *City:* Newfane *State:* NY *Phone:* 716-778-8531 *Visitors welcome?* Yes *Hours:* Daily *Admission:* FREE *Operated by:* Town of Newfane *NR?* No *NHL?* No *Year established/built:* 1873 *Latitude:* 43.2802 *Longitude:* -78.7069

OSWEGO HARBOR WEST PIERHEAD LIGHTHOUSE

Established in 1822, the current Oswego Harbor West Pierhead Lighthouse was built in 1924. Automated in 1968, it is still an active aid to navigation. *Address:* Oswego Harbor

West Pierhead Light *City:* Oswego *State:* NY *Visitors welcome?* No *Operated by:* U.S. Coast Guard (District 9) *NR?* Yes *NHL?* No *Year established/built:* 1934 *Latitude:* 43.4733 *Longitude:* -76.5168

PORT OF GENESSEE LIGHTHOUSE
Established and built in 1822, the Port of Genessee Lighthouse, also called the Charlotte-Genessee Lighthouse, was deactivated in 1881 and relighted in 1992. *Address:* 70 Lighthouse St. *City:* Rochester *State:* NY *Zip:* 14612 *Phone:* 585-621-6179 *Visitors welcome?* Yes *Hours:* May to October, Saturday and Sunday, 1 p.m. to 5 p.m. *Admission:* Donation requested *Operated by:* Charlotte-Genesee Lighthouse Historical Society *NR?* Yes *NHL?* No *Year established/built:* 1822 *Latitude:* 43.2529 *Longitude:* -77.6109

ROCHESTER HARBOR LIGHTHOUSE
First constructed in 1822 on a bluff overlooking Rochester Harbor on Lake Ontario, the lighthouse was moved to a pier extending into the lake in 1838, although the lighthouse on the bluff operated until 1881. The modern tower was on the pier in 1995. *Address:* Port of Rochester *City:* Rochester *State:* NY *Web:* www.geneseelighthouse.org *Visitors welcome?* Yes *Hours:* Daily *Admission:* FREE *Operated by:* U.S. Coast Guard (District 9) *NR?* No *NHL?* No *Year established/built:* 1822 *Latitude:* 43.25623 *Longitude:* -77.60744

ROCK ISLAND LIGHTHOUSE
Established in 1848, the current Rock Island Lighthouse was built in 1882 and deactivated in the 1930s and is now within a state park. *City:* Fishers Landing *State:* NY *Visitors welcome?* Yes *Hours:* Tower closed *Admission:* Tower closed *Operated by:* New York State Office of Parks, Recreation and Historic Preservation *NR?* Yes *NHL?* No *Year established/built:* 1848 *Latitude:* 44.2764 *Longitude:* -76.0080

SELKIRK LIGHTHOUSE
✦ Established and built in 1838, the Selkirk Lighthouse, also called the Salmon River Lighthouse, was automated in 1989 and is a private aid to navigation. *Address:* 6 Lake Road Ext *City:* Richland *State:* NY *Zip:* 13114 *Phone:* 315-298-6688 *Web:* www.salmonriverlighthousemarina.com *Visitors welcome?* Yes *Hours:* Contact attraction directly *Admission:* Contact attraction directly *Operated by:* Salmon River Lighthouse Marina *NR?* Yes *NHL?* No *Year established/built:* 1838 *Latitude:* 43.5763 *Longitude:* -76.2024 **Accommodations for overnight and/or long-term stays available.**

SODUS OUTER LIGHTHOUSE
First settled by Europeans in 1792, Sodus Bay is a the largest natural harbor on Lake Ontario. By 1824, a lighthouse was established on the bay to guide growing maritime traffic. A new structure was built in 1871. *Address:* Sodus Outer Light *City:* Sodus Point *State:* NY *Visitors welcome?* Yes *Hours:* No public access to structure, pier open *Admission:* No public access to structure, pier open *Operated by:* Sodus Bay Historical Society *NR?* No *NHL?* No *Year established/built:* 1901 *Latitude:* 43.2767 *Longitude:* -76.9750

SODUS POINT LIGHTHOUSE
First settled by Europeans in 1792, Sodus Bay is a the largest natural harbor on Lake Ontario. By 1824, a lighthouse was established on the bay to guide growing maritime traffic. *Address:* 7606 N. Ontario St. *City:* Sodus Point *State:* NY *Zip:* 14555 *Phone:* 315-483-4936 *Web:* www.soduspointlighthouse.org *Email:* bmccreary@soduspointlighthouse.org *Visitors welcome?* Yes *Hours:* May through October, Tuesday to Sunday, 10 a.m. to 5 p.m. *Admission:* $3 adults; $1 children 11 to 17 *Operated by:* Sodus Bay Historical Society *NR?* Yes *NHL?* No *Year established/built:* 1824 *Latitude:* 43.2738 *Longitude:* -76.9865

STONY POINT LIGHTHOUSE
Established in 1826, the current Stony Point Lighthouse, also known as the Henderson Lighthouse, was constructed in 1869 and deactivated in 1945. It is now in private hands. *Address:* Stony Point Light *City:* Henderson *State:* NY *Visitors welcome?* No *Operated by:* Private owner *NR?* No *NHL?* No *Year established/built:* 1826 *Latitude:* 43.8394 *Longitude:* -76.2983

SUNKEN ROCK LIGHTHOUSE
Established in 1847, the current Sunken Rock Lighthouse was constructed in 1884 and continues as a private aid to navigation. *Address:* Sunken Rock Light *City:* Alexandria Bay *State:* NY *Visitors welcome?* No *Operated by:* St. Lawrence Seaway Development Corp. *NR?* No *NHL?* No *Year established/built:* 1847 *Latitude:* 44.3456 *Longitude:* -75.9153

THIRTY MILE POINT LIGHTHOUSE
✦ Established and built in 1876, the Thirty Mile Point Lighthouse was automated in 1959 and is now a private aid to navigation within a state park. *Address:* Thirty Mile Point Light *City:* Lyndonville *State:* NY *Visitors welcome?* Yes *Hours:* Daily *Admission:* FREE *Operated by:* New York State Office of Parks, Recreation and Historic Preservation *NR?* Yes *NHL?* No *Year established/built:* 1876 *Latitude:* 43.3750 *Longitude:* -78.4864 **Accommodations for overnight and/or long-term stays available.**

THREE SISTERS ISLAND LIGHTHOUSE
Established and built in 1870, the Three Sisters Island Lighthouse was deactivated in the 1950s and is now privately owned. *Address:* Three Sisters Island *City:* Alexandria *State:* NY *Visitors welcome?* No *Operated by:* Private owner *NR?* No *NHL?* No *Year established/built:* 1870 *Latitude:* 44.3676 *Longitude:* -75.8594

TIBBETTS POINT LIGHTHOUSE
✦ Established in 1827, the current Tibbetts Point Lighthouse was constructed in 1854. Automated in 1981, it is still an active aid to navigation. The keepers house is used as a youth hostel. *Address:* Tibbetts Point Light *City:* Cape Vincent *State:* NY *Phone:* 315-654-2700 *Web:* www.capevincent.org/lighthouse/lighthouse_001.htm *Visitors welcome?* Yes *Hours:* Late May to early June: Friday to Monday, 10 a.m. to 7 p.m.; Late June through

early September: Daily, 10 a.m. to 7 p.m. ; Early September to early October: Friday to Monday, 10 a.m. to 7 p.m. *Admission:* Contact attraction directly *Operated by:* Tibbetts Point Lighthouse Society *NR?* Yes *NHL?* No *Year established/built:* 1827 *Latitude:* 44.1000 *Longitude:* -76.3700 **Accommodations for overnight and/or long-term stays available.**

OHIO

ASHTABULA LIGHTHOUSE
Established in 1836, the current Ashtabula Lighthouse was constructed in 1905 and automated in 1973. The lighthouse is still an active aid to navigation. The keepers quarters are now a maritime museum. *Address:* Ashtabula Light *City:* Ashtabula *State:* OH *Visitors welcome?* Yes *Hours:* Grounds only *Admission:* FREE *Operated by:* Ashtabula Lighthouse Restoration and Preservation Society *NR?* Yes *NHL?* No *Year established/built:* 1836 *Latitude:* 41.9186 *Longitude:* -80.7959

CEDAR POINT LIGHTHOUSE
Established in 1839, the current Cedar Point Lighthouse was constructed in 1862. The lighthouse is now within a resort that's part of an amusement park. *Address:* Cedar Point Amusement Park *City:* Sandusky *State:* OH *Zip:* 44870 *Phone:* 419-627-2350 *Visitors welcome?* Yes *Hours:* Contact attraction directly *Admission:* Contact attraction directly *Operated by:* Private owner *NR?* No *NHL?* No *Year established/built:* 1839 *Latitude:* 41.48611 *Longitude:* -82.68884

CELINA LIGHTHOUSE
The Celina Lighthouse is a private aid to navigation on Grand Lake St. Marys. *Address:* South Main Street and Lakeshore Drive *City:* Celina *State:* OH *Zip:* 45822 *Visitors welcome?* Yes *Hours:* Grounds only *Admission:* FREE *Operated by:* City of Celina *NR?* No *NHL?* No *Year established/built:* 1986 *Latitude:* 40.54894 *Longitude:* -84.57024

CLEVELAND EAST ENTRANCE LIGHTHOUSE
Established in 1915, the current Cleveland East Entrance light is a steel tower that guides vessels into Cleveland Harbor. *Address:* Cleveland Harbor *City:* Cleveland *State:* OH *Visitors welcome?* No *Operated by:* U.S. Coast Guard (District 9) *NR?* No *NHL?* No *Year established/built:* 1915 *Latitude:* 41.5195 *Longitude:* -81.6887

CLEVELAND HARBOR EAST PIERHEAD LIGHTHOUSE
Established in 1831, the current east and west pierhead lights that make up the Cleveland Harbor lighthouses were first lit in 1911. These lights are still active aids to naviga-

tion. *Address:* Cuyahoga River *City:* Cleveland *State:* OH *Visitors welcome?* No *Operated by:* U.S. Coast Guard (District 9) *NR?* No *NHL?* No *Year established/built:* 1831 *Latitude:* 41.50366 *Longitude:* -81.71236

CLEVELAND HARBOR WEST PIERHEAD LIGHTHOUSE
Established in 1831, the current east and west pierhead lights that make up the Cleveland Harbor lighthouses were first lit in 1911. These lights are still active aids to navigation. *Address:* Cuyahoga River *City:* Cleveland *State:* OH *Visitors welcome?* No *Operated by:* U.S. Coast Guard (District 9) *NR?* Yes *NHL?* No *Year established/built:* 1831 *Latitude:* 41.50366 *Longitude:* -81.71236

CONNEAUT HARBOR WEST BREAKWATER LIGHTHOUSE
Established in 1835, the current Art-Deco style Conneaut Lighthouse was constructed in 1936. Previous lighthouses were constructed of brick and steel in the coffee pot style. *Address:* Conneaut Harbor *City:* Conneaut *State:* OH *Visitors welcome?* Yes *Hours:* Grounds only *Admission:* FREE *Operated by:* U.S. Coast Guard (District 9) *NR?* Yes *NHL?* No *Year established/built:* 1835 *Latitude:* 41.9739 *Longitude:* -80.5536

FAIRPORT HARBOR WEST BREAKWATER LIGHTHOUSE
Established and built in 1925, the Fairport Harbor West Breakwater guards the entrance to the Grand River on Lake Erie. The lighthouse is still an active aid to navigation. *Address:* Fairport Harbor West Breakwater Light *City:* Fairport Harbor *State:* OH *Zip:* 44077 *Visitors welcome?* Yes *Hours:* Grounds only *Admission:* FREE *Operated by:* Private owner *NR?* Yes *NHL?* No *Year established/built:* 1925 *Latitude:* 41.7679 *Longitude:* -81.2812

GRAND RIVER LIGHTHOUSE
Established in 1825, the current Grand River Lighthouse, also called the Fairport Harbor Lighthouse, was constructed in 1871 and deactivated in 1925. It is now a maritime museum. *Address:* 129 Second Street *City:* Painsville *State:* OH *Zip:* 44077 *Phone:* 440-354-4825 *Web:* www.ncweb.com/org/fhlh/ *Email:* fhhs@ncweb.com *Visitors welcome?* Yes *Hours:* Memorial Day through September: Wednesdays, Saturdays, Sundays: 1 p.m. to 6 p.m. *Admission:* $3 adults, $2 seniors, $1 ages 6-12, under six FREE *Operated by:* Fairport Harbor Marine Museum *NR?* No *NHL?* No *Year established/built:* 1825 *Latitude:* 41.7571 *Longitude:* -81.2777

GREEN ISLAND LIGHTHOUSE
Established in 1851, the current light on Green Island is a skeletal tower. But the stone lighthouse built in 1864 is still on the island, though it's in ruinous condition. The island is now a wildlife refuge. *Address:* Green Island *City:* Put-in-Bay *State:* OH *Visitors welcome?* No *Operated by:* Ohio Dept. of Natural Resources *NR?* No *NHL?* No *Year established/built:* 1851 *Latitude:* 41.64588 *Longitude:* -82.86658

HURON HARBOR LIGHTHOUSE

Established in 1835, the current Art Moderne Huron Harbor Lighthouse was constructed in 1936. It is still an active aid to navigation. *Address:* Huron Harbor *City:* Huron *State:* OH *Visitors welcome?* Yes *Hours:* Grounds only *Admission:* **FREE** *Operated by:* U.S. Coast Guard (District 9) *NR?* Yes *NHL?* No *Year established/built:* 1835 *Latitude:* 41.4045 *Longitude:* -82.5442

LORAIN LIGHTHOUSE

Established in 1837, the current Lorain Lighthouse was constructed in 1917. The lighthouse was deactivated in 1966, but its exterior was restored in the 1990s. *Address:* Black River *City:* Lorain *State:* OH *Visitors welcome?* No *Operated by:* U.S. Coast Guard (District 9) *NR?* Yes *NHL?* No *Year established/built:* 1837 *Latitude:* 41.4728 *Longitude:* -82.1840

MANHATTAN FRONT AND REAR RANGE LIGHTHOUSES

The Manhattan Rear and Front Range Lighthouses guide ships up the Maumee River into the Port of Toledo. *Address:* North Summit Street and Troy Street *City:* Toledo *State:* OH *Visitors welcome?* No *Operated by:* Private owner *NR?* No *NHL?* No *Year established/built:* 1895 *Latitude:* 41.6772 *Longitude:* -83.4984

Marblehead Lighthouse, Marblehead, Ohio

MARBLEHEAD LIGHTHOUSE

Established in 1821, making it the oldest lighthouse in Ohio, the Marblehead Lighthouse, formerly the Sandusky Bay Lighthouse, is now within Marblehead Lighthouse State Park in Sandusky. The current structure was constructed in 1821 and is open for tours. *Address:* 110 Lighthouse Drive *City:* Marblehead *State:* OH *Zip:* 43440 *Phone:* 419-734-4424 *Web:* ohiodnr.com/?TabId=763 *Visitors welcome?* Yes *Hours:* Daily *Admission:* FREE *Operated by:* Ohio Dept. of Natural Resources *NR?* Yes *NHL?* No *Year established/built:* 1821 *Latitude:* 41.5367 *Longitude:* -82.7133

NORTHWOOD LIGHTHOUSE

Built in 1923, the Northwood Lighthouse is an inactive private aid to navigation. It was built to resemble the Eddystone Lighthouse in Cornwall, England. *Address:* State Highway 703 *City:* Northwood *State:* OH *Visitors welcome?* No *Operated by:* Private owner *NR?* No *NHL?* No *Year established/built:* 1923 *Latitude:* 40.4932 *Longitude:* -83.71085

PORT CLINTON LIGHTHOUSE

Established in 1832, the Port Clinton Lighthouse originally stood on a pier in the Port Clinton harbor. The 1896 structure was later moved to the entrance to Brands' Marina, where it sits today, still an active aid to navigation. *Address:* 451 W. Lakeshore Dr. *City:* Port Clinton *State:* OH *Zip:* 43452 *Phone:* 419-734-4212 *Visitors welcome?* Yes *Hours:* Grounds only *Admission:* FREE *Operated by:* Brands' Marina *NR?* No *NHL?* No *Year established/built:* 1832 *Latitude:* 41.5170 *Longitude:* -82.9485

SANDUSKY HARBOR BREAKWATER LIGHTHOUSE

The Sandusky Harbor Breakwater Lighthouse marks the entrance to Sandusky Bay. It was originally a range light. It's companion was discontinued in 1904. *Address:* Cedar Point *City:* Sandusky *State:* OH *Visitors welcome?* No *Operated by:* U.S. Coast Guard (District 9) *NR?* No *NHL?* No *Latitude:* 41.49418 *Longitude:* -82.68173

SOUTH BASS ISLAND LIGHTHOUSE

Established and built in 1897, the South Bass Island Lighthouse operated as an aid to navigation until it was deactivated in 1962. It is now a field research station operated by Ohio State University. *Address:* South Bass Island Light *City:* Put-in-Bay *State:* OH *Zip:* 43456 *Phone:* 419-285-2341 *Email:* southbasslighthouse@osu.edu *Visitors welcome?* Yes *Hours:* By appointment *Admission:* Contact attraction directly *Operated by:* Stone Laboratory, Ohio State University *NR?* Yes *NHL?* No *Year established/built:* 1897 *Latitude:* 41.6290 *Longitude:* -82.8415

TOLEDO HARBOR LIGHTHOUSE

Established and constructed in 1904 to guide ships into Toledo from Lake Erie, the Toledo Harbor Lighthouse was automated in 1966. Still an active aid to navigation, the lighthouse is now owned by a Toledo not-for-profit. *Address:* Toledo Harbor *City:* Toledo *State:* OH *Visitors welcome?* No *Operated by:* Toledo Harbor Lighthouse Preservation Society *NR?* Yes *NHL?* No *Year established/built:* 1904 *Latitude:* 41.7175 *Longitude:* -83.4315

TURTLE ISLAND LIGHTHOUSE

Established in 1831, the current Turtle Island Lighthouse structure, a remnant of the operating facility, was constructed in 1866. The light was decommissioned in 1904 and is no longer active. *Address:* Turtle Island *State:* OH *Visitors welcome?* No *Operated by:* Private owner *NR?* No *NHL?* No *Year established/built:* 1831 *Latitude:* 41.75254 *Longitude:* -83.39076

VERMILLION LIGHTHOUSE

Established in 1847, the Vermillion Lighthouse on the grounds of the Inland Seas Museum is a replica of the 1877 lighthouse that stood on a pier in Vermillion Harbor. *Address:* 480 Main Street *City:* Vermilion *State:* OH *Zip:* 44089 *Phone:* 440-967-3467 *Email:* glhs1@inlandseas.org *Visitors welcome?* Yes *Hours:* Grounds only *Admission:* FREE *Operated by:* Great Lakes Historical Society *NR?* No *NHL?* No *Year established/built:* 1847 *Latitude:* 41.4249 *Longitude:* -82.3668

WEST SISTER ISLAND LIGHTHOUSE

Established in 1821, the current West Sister Lighthouse was constructed in 1848, though the lantern is now missing. Still an active aid to navigation, the light is now in a wildlife refuge. *Address:* West Sister Island *City:* Jerusalem *State:* OH *Visitors welcome?* No *Operated by:* U.S. Coast Guard (District 9) *NR?* Yes *NHL?* No *Year established/built:* 1821 *Latitude:* 41.73921 *Longitude:* -83.10492

PENNSYLVANIA

ERIE LAND LIGHTHOUSE

Established in 1818, the current Erie Land Lighthouse, also called the Old Presque Isle Lighthouse, was constructed in 1867. The light was deactivated when the Presque Island Lighthouse went into service. *Address:* 2 Lighthouse Street *City:* Erie *State:* PA *Visitors welcome?* Yes *Hours:* Grounds only *Admission:* FREE *Operated by:* City of Erie *NR?* Yes *NHL?* No *Year established/built:* 1818 *Latitude:* 42.1443 *Longitude:* -80.0617

PRESQUE ISLE LIGHTHOUSE

Established in 1872 and lit a year later, the Presque Isle Lighthouse replaced the Erie Land Lighthouse on the mainland. Still an active aid to navigation, the lighthouse is now quarters for Presque Island State Park personnel. *Address:* Presque Isle Light *City:* Erie *State:* PA *Phone:* 814-833-0176 *Visitors welcome?* Yes *Hours:* Grounds only *Admission:* FREE *Operated by:* Pennsylvania Dept. of Conservation and Natural Resources *NR?* Yes *NHL?* No *Year established/built:* 1872 *Latitude:* 42.1634 *Longitude:* -80.1155

PRESQUE ISLE NORTH PIERHEAD LIGHTHOUSE

Established in 1857, the Presque Island North Pierhead Lighthouse, also known as the Erie Harbor Pierhead Lighthouse, is still an active aid to navigation. *Address:* Presque Isle

Peninsula *City:* Erie *State:* PA *Visitors welcome?* Yes *Hours:* Grounds only *Admission:* FREE *Operated by:* U.S. Coast Guard (District 9) *NR?* No *NHL?* No *Year established/built:* 1857 *Latitude:* 42.1481 *Longitude:* -80.0807

WISCONSIN

ALGOMA PIERHEAD LIGHTHOUSE
Established in 1893, the current Algoma Pierhead Lighthouse was constructed in 1932 and automated in 1973. *Address:* Algoma Pierhead Light *City:* Algoma *State:* WI *Visitors welcome?* Yes *Hours:* Grounds only *Admission:* FREE *Operated by:* U.S. Coast Guard (District 9) *NR?* No *NHL?* No *Year established/built:* 1893 *Latitude:* 44.60695 *Longitude:* -87.42944

ASHLAND BREAKWATER LIGHTHOUSE
Established in 1911 and first lit in 1915, the Ashland Breakwater Lighthouse is still an active aid to navigation. *Address:* Ashland Harbor Breakwater Light *City:* Ashland *State:* WI *Visitors welcome?* No *Operated by:* U.S. Coast Guard (District 9) *NR?* No *NHL?* No *Year established/built:* 1911 *Latitude:* 46.6283 *Longitude:* -90.8700

ASYLUM LIGHTHOUSE
Though never lit, the Asylum Point Lighthouse is a prominent landmark in the Oshkosh area. Located on the grounds of the Winnebago Mental Health Institute, the project was built by the Works Progress Administration in 1937. *Address:* Asylum Light *City:* Oshkosh *State:* WI *Visitors welcome?* Yes *Hours:* Grounds only *Admission:* FREE *Operated by:* Winnebago County *NR?* No *NHL?* No *Year established/built:* 1937 *Latitude:* 44.06236 *Longitude:* -88.51464

BAILEYS HARBOR LIGHTHOUSE
Established in 1853, the current skeletal tower Baileys Harbor Lighthouse was built in 1869 and deactivated in the 1960s. It is now privately owned. *Address:* Baileys Harbor Light *City:* Baileys Harbor *State:* WI *Visitors welcome?* No *Operated by:* Private owner *NR?* No *NHL?* No *Year established/built:* 1853 *Latitude:* 45.05583 *Longitude:* -87.09695

BAILEY'S HARBOR RANGE LIGHTHOUSE
Established in 1853, the historic Baileys Harbor Range Lighthouses are now within a state park. The range lights themselves were moved to a different location in 1969. *Address:* Baileys Harbor Range Lights *City:* Baileys Harbor *State:* WI *Visitors welcome?* Yes *Hours:* Grounds only *Admission:* FREE *Operated by:* Door County Maritime Museum & Lighthouse Preservation Society *NR?* Yes *NHL?* No *Year established/built:* 1853 *Latitude:* 45.0700 *Longitude:* -87.1200

BOYER BLUFF LIGHTHOUSE

The Boyer Bluff Lighthouse is a steel skeletal tower on Washington Island. *Address:* Washington Island *City:* Detroit Harbor *State:* WI *Visitors welcome?* No *Operated by:* U.S. Coast Guard (District 9) *NR?* No *NHL?* No *Latitude:* 45.3567 *Longitude:* -86.9307

BRAY'S POINT LIGHTHOUSE

The Bray's Point Lighthouse is a private aid to navigation built in 1909. The grounds and tower are closed to visitors, but the site can be see clearly from a street. *Address:* Bay Shore Drive and Lake Street *City:* Oshkosh *State:* WI *Visitors welcome?* Yes *Operated by:* Private owner *NR?* No *NHL?* No *Year established/built:* 1909 *Latitude:* 44.0076 *Longitude:* -88.5199

CALUMET HARBOR LIGHTHOUSE

Originally built as a water tower, the Calumet Lighthouse was first lit in 1936 and deactivated in the 1980s. It is now used as a public observation tower. *Address:* Calumet Light *City:* Pipe *State:* WI *Visitors welcome?* Yes *Hours:* Daily *Admission:* FREE *Operated by:* Fond du Lac County *NR?* No *NHL?* No *Year established/built:* 1936 *Latitude:* 43.9150 *Longitude:* -88.3324

CANA ISLAND LIGHTHOUSE

Established and built in 1870, the Cana Island Lighthouse was automated in 1945, and it is still an active aid to navigation. Now managed by the Door County Museum, visitors are allowed to climb the historic tower. *Address:* Cana Island Light *City:* Baileys Harbor *State:* WI *Phone:* 920-743-5958 *Web:* www.dcmm.org *Email:* info@dcmm.org *Visitors welcome?* Yes *Hours:* May to October, daily, 10 a.m. to 5 p.m. *Admission:* $4 adults, $2 children, additional $2 to climb the tower *Operated by:* Door County Maritime Museum & Lighthouse Preservation Society *NR?* Yes *NHL?* No *Year established/built:* 1870 *Latitude:* 45.0883 *Longitude:* -87.0467

CHAMBERS ISLAND LIGHTHOUSE

Established and built in 1868, the Chambers Island Lighthouse was deactivated in 1961. *Address:* Chambers Island Light *State:* WI *Visitors welcome?* Yes *Hours:* Grounds only *Admission:* FREE *Operated by:* Town of Gibralter *NR?* Yes *NHL?* No *Year established/built:* 1868 *Latitude:* 45.2025 *Longitude:* -87.3647

CHEQUAMEGON POINT LIGHTHOUSE

Established in 1858, the Chequamegon Lighthouse skeletal tower was constructed in 1896 and suplemeted by a nearby modern tower in 1987. *Address:* Chequamegon Point Light *City:* Ashland *State:* WI *Phone:* 715-779-3397 *Web:* www.nps.gov/apis/historyculture/lighthouses.htm *Visitors welcome?* Yes *Hours:* Grounds only *Admission:* FREE *Operated by:* Apostle Islands National Lakeshore *NR?* Yes *NHL?* No *Year established/built:* 1858 *Latitude:* 46.7283 *Longitude:* -90.8094

Devils Island Lighthouse, Ashland, Wisconsin

DEVILS ISLAND LIGHTHOUSE

✦ Established in 1891, the current Devils Island Lighthouse was constructed in 1898 with extra reinforcing added in 1914. The lighthouse is now part of the Apostle Islands National Lakeshore. *Address:* Devils Island Light *City:* Ashland *State:* WI *Phone:* 715-779-3397 *Web:* www.nps.gov/apis/historyculture/lighthouses.htm *Visitors welcome?* Yes *Hours:* Grounds only *Admission:* FREE *Operated by:* Apostle Islands National Lakeshore *NR?* Yes *NHL?* No *Year established/built:* 1891 *Latitude:* 47.0800 *Longitude:* -90.7283 **Accommodations for overnight and/or long-term stays available.**

EAGLE BLUFF LIGHTHOUSE

Established and built in 1868, the Eagle Bluff Lighthouse was automated in 1926. Still an active aid to navigation, the lighthouse is now within a state park. *Address:* Eagle Bluff Light

121

State: WI *Phone:* 920-868-3258 *Visitors welcome?* Yes *Hours:* Contact attraction directly *Admission:* Contact attraction directly *Operated by:* Wisconsin Dept. of Natural Resources *NR?* Yes *NHL?* No *Year established/built:* 1868 *Latitude:* 45.1683 *Longitude:* -87.2367

FISHERMANS ROAD LIGHTHOUSE

The Fishermans Road Lighthouse is a private aid to navigation owned by the Fishermans Road Fishing Club. *Address:* Fishermans Road and Willow Lane Beach Road *City:* Pipe *State:* WI *Visitors welcome?* Yes *Hours:* Grounds only *Admission:* FREE *Operated by:* Private owner *NR?* No *NHL?* No *Latitude:* 43.9142 *Longitude:* -88.3126

GRASSY ISLAND RANGE LIGHTHOUSES

The Grassy Island Range Lighthouses once stood on an island in Green Bay, Lake Michigan. *Address:* Grassy Island Range Lights *City:* Green Bay *State:* WI *Phone:* 920-432-0168 *Visitors welcome?* No *Operated by:* Green Bay Yacht Club *NR?* No *NHL?* No *Year established/built:* 1872 *Latitude:* 44.5361 *Longitude:* -88.0051

GREEN BAY HARBOR ENTRANCE LIGHTHOUSE

Built in 1935, the Green Bay Harbor Lighthouse is nine miles north of Green Bay in the middle of Green Bay itself. *Address:* Green Bay Harbor *City:* Green Bay *State:* WI *Visitors welcome?* No *Operated by:* U.S. Coast Guard (District 9) *NR?* No *NHL?* No *Year established/built:* 1935 *Latitude:* 44.6628 *Longitude:* -87.9126

GREEN ISLAND LIGHTHOUSE

Established in 1863, the original Green Island Lighthouse is now a ruin, although the light is still operational atop a skeletal tower. *Address:* Green Island *City:* Marinette *State:* WI *Visitors welcome?* No *Operated by:* Private owner *NR?* No *NHL?* No *Year established/built:* 1863 *Latitude:* 45.05943 *Longitude:* -87.50094

GULL ISLAND LIGHTHOUSE

Established and built in 1928, the skeletal steel tower of the Gull Island Lighthouse is off Michigan Island, which is part of the Apostle Islands National Lakeshore. *Address:* Gull Island Light *City:* Bayfield *State:* WI *Visitors welcome?* No *Operated by:* U.S. Coast Guard (District 9) *NR?* No *NHL?* No *Year established/built:* 1928 *Latitude:* 46.9069 *Longitude:* -90.4422

KENOSHA NORTH PIER LIGHTHOUSE

Address: Kenosha North Pier Light *City:* Kenosha *State:* WI *Visitors welcome?* Yes *Hours:* Grounds only *Admission:* FREE *Operated by:* U.S. Coast Guard (District 9) *NR?* No *NHL?* No *Latitude:* 42.58883 *Longitude:* -87.80864

KENOSHA-SOUTHPORT LIGHTHOUSE

Established in 1848, the current Kenosha Lighthouse, also called the Southport Lighthouse, was constructed in 1866 and automated in 1996 after it was re-lighted. It is now part of a museum. *Address:* 220 51st Place *City:* Kenosha *State:* WI *Zip:* 53140 *Phone:* 262-654-5770 *Web:* www.kenoshahistorycenter.org *Email:* kchs@kenoshahistorycenter. org *Visitors welcome?* Yes *Hours:* Tuesday to Friday, 10 a.m. to 4:30 p.m.; Saturday, 10 a.m. to 4 p.m.; Sunday, noon to 4 p.m. *Admission:* $10 adults, $5 children *Operated by:* Kenosha History Center *NR?* Yes *NHL?* No *Year established/built:* 1866 *Latitude:* 42.5891 *Longitude:* -87.8154

KEVICH LIGHTHOUSE

Built as a private aid to navigation, Kevich Lighthouse sits on a bluff overlooking Lake Michigan. *Address:* Kevich Light *City:* Grafton *State:* WI *Visitors welcome?* No *Operated by:* Private owner *NR?* No *NHL?* No *Year established/built:* 1981 *Latitude:* 43.3240 *Longitude:* -87.8889

KEWAUNEE PIERHEAD LIGHTHOUSE

Established in 1891, the current Kewaunee Pierhead Lighthouse was constructed in 1931 and is still an active aid to navigation. *Address:* Kewaunee Pierhead Light *City:* Kewaunee *State:* WI *Visitors welcome?* Yes *Hours:* Grounds only *Admission:* FREE *Operated by:* U.S. Coast Guard (District 9) *NR?* No *NHL?* No *Year established/built:* 1891 *Latitude:* 44.4512 *Longitude:* -87.4931

LA POINT LIGHTHOUSE

Established in 1858, the current skeletal tower was built in 1896 and automated in 1964. Still an active aid to navigation, the lighthouse is one of the oldest skeletal lighthouses in the Great Lakes. *Address:* Chequamegon Bay *State:* WI *Phone:* 715-779-3397 *Visitors welcome?* Yes *Hours:* Grounds only *Admission:* FREE *Operated by:* Apostle Islands National Lakeshore *NR?* Yes *NHL?* No *Year established/built:* 1858 *Latitude:* 46.7290 *Longitude:* -90.7852

LONG TAIL POINT LIGHTHOUSE

Now in ruins, the Long Tail Point Lighthouse is within a state wildlife refuge. *Address:* Long Tail Point *City:* Suamico *State:* WI *Visitors welcome?* Yes *Hours:* Grounds only *Admission:* FREE *Operated by:* Wisconsin Dept. of Natural Resources *NR?* No *NHL?* No *Latitude:* 44.5867 *Longitude:* -87.9804

MANITOWOC BREAKWATER LIGHTHOUSE

Established in 1895, the current Manitowoc Breakwater Lighthouse was constructed in 1918. Automated in 1971, it is still an active aid to navigation. *Address:* Manitowoc Breakwater Light *City:* Manitowoc *State:* WI *Visitors welcome?* No *Operated by:* Private owner *NR?* No *NHL?* No *Year established/built:* 1895 *Latitude:* 44.09278 *Longitude:* -87.64361

MICHIGAN ISLAND (NEW)

✦ Established in 1856, the current skeletal tower of the Michigan Island Lighthouse was built in 1880 where it guided mariners in the Delaware River before it was taken down and reassembled at Michigan Island in 1929. The light is still an active aid to navigation. *Address:* Michigan Island Light *State:* WI *Phone:* 715-779-3397 *Web:* www.nps.gov/apis/ historyculture/lighthouses.htm *Visitors welcome?* Yes *Hours:* Grounds only *Admission:* **FREE** *Operated by:* Apostle Islands National Lakeshore *NR?* Yes *NHL?* No *Year established/built:* 1856 *Latitude:* 46.8717 *Longitude:* -90.4967 **Accommodations for overnight and/or long-term stays available.**

MICHIGAN ISLAND (OLD)

✛ Established in 1856, the first Michigan Island lighthouse was built in error; the contractors picked the wrong island and the lighthouse was closed a year later. Restarted in 1869, it was again closed down in favor of a replacement skeletal tower. *Address:* Michigan Island Light *State:* WI *Phone:* 715-779-3397 *Web:* www.nps.gov/apis/historyculture/ lighthouses.htm *Visitors welcome?* Yes *Hours:* Grounds only *Admission:* **FREE** *Operated by:* Apostle Islands National Lakeshore *NR?* Yes *NHL?* No *Year established/built:* 1856 *Latitude:* 46.8717 *Longitude:* -90.4967 **Accommodations for overnight and/or long-term stays available.**

MILWAUKEE BREAKWATER LIGHTHOUSE

Established and buit in 1926, the Milwaukee Breakwater Lighthouse is still an active aid to navigation. *Address:* Milwaukee Breakwater Light *City:* Milwaukee *State:* WI *Visitors welcome?* No *Operated by:* U.S. Coast Guard (District 9) *NR?* No *NHL?* No *Year established/ built:* 1926 *Latitude:* 43.0270 *Longitude:* -87.8820

MILWAUKEE PIERHEAD LIGHTHOUSE

Established in 1872, the current Milwaukee Pierhead Lighthouse was constructed in 1906 and is still an active aid to navigation. *Address:* Milwaukee Pierhead Light *City:* Milwaukee *State:* WI *Visitors welcome?* Yes *Hours:* Grounds only *Admission:* **FREE** *Operated by:* U.S. Coast Guard (District 9) *NR?* No *NHL?* No *Year established/built:* 1872 *Latitude:* 43.02601 *Longitude:* -87.89535

NEENAH LIGHTHOUSE

The Neenah Lighthouse at Kimberly Point on the shore of Lake Winnebago in Neenah, Wisconsin has stood for the last 50 years in a place where local Native American tribes met for pow-wows 150 years ago at the mouth of the Fox River. *Address:* Neenah Light *City:* Neenah *State:* WI *Zip:* 54956 *Visitors welcome?* Yes *Hours:* Grounds only *Admission:* **FREE** *Operated by:* City of Neenah *NR?* No *NHL?* No *Year established/built:* 1947 *Latitude:* 44.1855 *Longitude:* -88.44139

NORTH POINT LIGHTHOUSE

Established in 1855, the current North Point Lighthouse, also known as the Milwaukee Lighthouse, was constructed in 1888 and deactivated in 1994. In 2007, local residents completed a restoration of the lighthouse, which is now in a public park. *Address:* 2650

N. Wahl Ave. *City:* Milwaukee *State:* WI *Zip:* 53211 *Phone:* 414-332-6754 *Web:* www. northpointlighthouse.org *Email:* keeper@northpointlighthouse.org *Visitors welcome?* Yes *Hours:* May to October, Saturdays, 1 p.m. to 4 p.m.; November to April, first Saturday of the month, 1 p.m. to 4 p.m. *Admission:* $5 adults, $3 children, under five FREE *Operated by:* North Point Lighthouse Friends *NR?* Yes *NHL?* No *Year established/built:* 1855 *Latitude:* 43.0656 *Longitude:* -87.8700

OUTER ISLAND LIGHTHOUSE

Established and built in 1874, the Outer Island Lighthouse is within the Apostle Islands National Lakeshore and is still an active aid to navigation. *Address:* Outer Island Light *City:* Bayfield *State:* WI *Phone:* 715-779-3397 *Web:* www.nps.gov/apis/historyculture/ lighthouses.htm *Visitors welcome?* Yes *Hours:* Contact attraction directly *Admission:* **FREE** *Operated by:* Apostle Islands National Lakeshore *NR?* Yes *NHL?* No *Year established/built:* 1874 *Latitude:* 41.0767 *Longitude:* -90.4167

PESHTIGO REEF LIGHTHOUSE

Built in 1934 to replace a lightship, the Peshtigo Reef Lighthouse is still an active aid to navigation. *Address:* Peshtigo Harbor *City:* Peshtigo *State:* WI *Visitors welcome?* No *Operated by:* U.S. Coast Guard (District 9) *NR?* No *NHL?* No *Year established/built:* 1934 *Latitude:* 44.97239 *Longitude:* -87.64948

PILOT ISLAND LIGHTHOUSE

Established and built in 1858, the Pilot Island Lighthouse is within a wildlife refuge. Automated in 1962, it is still an active aid to navigation. *Address:* Pilot Island Light *State:* WI *Visitors welcome?* No *Operated by:* U.S. Coast Guard (District 9) *NR?* Yes *NHL?* No *Year established/built:* 1858 *Latitude:* 45.28443 *Longitude:* -86.91928

PLUM ISLAND REAR RANGE LIGHTHOUSE

Established and built in 1897, the skeletal tower of the Plum Island Rear Range Lighthouse was automated in 1969 and it is still an active aide to navigation. *Address:* Plum Island Range Rear Light *State:* WI *Visitors welcome?* No *Operated by:* U.S. Coast Guard (District 9) *NR?* Yes *NHL?* No *Year established/built:* 1897 *Latitude:* 45.3078 *Longitude:* -86.9581

PORT WASHINGTON BREAKWATER LIGHTHOUSE

Established in 1889 to supplement and then replace the on-shore Port Washington Lighthouse, the current Port Washington Breakwater Lighthouse was built in the 1935 and is still an active aid to navigation. *Address:* Port Washington Harbor *City:* Port Washington *State:* WI *Zip:* 53074 *Visitors welcome?* Yes *Hours:* Grounds only *Admission:* FREE *Operated by:* U.S. Coast Guard (District 9) *NR?* No *NHL?* No *Year established/built:* 1889 *Latitude:* 43.38534 *Longitude:* -87.86007

Port Washington Lighthouse, Port Washington, Wisconsin

PORT WASHINGTON LIGHTHOUSE

Established in 1848, the current Port Washington Lighthouse was constructed in 1860 and deactivated in 1903. *Address:* 311 Johnson St. *City:* Port Washington *State:* WI *Zip:* 53074 *Phone:* 262-284-7240 *Web:* www.portlightstation.org *Email:* 1860lightstation@ sbcglobal.net *Visitors welcome?* Yes *Hours:* Summer: Saturdays, 11 a.m. to 4 p.m., Sunday, noon to 4 p.m. *Admission:* Contact attraction directly *Operated by:* Port Washington Historical Society *NR?* Yes *NHL?* No *Year established/built:* 1849 *Latitude:* 43.3912 *Longitude:* -87.8684

POTTAWATOMIE LIGHTHOUSE

✦ Established in 1837, the current Pottawatomie Lighthouse, also called the Rock Island Lighthouse, was constructed in 1858 and automated in 1966. *Address:* Pottawatomie Light *State:* WI *Email:* kirby.foss@wisconsin.gov *Visitors welcome?* Yes *Hours:* Contact attraction directly *Admission:* Contact attraction directly *Operated by:* Friends of Rock Island State Park *NR?* Yes *NHL?* No *Year established/built:* 1837 *Latitude:* 45.4275 *Longitude:* -86.8281 **Accommodations for overnight and/or long-term stays available.**

RACINE BREAKWATER LIGHTHOUSE

Established in 1872 shortly after the construction of a breakwater, the current Racine Breakwater Lighthouse is inactive, although it is beloved by the community as a marker of its maritime heritage. *City:* Racine *State:* WI *Visitors welcome?* No *Operated by:* City of Racine *NR?* No *NHL?* No *Year established/built:* 1872 *Latitude:* 42.72613 *Longitude:* -87.78285

The interior of the Raspberry Island Lighthouse near Bayfield, Wisconsin

RASPBERRY ISLAND LIGHTHOUSE

Established and built in 1863, the Raspberry Island Lighthouse was deactivated in 1957. The light station is now part of the Apostle Islands National Lakeshore. *Address:* Raspberry Island Light *City:* Bayfield *State:* WI *Phone:* 715-779-3397 *Web:* www.nps.gov/apis/historyculture/lighthouses.htm *Visitors welcome?* Yes *Hours:* Contact attraction directly *Admission:* Contact attraction directly *Operated by:* Apostle Islands National Lakeshore *NR?* Yes *NHL?* No *Year established/built:* 1863 *Latitude:* 46.9706 *Longitude:* -90.8050

RAWLEY POINT LIGHTHOUSE

Established in 1853, the current cast-iron skeletal tower of the Rawley Point Lighthouse, also called the Twin River Lighthouse, was constructed in 1894. Automated in 1979, the light is still an active aid to navigation. *Address:* Rawley Point *City:* Two Rivers *State:* WI *Visitors welcome?* Yes *Hours:* Grounds only *Admission:* FREE *Operated by:* U.S. Coast Guard (District 9) *NR?* Yes *NHL?* No *Year established/built:* 1853 *Latitude:* 44.2125 *Longitude:* -87.5079

Sand Island Lighthouse, Bayfield, Wisconsin

SAND ISLAND LIGHTHOUSE

✦ Established and buit in 1881, the Sand Point Lighthouse is an active aid to navigation within the Apostle Islands National Lakeshore. *Address:* Sand Island Light *City:* Bayfield *State:* WI *Phone:* 715-779-3397 *Web:* www.nps.gov/apis/historyculture/lighthouses.htm *Visitors welcome?* Yes *Hours:* Grounds only *Admission:* **FREE** *Operated by:* Apostle Islands National Lakeshore *NR?* Yes *NHL?* No *Year established/built:* **1881** *Latitude:* 47.0033 *Longitude:* -90.9367 **Accommodations for overnight and/or long-term stays available.**

SHEBOYGAN BREAKWATER LIGHTHOUSE

Established in 1905, the current Sheboygan Breakwater Lighthouse was installed in 1915 and is still an active aid to navigation. *Address:* Sheboygan Harbor *City:* Sheboygan *State:* WI *Visitors welcome?* Yes *Hours:* Grounds only *Admission:* **FREE** *Operated by:* U.S. Coast Guard (District 9) *NR?* No *NHL?* No *Year established/built:* 1905 *Latitude:* 43.7496 *Longitude:* -87.6930

SHERWOOD POINT LIGHTHOUSE

Established and built in 1883, the Sherwood Point Lighthouse is used as recreational facilities for U.S. Coast Guard personnel. The light is still an active aid to navigation. *Address:* Sherwood Point Light *City:* Idlewild *State:* WI *Visitors welcome?* No *Operated by:* U.S. Coast Guard (District 9) *NR?* Yes *NHL?* No *Year established/built:* 1883 *Latitude:* 44.89333 *Longitude:* -87.43333

STURGEON BAY SHIP CANAL LIGHTHOUSE

Established and built in 1899, the Sturgeon Bay Ship Canal Lighthouse is still an active aid to navigation. *Address:* Sturgeon Bay Canal Light *City:* Sturgeon Bay *State:* WI

Visitors welcome? Yes *Hours:* Grounds only *Admission:* FREE *Operated by:* U.S. Coast Guard (District 9) *NR?* Yes *NHL?* No *Year established/built:* 1899 *Latitude:* 44.7950 *Longitude:* -87.31333

STURGEON BAY SHIP CANAL PIERHEAD LIGHTHOUSE
Established in 1882, the current Sturgeon Bay Ship Canal North Pierhead Lighthouse was constructed in 1903 and is still an active aid to navigation. *Address:* Sturgeon Bay Ship Canal *City:* Sturgeon Bay *State:* WI *Visitors welcome?* Yes *Hours:* Grounds only *Admission:* FREE *Operated by:* U.S. Coast Guard (District 9) *NR?* No *NHL?* No *Year established/built:* 1882 *Latitude:* 44.79202 *Longitude:* -87.30943

TWO RIVERS LIGHTHOUSE
The Two Rivers Lighthouse, now on the site of the Rogers Street Fishing Village, once sat on a breakwater guiding mariners into Two Rivers Harbor. *Address:* 2010 Rogers St. *City:* Two Rivers *State:* WI *Zip:* 54241 *Phone:* 920-793-5905 *Web:* www.rogersstreet.com *Email:* szippercr@rogersstreet.com *Visitors welcome?* Yes *Hours:* May to October: Daily, 10 a.m. to 4 p.m. *Admission:* $4 adults, $2 children under 16 *Operated by:* Rogers Street Fishing Village & Great Lakes Coast Guard Museum *NR?* No *NHL?* No *Year established/built:* 1886 *Latitude:* 44.1518 *Longitude:* -87.5626

WIND POINT LIGHTHOUSE
Established and built in 1880, the Wind Point Lighthouse was automated in 1964 and is still an active aid to navigation. It is now cared for by the City of Wind Point and a local not-for-profit organization. *Address:* Wind Point Light *City:* Wind Point *State:* WI *Phone:* 262-639-2026 *Visitors welcome?* Yes *Hours:* July to October, First Sunday *Admission:* Contact attraction directly *Operated by:* Friends of Wind Point Lighthouse *NR?* Yes *NHL?* No *Year established/built:* 1880 *Latitude:* 42.78111 *Longitude:* -87.75833

WISCONSIN POINT LIGHTHOUSE
Established and built in 1913, the Wisconsin Point Lighthouse is still an active aid to navigation. *Address:* Wisconsin Point Light *City:* Superior *State:* WI *Visitors welcome?* Yes *Hours:* Grounds only *Admission:* FREE *Operated by:* U.S. Coast Guard (District 9) *NR?* No *NHL?* No *Year established/built:* 1913 *Latitude:* 46.71014 *Longitude:* -92.00639

Check your attraction's listing on www.fyddeye.com for any updates to contact information.

CHAPTER 3

GULF COAST LIGHTHOUSES

Sanibel Island Lighthouse, Sanibel Island, Florida

Lighthouses you can visit today in Alabama, Florida, Louisiana, Mississippi, Nebraska, and Texas. Use your smart phone QR or bar code reader to visit this Fyddeye web page.

FYDDEYE RECOMMENDS:

Mobile Point Lighthouse, Fort Morgan, Alabama	Tchefuncte River Lighthouse, Madisonville, Louisiana
Pensacola Lighthouse, Pensacola, Florida	Port Isabel Lighthouse, Port Isabel, Texas

Lighthouse keeping, then and now

Ida Lewis maintained the Lime Rock Lighthouse in Newport, R.I. from 1857 to 1911. The lighthouse was later renamed the Ida Lewis Rock Lighthouse by the government.

During the heyday of the American lighthouse from the late 18th century through the middle of the 20th century, a cadre of men—and a small but significant number of women—kept thousands of lighthouses and smaller navigational aids in working order. It was an age before automation and electronics, when human beings were asked to keep life-saving mechanisms operating at peak performance 24 hours a day, seven days a week, all year long. These demands fostered a unique lighthouse culture that held a singular place in the popular mind. Lighthouse keepers were folk heroes, despite their isolation, loneliness, and sometimes, madness.

The first duty of the lighthouse keeper was to keep the light and other mechanical devices in good working order and operating at all times. He or she lit the light at sunset and doused it at sunrise. Keepers refilled the kerosene reservoir, trimmed the wicks, cleaned the prisms of the Fresnel lens, washed the windows of the lantern, and polished the carbon off the mirrors. If a light spun slowly in the lantern, the keeper lubricated the cast-iron mechanisms, driven by weights similar to a pendulum clock, and reset the weights every two hours. All these tasks were done each day, and everything important was noted in a logbook. If the light station had a mechanical foghorn, the keeper was expected to keep its lowing sound going until the fog lifted, occasionally for days at a time. In addition to the navigational aids, the keeper was responsible for maintaining his quarters, small boats at the station, a dock, and the grounds around the lighthouse, which could be several dozen acres, even an entire island. Vegetable gardens and pens for small animals were common.

Depending on the size and importance of the station, the lighthouse keeper had help. One or two assistants might be assigned to his station, and if the keeper's family lived with him, his wife and older children would help with daily operations. In the case of the Raspberry Island Lighthouse in Wisconsin's Apostle Islands, two families shared the responsibility for maintaining the large station. In addition to the keeper's responsibilities for maintaining the light station, he was also expected to assist ships in trouble. Captain William Tate, who oversaw 42 navigation aids on North Carolina's Outer Banks, was involved in a dozen rescues and assists in 1917 alone. He also assisted aviation pioneers Orville and Wilbur Wright as they prepared their test flights near Kitty Hawk. In April, 1920, Tate made the first inspection of navigation lights from the air.

The presence of families at many light stations led to one of the most unique aspects of lighthouse culture, the prominence of women. In an age when women's roles were limited to the home, or perhaps teaching and nursing, women at lighthouses were often called to perform the same duties as their keeper husbands, fathers, or brothers, particularly if he was sick or had died. The most famous of the female lighthouse keepers in America was Ida Lewis, the daughter of Captain Hosea Lewis, the keeper of Lime Rock Light in Newport, Rhode Island. In 1854, he suffered a debilitating stroke, and Ida took up her father's duties, hoping perhaps that her father would soon be back at work. But he never fully recovered, and over the next 15 years, until he died, Ida and her mother become known far and wide for their dedication to the light. Ida was appointed keeper in 1879, and as the highest paid lighthouse keeper in America ($750 a year), she held a unique spot in a time when most women could never imagine earning as much as men for the same job. Lewis also performed several daring rescues that brought her to the attention of the media and important politicians, such as President U.S. Grant. Thousands of visitors flocked to her lighthouse to meet her, and in 1924, thirteen years after her death, the government renamed the lighthouse from Lime Rock to Ida Lewis Lighthouse. The site is now home to a yacht club.

In some cases, the exploits of female lighthouse keepers became the stuff of legend. On September 7, 1838, 23-year-old Grace Darling and her father William tended the Longstone Lighthouse off the Northumberland coast of England. Glancing out the lighthouse's window, Grace spotted a ship broken in half on one of the islands marked by the lighthouse. Survivors clung to the rocks as the storm that destroyed their ship raged all around. Grace and her father climbed into a 21-foot, four-person rowboat and rowed nearly a mile to the wreck. She and her father carried five survivors to shore. The story of a young woman rowing out in storm to rescue strangers captivated intellectuals in the Romantic Age, when many artists and writers focused on the natural world and women were seen as the guardians of virtue. Fictional retellings of Grace Darling's story appeared as early as 1839, a popular song was written, and the poet laureate William Wordsworth immortalized her exploits in an 1843 poem, "Grace Darling."

> *Pious and pure, modest and yet so brave,*
> *Though young so wise, though meek so resolute.*

The story of Grace Darling still influences English culture: A musical based on her life was produced in York, England in 2010.

While artists and writers celebrated lighthouse keepers as heroes, the loneliness, danger, and isolation of life at these coastal outposts also penetrated the popular culture, often in stories of madness and ghosts. The history of lighthouse keepers is peppered with tales of extreme loneliness driving people—especially women—to insanity, even murder. Numerous lighthouses in Door County, Wisconsin, are said to be haunted, including Pottawatomie Lighthouse. It's said that in 1840, the wife of the keeper went mad and tried to kill her husband. Unable to commit the woman he loved to an asylum, he locked her in a basement room where she raved until her death. At the Chambers Island Lighthouse, the keeper murdered his new bride, who drove him crazy by playing the same piece of sheet music on their piano day after day. In both cases, present day visitors and caretakers swear they can hear the ghosts of these tortured people wandering the buildings and grounds.

Historians dispute the facts of these stories, but the tales reflect the nature of the job, especially in winter, when blizzards, endless storms, long hours of darkness, and the lack of social contact could strain the nerves of the most stable man or woman. And savvy modern lighthouse promoters are eager to stoke the imagination of visitors; in recent years "paranormal explorations" of lighthouses have become popular. In reality, the lives of keepers were usually threatened far more by nature than by madness; hardly a year went by when a keeper, an assistant, or a family member somewhere wasn't swept away by a powerful wave pounding the rocky shore around a lighthouse.

By the end of World War II, the traditional life of the lighthouse keeper was doomed by automation and the need for efficiency. The U.S. Coast Guard, in charge of lighthouses since 1938, accelerated plans to replace hand-operated equipment with machines that could operate independently with only occasional visits by a maintenance team. By the end of the century, the last lighthouse keeper had retired. But throughout history, visitors were welcomed at lighthouses, and in the early 21st century, lighthouse owners began to advertise an experience that offered a taste of the old way of life. For example, the New Dungeness Lighthouse in Washington state invites families to stay at the light station for as long as a week maintaining the grounds and conducting tours of the lighthouse. Some Great Lakes lighthouses on island outposts welcome volunteer keepers for as long as a month with only one visit allowed to shore. Other lighthouses have been converted into bed and breakfasts for overnight visitors. Members of the United States Lighthouse Society, a non-profit association of lighthouse aficionados, receive discounts at many of these sites. For lovers of maritime history and lighthouses in particular, it's a chance to live a life that's disappeared from America.

Look for notes in the Guide's listings that indicate whether the lighthouse welcomes extended stays by visitors.

ALABAMA

MOBILE BAY LIGHT

Established and built in 1885, the Mobile Bay Lighthouse,also called Middle Bay Light, is an example of a screw-pile lighthouse, in which pilings with screw-like head are driven into the sand. Deactivated in 1967, the lighthouse is now under the care of a not-for-profit organization. *Address:* Middle Bay Light *City:* Mobile *State:* AL *Visitors welcome?* No *Operated by:* Alabama Lighthouse Association *NR?* Yes *NHL?* No *Year established/built:* 1885 *Latitude:* 30.4375 *Longitude:* -88.0114

MOBILE POINT LIGHTHOUSE

Established and built in 1822, the remains of the Mobile Point Lighthouse are at Fort Morgan, a memorial to the Civil War Battle of Mobile Bay. *Address:* Mobile Point Lighthouse *State:* AL *Zip:* 36542 *Visitors welcome?* Yes *Hours:* Daily *Admission:* FREE *Operated by:* Alabama Lighthouse Association *NR?* No *NHL?* No *Year established/built:* 1822 *Latitude:* 30.2278 *Longitude:* -88.0239

SAND ISLAND LIGHTHOUSE

Established in 1837, the current Sand Island Lighthouse was constructed in 1873, replaced an 1859 tower destroyed during the Civil War. Residents of nearby Dauphin Island are leading a project to restore the now automated lighthouse. *Address:* Dauphin Island *City:* Mobile *State:* AL *Visitors welcome?* No *Operated by:* Alabama Lighthouse Association *NR?* Yes *NHL?* No *Year established/built:* 1837 *Latitude:* 30.25548 *Longitude:* -88.10972

FLORIDA

ALLIGATOR REEF LIGHTHOUSE

Established and built in 1873, the cast-iron Alligator Reef Lighthouse was automated in 1963 and is still an active aid to navigation. *Address:* Alligator Reef Light *State:* FL *Visitors welcome?* No *Operated by:* U.S. Coast Guard (District 7) *NR?* No *NHL?* No *Year established/built:* 1873 *Latitude:* 24.8517 *Longitude:* -80.6183

AMERICAN SHOAL LIGHTHOUSE

Established and built in 1880, the American Shoal Lighthouse was automated in 1963 and is still an active aid to navigation. *Address:* American Shoal Light *State:* **FL** *Visitors welcome?* No *Operated by:* U.S. Coast Guard (District 7) *NR?* No *NHL?* No *Year established/built:* 1880 *Latitude:* 24.5250 *Longitude:* -81.5200

ANCLOTE KEY LIGHTHOUSE

Established and built in 1887, the Anclote Key Lighthouse was deactivated in 1985 and is now within a wildlife refuge. *Address:* Anclote Key Preserve State Park *State:* **FL** *Visitors welcome?* Yes *Hours:* Grounds only *Admission:* **FREE** *Operated by:* Florida Division of Recreation and Parks *NR?* Yes *NHL?* No *Year established/built:* 1887 *Latitude:* 28.1726 *Longitude:* -82.8466

CAPE SAN BLAS LIGHTHOUSE

Established in 1848, the current Cape San Blas Lighthouse was constructed in 1885 and deactivated in 1996. *Address:* Cape San Blas Light *City:* Port St. Joe *State:* **FL** *Visitors welcome?* Yes *Hours:* Daily, grounds only *Admission:* **FREE** *Operated by:* Gulf County *NR?* Yes *NHL?* No *Year established/built:* 1848 *Latitude:* 29.6712 *Longitude:* -85.3563

CAPE ST. GEORGE LIGHTHOUSE

Established in 1833, the current Cape St. George Lighthouse was constructed in 1852. Deactivated in 1994, the lighthouse is now a museum. *Address:* Franklin Boulevard and West Gulf Beach Drive *City:* St. George Island *State:* **FL** *Phone:* 850-927-7744 *Web:* www.stgeorgelight.org *Visitors welcome?* Yes *Hours:* Monday, Tuesday, Wednesday: 9 a.m. to noon and 1 p.m. to 3 p.m.; Saturday: 9 a.m. to 1 p.m.; Sunday: 1 p.m. to 3 p.m. *Admission:* $5 adults, $3 six to 16, under six FREE *Operated by:* St. George Lighthouse Association *NR?* Yes *NHL?* No *Year established/built:* 1833 *Latitude:* 29.6408 *Longitude:* -84.9124

CEDAR KEYS LIGHTHOUSE

Established and built in 1854, the Cedar Keys Lighthouse was deactivated in 1915. Also known as Seahorse Key Lighthouse, the site is now used by the University of Florida as a marine lab. *Address:* Seahorse Key *City:* Cedar Key *State:* **FL** *Phone:* 352-392-1101 *Web:* www.zoology.ufl.edu *Email:* hbl@zoology.ufl.edu *Visitors welcome?* Yes *Hours:* Contact attraction directly *Admission:* Contact attraction directly *Operated by:* Seahorse Key Marine Laboratory (University of Florida) *NR?* Yes *NHL?* No *Year established/built:* 1854 *Latitude:* 29.0972 *Longitude:* -83.0660

CROOKED RIVER LIGHTHOUSE

Established and built in 1895, the Crooked River Lighthouse, also known as Carrabelle Lighthouse, was deactivated in 1995 and is now in a public park. *Address:* Crooked River Light *City:* Franklin *State:* **FL** *Visitors welcome?* Yes *Hours:* Daily *Admission:* **FREE** *Operated* *by:* Carrabelle Lighthouse Association *NR?* Yes *NHL?* No *Year established/built:* 1895 *Latitude:* 29.8275 *Longitude:* -84.7011

EGMONT KEY LIGHTHOUSE

Established in 1848, the current Egmont Key Lighthouse was constructed in 1858. Automated in 1989, the lighthouse is still an active aid to navigation within a wildlife refuge. *Address:* Egmont Key Light *City:* Anna Maria *State:* FL *Visitors welcome?* Yes *Hours:* Daily, grounds only *Admission:* FREE *Operated by:* Florida Division of Recreation and Parks *NR?* Yes *NHL?* No *Year established/built:* 1848 *Latitude:* 27.6008 *Longitude:* -82.7608

GASPARILLA ISLAND RANGE LIGHTHOUSE

Established in 1890, the front range Gasparilla Island Lighthouse was constructed in 1890, and the rear range tower was built in 1932. Both lights, as known as the Boca Grande Range Lighthouses, are still active aids to navigation. *Address:* Gasparilla Island Lights *City:* Boca Grande *State:* FL *Visitors welcome?* No *Operated by:* Florida Division of Recreation and Parks *NR?* Yes *NHL?* No *Year established/built:* 1890 *Latitude:* 26.7419 *Longitude:* -82.2633

KEY LARGO LIGHTHOUSE

Address: Oleander Circle *City:* Key Largo *State:* FL *Visitors welcome?* No *Operated by:* Private owner *NR?* No *NHL?* No *Year established/built:* 1953 *Latitude:* 25.0921 *Longitude:* -80.4346

KEY WEST LIGHTHOUSE

Established in 1825, the current Key West Lighthouse was constructed in 1847. Deactivated in 1969, the lighthouse is within the Key West National Historic District. *Address:* 938 Whitehead Street *City:* Key West *State:* FL *Zip:* 33040 *Phone:* 305-294-0012 *Web:* www.kwahs.com *Email:* cpennington@kwahs.org *Visitors welcome?* Yes *Hours:* Daily, 9:30 a.m. to 4:30 p.m. *Admission:* Contact attraction directly *Operated by:* Key West Art & Historical Society *NR?* Yes *NHL?* No *Year established/built:* 1825 *Latitude:* 24.55046 *Longitude:* -81.80085

Pensacola Lighthouse, Pensacola Naval Air Station

PENSACOLA LIGHTHOUSE
Established in 1824, the current Pensacola Lighthouse was constructed in 1859 and is still an active aid to navigation within the Pensacola Naval Air Station. *Address:* 2081 Radford Blvd. *City:* Pensacola *State:* FL *Zip:* 32508 *Phone:* 850-393-1561 *Web:* pensacolalighthouse. org *Email:* info@pensacolalighthouse.org *Visitors welcome?* Yes *Hours:* Monday through Saturday: 10 a.m. to 5:30 p.m. *Admission:* Adults, $5; seniors and children six to 11, $3; under six FREE *Operated by:* Pensacola Lighthouse and Museum *NR?* Yes *NHL?* No *Year established/built:* 1824 *Latitude:* 30.34814 *Longitude:* -87.30219

PORT BOCA GRANDE LIGHTHOUSE
Built in 1890 by the U.S. Lighthouse Service to mark the entrance into Charlotte Harbor from the Gulf of Mexico, the Boca Grande Lighthouse is the oldest building on Gasparilla Island and its most recognized landmark. *Address:* Port Boca Grande Light *City:* Boca Grande *State:* FL *Phone:* 941-964-0060 *Web:* www.barrierislandparkssociety. org *Email:* barrierislandparkssociety@yahoo.com *Visitors welcome?* Yes *Hours:* Contact attraction directly *Admission:* Contact attraction directly *Operated by:* Barrier Islands Park Society *NR?* Yes *NHL?* No *Year established/built:* 1890 *Latitude:* 26.7419 *Longitude:* -82.2633

SAND KEY LIGHTHOUSE
Established in 1826, the Sand Key Lighthouse was constructed in 1853. Automated in 1938, the lighthouse is still an active aid to navigation. *Address:* Sand Key *State:* FL *Visitors*

welcome? No *Operated by:* U.S. Coast Guard (District 7) *NR?* Yes *NHL?* No *Year established/built:* 1826 *Latitude:* 27.9591 *Longitude:* -82.8277

SANIBEL ISLAND LIGHTHOUSE

Established and built in 1884, the Sanibel Island Lighthouse was automated in 1949 and is still an active aid to navigation. *Address:* Sanibel Light *City:* Sanibel Island *State:* FL *Visitors welcome?* Yes *Hours:* Daily, grounds only *Admission:* FREE *Operated by:* U.S. Coast Guard (District 7) *NR?* Yes *NHL?* No *Year established/built:* 1884 *Latitude:* 26.4540 *Longitude:* -82.0137

Sombrero Key Lighthouse, Florida

SOMBRERO KEY LIGHTHOUSE

Established and built in 1858, the Sombrero Key Lighthouse was automated in 1960 and is still an active aid to navigation. *Address:* Sombrero Key Light *City:* Marathon *State:* FL *Visitors welcome?* No *Operated by:* U.S. Coast Guard (District 7) *NR?* No *NHL?* No *Year established/built:* 1858 *Latitude:* 24.6279 *Longitude:* -81.1116

ST. MARKS REAR RANGE LIGHTHOUSE

Established in 1831, the current St. Marks Rear Range Lighthouse was constructed in 1842. Automated in 1960, the lighthouse is still an active aid to navigation in a national wildlife refuge. *Address:* St. Marks National Wildlife Refuge *City:* St. Marks *State:* FL *Visitors welcome?* Yes *Hours:* Grounds only *Admission:* Refuge entrance fee *Operated by:* U.S.

Coast Guard (District 7) *NR?* Yes *NHL?* No *Year established/built:* 1831 *Latitude:* 30.1610 *Longitude:* -84.2063

Tortugas Harbor Lighthouse, Dry Tortugas National Park

TORTUGAS HARBOR LIGHTHOUSE

⤙ Established in 1825, the current Tortugas Harbor Lighthouse, also known as the Fort Jefferson Lighthouse or Garden Key Lighthouse, was deactivated in 1921. It is now part of Fort Jefferson National Monument. *Address:* Garden Key Light *State:* FL *Phone:* 305-242-7700 *Visitors welcome?* Yes *Hours:* Contact attraction directly *Admission:* Contact attraction directly *Operated by:* Dry Tortugas National Park *NR?* Yes *NHL?* No *Year established/built:* 1825 *Latitude:* 24.6281 *Longitude:* -82.8722 **Accommodations for overnight and/or long-term stays available.**

LOUISIANA

CHANDELEUR ISLAND LIGHTHOUSE

Established and built in 1896, the Chandeleur Island Lighthouse was destroyed by Hurricane Katrina in 2005. *Address:* Chandeleur Islands *City:* New Orleans *State:* LA *Visitors welcome?* No *Operated by:* Breton National Wildlife Refuge *NR?* No *NHL?* No *Year established/built:* 1896 *Latitude:* 29.83625 *Longitude:* -88.8387

NEW CANAL LIGHTHOUSE
Established in 1838, the current 1890 New Canal Lighthouse is undergoing reconstruction after it was destroyed by Hurricane Katrina in 2005. It will be used as an environmental education center. *Address:* Lakeshore Drive *City:* Metairie *State:* LA *Phone:* 504-836-2215 *Visitors welcome?* No *Operated by:* Lake Pontchartrain Basin Foundation *NR?* Yes *NHL?* No *Year established/built:* 1838 *Latitude:* 30.02062 *Longitude:* -90.17053

PASS A L'OUTRE LIGHTHOUSE
Established and built in 1855, the Pass a l'Outre Lighthouse was decommissioned in 1930 and is now in a decaying condition. *Address:* Pass A Loutre Wildlife Management Area *City:* New Iberia *State:* LA *Visitors welcome?* Yes *Hours:* Grounds only *Admission:* FREE *Operated by:* Pass A Loutre Wildlife Management Area *NR?* No *NHL?* No *Year established/built:* 1855 *Latitude:* 30.00354 *Longitude:* -91.81873

PASS MANCHAC LIGHTHOUSE
Established in 1839, the current Pass Manchac Lighthouse was deactivated in 1987. *Address:* Lake Ponchartrain *City:* New Orleans *State:* LA *Visitors welcome?* Yes *Hours:* Grounds only *Admission:* Grounds only *Operated by:* Lake Maurepas Society *NR?* Yes *NHL?* No *Year established/built:* 1839 *Latitude:* 30.20506 *Longitude:* -90.11207

POINT AU FER REEF LIGHTHOUSE
Established and built in 1916, the Point Au Fer Reef Lighthouse was automated in 1975. *Address:* Eugene Island, Atchafalaya Bay *City:* Berwick *State:* LA *Visitors welcome?* No *Operated by:* U.S. Coast Guard (District 8) *NR?* No *NHL?* No *Year established/built:* 1916 *Latitude:* 29.6947 *Longitude:* -91.2190

PORT PONTCHARTRAIN LIGHTHOUSE
Established in 1832, the current Port Pontchartrain Lighthouse was constructed in 1855 and deactivated in 1929. *Address:* Lakeshore Drive *City:* New Orleans *State:* LA *Visitors welcome?* Yes *Hours:* Grounds only *Admission:* FREE *Operated by:* University of New Orleans *NR?* Yes *NHL?* No *Year established/built:* 1832 *Latitude:* 30.0307 *Longitude:* -90.06016

SABINE PASS LIGHTHOUSE
Established and built in 1856, the Sabine Pass Lighthouse was deactivated in 1952. *City:* Sabine Pass *State:* LA *Visitors welcome?* Yes *Hours:* Grounds only *Admission:* FREE *Operated by:* Cameron Preservation Alliance - Sabine Pass Lighthouse *NR?* Yes *NHL?* No *Year established/built:* 1856 *Latitude:* 29.73309 *Longitude:* -93.89442

SHIP SHOAL LIGHTHOUSE

Established and built in 1858, the Ship Shoal Lighthouse was deactivated in 1965. The Town of Berwich hopes to bring the structure ashore to a city park. *City:* Cocodrie *State:* LA *Visitors welcome?* No *Operated by:* U.S. Coast Guard (District 8) *NR?* No *NHL?* No *Year established/built:* 1858 *Latitude:* 29.24689 *Longitude:* -90.66148

SOUTH PASS RANGE LIGHTHOUSES

Also called the Port Eads Lighthouse, the South Pass Rear Range Lighthouse was built in 1881 and is still an active aid to navigation. The companion front range light was constructed in 1947. *Address:* South Pass *State:* LA *Visitors welcome?* Yes *Hours:* Grounds only *Admission:* FREE *Operated by:* U.S. Coast Guard (District 8) *NR?* Yes *NHL?* No *Year established/built:* 1832 *Latitude:* 28.99468 *Longitude:* -89.14282

SOUTHWEST PASS LIGHTHOUSE 1

Several lighthouses have marked Southwest Pass, the major shipping entrance to the Mississippi River, including one built in 1871. The first lighthouse to mark the entrance was constructed in 1832, and the last one built in 1953 on the end of a jetty. *Address:* Southwest Pass *City:* New Orleans *State:* LA *Visitors welcome?* No *Operated by:* Private owner *NR?* No *NHL?* No *Year established/built:* 1839 *Latitude:* 29.0141 *Longitude:* -89.3442

SOUTHWEST PASS LIGHTHOUSE 2

Several lighthouses have marked Southwest Pass, the major shipping entrance to the Mississippi River, including one built in 1871. The first lighthouse to mark the entrance was constructed in 1832, and the last one built in 1953 on the end of a jetty. *Address:* Southwest Pass, Mississippi River *City:* New Orleans *State:* LA *Visitors welcome?* No *Operated by:* U.S. Coast Guard (District 8) *NR?* No *NHL?* No *Year established/built:* 1871 *Latitude:* 30.1144 *Longitude:* -89.7039

SOUTHWEST PASS LIGHTHOUSE 3

Several lighthouses have marked Southwest Pass, the major shipping entrance to the Mississippi River, including one built in 1871. The first lighthouse to mark the entrance was constructed in 1832, and the last one built in 1953 on the end of a jetty. *Address:* Southwest Pass *City:* New Orleans *State:* LA *Visitors welcome?* No *Operated by:* U.S. Coast Guard (District 8) *NR?* No *NHL?* No *Year established/built:* 1871 *Latitude:* 29.0141 *Longitude:* -89.3442

SOUTHWEST REEF LIGHTHOUSE

Established and built in 1858, the Southwest Reef Lighthouse was deactivated in 1916. It is now located in a city park in the Town of Berwick. *Address:* Atchafalaya River *City:* Berwick *State:* LA *Zip:* 70342 *Phone:* 985-384-8858 *Visitors welcome?* Yes *Hours:* Grounds only *Admission:* FREE *Operated by:* Town of Berwick *NR?* Yes *NHL?* No *Year established/built:* 1858 *Latitude:* 29.69465 *Longitude:* -91.21899

TCHEFUNCTE RIVER LIGHTHOUSE

Established in 1838, the current Tchefuncte River Lighthouse was constructed in 1868 and is still an active aid to navigation. It is operated as a museum by a local historical society. *Address:* Tchefuncte River *City:* Madisonville *State:* LA *Zip:* 70447 *Phone:* 985-845-9200 *Web:* www.lpbmaritimemuseum.org *Visitors welcome?* Yes *Hours:* Contact attraction directly *Admission:* Contact attraction directly *Operated by:* Lake Pontchartrain Basin Maritime Museum *NR?* Yes *NHL?* No *Year established/built:* 1838 *Latitude:* 30.37761 *Longitude:* -90.16342

WEST RIGOLETS LIGHTHOUSE

Established and built in 1855, the West Rigolets Lighthouse was destroyed by Hurricane Katrina in 2005. *Address:* Fort Pike Historic Site *City:* New Orleans *State:* LA *Zip:* 70129 *Phone:* 504-255-9171 *Toll-free:* 888-662-5703 *Visitors welcome?* No *Operated by:* Fort Pike Historic Site *NR?* No *NHL?* No *Year established/built:* 1855 *Latitude:* 30.16625 *Longitude:* -89.73711

MISSISSIPPI

BILOXI LIGHTHOUSE

Built in 1848, the Biloxi Lighthouse was one of the original cast-iron lighthouses constructed in the U.S. It is believed to be the only remaining lighthouse marking the Mississippi shore. *Address:* State Highway 90 *City:* Biloxi *State:* MS *Zip:* 39533 *Phone:* 228-435-6305 *Visitors welcome?* Yes *Hours:* Grounds only *Admission:* FREE *Operated by:* City of Biloxi *NR?* No *NHL?* No *Year established/built:* 1848 *Latitude:* 30.39438 *Longitude:* -88.92143

ROUND ISLAND LIGHTHOUSE

Established in 1833, the current Round Island Lighthouse was constructed in 1859. Decommissioned in the 1940s, the lighthouse was toppled by a hurricane in 1998. *Address:* Round Island *State:* MS *Phone:* 228-938-2356 *Visitors welcome?* Yes *Hours:* Grounds only *Admission:* FREE *Operated by:* City of Pascagoula *NR?* Yes *NHL?* No *Year established/built:* 1833 *Latitude:* 30.29492 *Longitude:* -88.58669

SHIP ISLAND LIGHTHOUSE

Established in 1853, the original Ship Island Lighthouse tower was destroyed by Confederate troops during the Civil War. It was rebuilt by Union troops in 1862. *Address:* Ship Island *State:* MS *Visitors welcome?* Yes *Hours:* Grounds only *Admission:* FREE *Operated by:* U.S. Coast Guard (District 8) *NR?* No *NHL?* No *Year established/built:* 1853 *Latitude:* 30.2082 *Longitude:* -88.95695

NEBRASKA

LINOMA LIGHTHOUSE
The Linoma Lighthouse is located at Linoma Beach, a resort opened in 1926 on the east bank of the Platte River. The lighthouse itself was lit in 1939. *Address:* 17106 S. 255th St. *City:* Gretna *State:* NE *Zip:* 68028 *Phone:* 402-944-3383 *Web:* www.linomalighthouse. com *Email:* support@linomalighthouse.com *Visitors welcome?* Yes *Hours:* Grounds only *Admission:* Contact attraction directly *Operated by:* Private owner *NR?* No *NHL?* No *Year established/built:* 1939 *Latitude:* 41.06222 *Longitude:* -96.32022

TEXAS

GALVESTON JETTY LIGHTHOUSE
Established and built in 1918, the Galveston Jetty Lighthouse was deactivated in 1972 and collapsed in 2000. The lantern room, rescued before the collapse, is now on display at Galveston College. *Address:* Galveston College *City:* Galveston *State:* TX *Visitors welcome?* Yes *Hours:* Grounds only *Admission:* **FREE** *Operated by:* Private owner *NR?* No *NHL?* No *Year established/built:* 1904 *Latitude:* 29.28415 *Longitude:* -94.80833

HALF MOON REEF LIGHTHOUSE
Established in 1858, the Half Moon Reef Lighthouse originally guided mariners through Matagorda Bay. The lighthouse survived several hurricanes, only to be threatened by bombing practice in 1942. The now deactivated lighthouse was moved ashore in 1978. *Address:* 301 South Ann Street *City:* Port Lavaca *State:* TX *Phone:* 361-552-9793 *Visitors welcome?* Yes *Hours:* Contact attraction directly *Admission:* Contact attraction directly *Operated by:* City of Port Lavaca *NR?* No *NHL?* No *Year established/built:* 1858 *Latitude:* 28.61278 *Longitude:* -96.6255

LYDIA ANN LIGHTHOUSE
Established in 1855 and built in 1857, the Lydia Ann Lighthouse, originally called the Aransas Pass Lighthouse, was destroyed by Confederate soldiers during the Civil War. The second, current structure was built in 1867, was deactivated in 1952. *Address:* Lydia Ann Channel *City:* Port Aransas *State:* TX *Visitors welcome?* No *Operated by:* Private owner *NR?* Yes *NHL?* No *Year established/built:* 1855 *Latitude:* 27.7151 *Longitude:* -97.1425

MATAGORDA ISLAND LIGHTHOUSE
Established and built in 1852, the cast-iron Matagorda Island Lighthouse was damaged during the Civil War. After the war, it was moved to avoid encroachment by the Gulf of Mexico. The lighthouse is now within a state park. *Address:* Matagorda Island State

Park *State:* TX *Phone:* 979-244-7697 *Visitors welcome?* Yes *Hours:* Grounds only *Admission:* FREE *Operated by:* Matagorda Island Foundation *NR?* Yes *NHL?* No *Year established/built:* 1852 *Latitude:* 28.1689 *Longitude:* -96.7387

POINT BOLIVAR LIGHTHOUSE

Established in 1852, the cast-iron Point Bolivar Lighthouse was dismantled at the beginning of the Civil War so that its plating could be used for armaments. A new iron tower was lit in 1872 and remained active until 1933. The lighthouse is now in private hands. *City:* Port Bolivar *State:* TX *Visitors welcome?* No *Operated by:* Private owner *NR?* Yes *NHL?* No *Year established/built:* 1852 *Latitude:* 29.38079 *Longitude:* -94.76436

PORT ISABEL LIGHTHOUSE

The Port Isabel Lighthouse, also called the Point Isabel Lighthouse, was built in 1852 in response to requests from sea captains for help in navigating around the low-lying Texas coast. *Address:* 421 East Queen Isabella Blvd *City:* Port Isabel *State:* TX *Zip:* 78578 *Phone:* 956-943-2262 *Visitors welcome?* Yes *Hours:* Sunday to Thursday, 10 a.m. to 6 p.m.; Friday and Saturday, 11 a.m. to 8 p.m. *Admission:* Contact attraction directly *Operated by:* Museums of Port Isabel *NR?* Yes *NHL?* No *Year established/built:* 1852 *Latitude:* 26.0774 *Longitude:* -97.2076

SABINE PASS LIGHTHOUSE

Established in 1906, the coffee pot-style Sabine Pass Lighthouse is located 15 miles from the mouth of the Sabine River in the Gulf of Mexico. The lighthouse's lantern was removed in 2002 and placed on shore as an exhibit. *Address:* Lions Park *City:* Sabine *State:* TX *Visitors welcome?* Yes *Hours:* Grounds only *Admission:* FREE *Operated by:* Private owner *NR?* No *NHL?* No *Year established/built:* 1906 *Latitude:* 29.87644 *Longitude:* -93.92761

Some lighthouses limit kid access to those taller than four feet, sometimes more. Call first!

CHAPTER 4

WEST COAST, ALASKA, AND HAWAII LIGHTHOUSES

Grays Harbor Lighthouse, Westport, Washington

Lighthouses you can visit today in Alaska, California, Hawaii, Oregon, and Washington state. Use your smart phone QR or bar code reader to visit this Fyddeye web page.

FYDDEYE RECOMMENDS:	
Alcatraz Island Lighthouse, San Francisco, California	Pigeon Point Lighthouse, Pescadero, California
Grays Harbor Lighthouse, Westport, Washington	Point Arena Lighthouse, Point Arena, California
Heceta Head Lighthouse, Florence, Oregon	Point Fermin Lighthouse, San Pedro, California
Molokai Lighthouse, Kalaupapa, Hawaii	Yaquina Bay Lighthouse, Newport, Oregon
Mukilteo Lighthouse, Mukilteo, Washington	Yaquina Head Lighthouse, Agate Beach, Oregon

ALASKA

CAPE DECISION LIGHTHOUSE

Established and built in 1932, the Cape Decision Lighthouse was the last constructed in Alaskan waters. Still an active aid to navigation, it is now managed by a not-for-profit. *Address:* Cape Decision *State:* AK *Visitors welcome?* Yes *Hours:* By appointment *Admission:* Contact attraction directly *Operated by:* Cape Decision Lighthouse Society *NR?* Yes *NHL?* No *Year established/built:* 1932 *Latitude:* 56.00555 *Longitude:* -134.13251

CAPE HINCHINBROOK LIGHTHOUSE

Established in 1910, the current Cape Hinchinbrook Lighthouse was constructed in 1934. The light was automated in 1974 and is still an active aid to navigation at the entrance to Prince William Sound. *Address:* Cape Hinchinbrook Light *City:* Cordova *State:* AK *Visitors welcome?* No *Operated by:* U.S. Coast Guard (District 17) *NR?* No *NHL?* No *Year established/built:* 1910 *Latitude:* 60.2375 *Longitude:* -146.6470

CAPE SPENCER LIGHTHOUSE

Established in 1913, the current Cape Spencer Lighthouse was constructed in 1925 and automated in 1974. The light is still an active aid to navigation. *Address:* Cape Spencer Light *State:* AK *Visitors welcome?* No *Operated by:* U.S. Coast Guard (District 17) *NR?* Yes *NHL?* No *Year established/built:* 1913 *Latitude:* 58.19889 *Longitude:* -136.64444

CAPE ST. ELIAS LIGHTHOUSE

Established and built in 1916, the Cape St. Elias lighthouse is at the south end of Kodiak Island and is still an active aid to navigation. *Address:* Cape St. Elias Light *City:* Cordova *State:* AK *Visitors welcome?* Yes *Hours:* Contact attraction directly *Admission:* Contact attraction directly *Operated by:* Cape Saint Elias Lighthouse Keepers Association *NR?* Yes *NHL?* No *Year established/built:* 1916 *Latitude:* 59.79833 *Longitude:* -144.59889

ELDRED ROCK LIGHTHOUSE

Established and built in 1905, the Eldred Rock Lighthouse was renovated in 1996 and leased to a local museum. It is still an active aid to naviation. *Address:* Eldred Rock Light *City:* Haines *State:* AK *Visitors welcome?* No *Operated by:* U.S. Coast Guard (District 17) *NR?* Yes *NHL?* No *Year established/built:* 1905 *Latitude:* 58.97167 *Longitude:* -135.22084

FIVE FINGERS ISLAND LIGHTHOUSE

Established in 1902, the Five Fingers Island Lighthouse is the first Alaskan lighthouse. The current structure was built in 1935 and is now managed by a not-for-profit organization. *Address:* Five Finger Islands Light *State:* AK *Visitors welcome?* Yes *Hours:* Contact attraction directly *Admission:* Contact attraction directly *Operated by:* Juneau Lighthouse Association *NR?* Yes *NHL?* No *Year established/built:* 1902 *Latitude:* 57.27028 *Longitude:* -133.63139

GUARD ISLAND LIGHTHOUSE

Established in 1904, the current Guard Island Lighthouse was built in 1924 and automated in 1969. It is still an active aid to navigation. *Address:* Guard Island Light *State:* AK *Visitors welcome?* No *Operated by:* U.S. Coast Guard (District 17) *NR?* Yes *NHL?* No *Year established/built:* 1905 *Latitude:* 55.44584 *Longitude:* -131.8811

MARY ISLAND LIGHTHOUSE

Established in 1903, the current Mary Island Lighthouse was constructed in 1937 and is still an active aid to navigation. *Address:* Mary Island *City:* Ketchikan *State:* AK *Visitors welcome?* No *Operated by:* U.S. Coast Guard (District 17) *NR?* No *NHL?* No *Year established/built:* 1903 *Latitude:* 55.0985 *Longitude:* -131.18401

ODIAK PHAROS

The Odiak Pharos is a small, privately owned navigation aid. *Address:* 1315 Whitshed Rd. *City:* Cordova *State:* AK *Visitors welcome?* Yes *Hours:* Daily *Admission:* FREE *Operated by:* Cordova Rose Lodge *NR?* No *NHL?* No *Year established/built:* 1992 *Latitude:* 60.53907 *Longitude:* -145.75258

POINT RETREAT LIGHTHOUSE

Established in 1903, the current Point Retreat Lighthouse was constructed in 1924 and is still an active aid to navigation. It is now managed by a not-for-profit. *Address:* Admirality Island *City:* Douglas *State:* AK *Visitors welcome?* Yes *Hours:* By appointment *Admission:* Contact attraction directly *Operated by:* Alaska Lighthouse Association *NR?* Yes *NHL?* No *Year established/built:* 1903 *Latitude:* 57.6269 *Longitude:* -134.36301

POINT SHERMAN LIGHTHOUSE

Established in 1904, the Point Sherman Lighthouse was downgraded to a minor light by World War I. Today, only a dayboard and a light mark the location of the original structures. *Address:* Point Sherman Light *City:* Juneau *State:* AK *Visitors welcome?* No *Operated by:* U.S. Coast Guard (District 17) *NR?* No *NHL?* No *Year established/built:* 1904 *Latitude:* 58.8550 *Longitude:* -135.1517

SENTINEL ISLAND LIGHTHOUSE

Established in 1902. the current Sentinel Island Lighthouse was constructed in 1935 and automated in 1966. It is still an active aid to navigation and managed by a local historical society. *Address:* Sentinel Island Light *State:* AK *Phone:* 907-586-5338 *Visitors welcome?* Yes *Hours:* Contact attraction directly *Admission:* Contact attraction directly *Operated by:* Gastineau Channel Historical Society *NR?* Yes *NHL?* No *Year established/built:* 1902 *Latitude:* 58.54611 *Longitude:* -134.92278

TREE POINT LIGHTHOUSE

Established in 1903, the current Tree Point Lighthouse was constructed in 1935 and automated in 1969. It is still an active aid to navigation. *Address:* Misty Fjords National Monument *City:* Ketchikan *State:* AK *Visitors welcome?* No *Operated by:* U.S. Coast Guard (District 17) *NR?* No *NHL?* No *Year established/built:* 1903 *Latitude:* 55.62167 *Longitude:* -130.60722

Cape Decision Lighthouse, Alaska

CALIFORNIA

ALCATRAZ ISLAND LIGHTHOUSE

Established in 1853, the original tower of the Alcatraz Lighthouse was destroyed by the 1906 San Francisco Earthquake. The replacement tower was constructed shortly afterward, and it is now part of the Alcatraz Island National Historic Landmark. *Address:* Alcatraz Island Light *City:* San Francisco *State:* CA *Visitors welcome?* Yes *Hours:* By appointment *Admission:* FREE *Operated by:* Golden Gate National Parks *NR?* Yes *NHL?* No *Year established/built:* 1853 *Latitude:* 37.82623 *Longitude:* -122.4222

ANACAPA ISLAND LIGHTHOUSE

Established in 1930 and built in 1932, the Anacapa Island Lighthouse is now part of Channels Islands National Park. *Address:* Anacapa Island Light *State:* CA *Zip:* 93001 *Visitors welcome?* Yes *Hours:* Grounds open, tower closed *Admission:* FREE *Operated by:* Channel Islands National Park *NR?* Yes *NHL?* No *Year established/built:* 1930 *Latitude:* 34.0156 *Longitude:* -119.3580

ANO NUEVO LIGHTHOUSE

Established in 1872, the tower for Ano Nuevo Lighthouse off Pigeon Point near Santa Cruz was first lit in 1890, but the Coast Guard shut it down in 1948. The ruins are now in the Ano Nuevo State Reserve. *Address:* New Years Creek Road *City:* Pescadero *State:* CA *Visitors welcome?* No *Operated by:* California Dept. of Parks and Recreation *NR?* No *NHL?* No *Year established/built:* 1872 *Latitude:* 37.10818 *Longitude:* -122.33672

BATTERY POINT LIGHTHOUSE

Established and built in 1855, the Battery Point Lighthouse was named for cannon salvaged from a nearby wreck. Automated in 1953, the lighthouse, known officially as the Crescent City Lighthouse, is now operated by the Del Norte Historical Society as a museum. *Address:* Battery Point Light *City:* Crescent City *State:* CA *Visitors welcome?* Yes *Hours:* 10 a.m. to 4 p.m., Wednesday through Sunday, April through September *Admission:* Contact attraction directly *Operated by:* Del Norte County Historical Society *NR?* Yes *NHL?* No *Year established/built:* 1855 *Latitude:* 41.7440 *Longitude:* -124.2030

California Coastal Lighthouse Tour Itvinerary

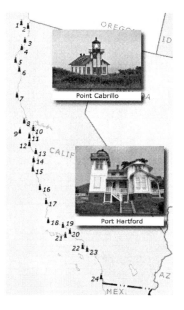

1. St. George Reef	13. Walton (Santa Cruz)
2. Battery Point (Crescent City)	14. Point Pinos (Pacific Grove)
3. Trinidad Head (Trinidad)	15. Point Sur (Carmel)
4. Old Table Bluff (Eureka)	16. Piedras Blancas
5. Punta Gorda	17. Port Hartford (San Luis Obispo)
6. Cape Mendocino	18. Point Conception (Concepcion)
7. Point Cabrillo (Mendocino)	19. Santa Barbara
8. Point Reyes (Point Reyes Station)	20. Port Hueneme
9. Farallon Islands	21. Anacapa Island
10. Alcatraz Island (San Francisco Bay)	22. Point Vicente (Rancho Palos Verdes)
11. Point Montara (Moss Beach)	23. Point Fermin (San Pedro)
12. Pigeon Point (Pescadero)	24. Old Point Loma (San Diego)

California lighthouses mark some of the most spectacular maritime scenery in the country. Begin with Battery Point in Crescent City and follow U.S. Highway 101 to the California Highway 1 cutoff. Then follow Highway 1 all the way to where it joins Interstate 5 near Dana Point. Then make your way to San Diego and Old Point Loma at the Cabrillo National Monument. It's a five to ten day trip--and unforgettable.

California lighthouses mark some of the most spectacular maritime scenery in the country. Begin with Battery Point in Crescent City and follow U.S. Highway 101 to the California Highway 1 cutoff. Then follow Highway 1 all the way to where it joins Interstate 5 near Dana Point. Then make your way to San Diego and Old Point Loma at the Cabrillo National Monument. It's a five- to ten-day trip--and unforgettable.
BOX ENDS

CAPE MENDOCINO LIGHTHOUSE

Constructed in 1867 and 1868 on the westernmost tip of California, Cape Mendocino Lighthouse warned mariners away from one of the most dangerous shorelines in the state. *Address:* Cape Medocino *State:* CA *Visitors welcome?* Yes *Hours:* Grounds open, tower closed *Admission:* FREE *Operated by:* Cape Mendocino Lighthouse Preservation Society - Shelter Cove *NR?* No *NHL?* No *Year established/built:* 1867 *Latitude:* 40.44013 *Longitude:* -124.4095

CARQUINEZ STRAIT LIGHTHOUSE

Built in 1910, the lighthouse was one of seventeen stations in the San Francisco Bay Area, In 1955, the U.S. Coast Guard automated the light and fog horn, and the light station residence was sold to a private owner who moved the building to its present position. *Address:* 2000 Glen Cove Marina Rd *City:* Vallejo *State:* CA *Zip:* 94591 *Phone:* 707-552-3236 *Web:* www.glencovemarina.net *Email:* glencovemarina@gmail.com *Visitors welcome?* Yes *Hours:* Contact attraction directly *Admission:* Contact attraction directly *Operated by:* Glen Cove Marina *NR?* No *NHL?* No *Year established/built:* 1910 *Latitude:* 38.0693 *Longitude:* -122.2130

EAST BROTHER ISLAND LIGHTHOUSE

✦ Built on San Pablo Strait in 1874 at the request of ship captains, East Brother Island Lighthouse is at the point where the San Francisco and San Pablo bays meet. It is now a bed and breakfast. *Address:* East Brother Island Light *City:* North Richmond *State:* CA *Visitors welcome?* Yes *Hours:* By appointment *Admission:* Contact attraction directly *Operated by:* East Brother Light Station, Inc. *NR?* Yes *NHL?* No *Year established/built:* 1874 *Latitude:* 37.9633 *Longitude:* -122.4330 **Accommodations for overnight and/or long-term stays available.**

FARALLON ISLAND LIGHTHOUSE

Established and built in 1855, the Farallon Islands Lighthouse was constructed on the tallest point of the rocky, lonely Farallon Islands. The station was automated in 1972, and the islands are now part of the Farallon Islands National Wildlife Refuge. *Address:* Farallon Islands *City:* San Francisco *State:* CA *Zip:* 94560 *Visitors welcome?* No *Operated by:* U.S. Coast Guard (District 11) *NR?* No *NHL?* No *Year established/built:* 1855 *Latitude:* 37.6993 *Longitude:* -123.0040

FORT POINT LIGHTHOUSE

Established in 1853, the current Fort Point Lighthouse was built two years later and served until 1934, when navigational aids on the Golden Gate Bridge replaced it. The lighthouse is now part of Fort Point National Historic Site. *Address:* Fort Point Light *City:* San Francisco *State:* CA *Visitors welcome?* Yes *Hours:* Thursday through Monday, 10 a.m. to 5 p.m. *Admission:* FREE *Operated by:* Golden Gate National Parks *NR?* Yes *NHL?* No *Year established/built:* 1853 *Latitude:* 37.8110 *Longitude:* -122.4770

HUMBOLDT HARBOR LIGHTHOUSE

Established and built in 1856, the Humboldt Harbor Lighthouse served until 1896, when the site was abandoned by the Coast Guard. Only the ruins of the lighthouse remains, although the original Fresnel lens is at the nearby Humboldt Bay Maritime Museum. *City:* Samoa *State:* CA *Visitors welcome?* Yes *Hours:* Dawn to dusk *Admission:* FREE *Operated by:* Samoa Dunes Recreation Area *NR?* No *NHL?* No *Year established/built:* 1856 *Latitude:* 40.81874 *Longitude:* -124.18646

LIME POINT LIGHTHOUSE

Established in 1833, the original tower, now gone, was built in 1900. Only the fog signal building remains of the automated station. *Address:* Lime Point Light *City:* Sausalito *State:* CA *Visitors welcome?* No *Operated by:* Golden Gate National Parks *NR?* No *NHL?* No *Year established/built:* 1833 *Latitude:* 37.82554 *Longitude:* -122.47841

LONG BEACH HARBOR LIGHTHOUSE

Completed in 1949, the Long Beach Harbor Lighthouse guides container ships into one of the busiest container shipping facilities in the world. *Address:* Long Beach Light *City:* Long Beach *State:* CA *Visitors welcome?* No *Operated by:* U.S. Coast Guard (District 11) *NR?* No *NHL?* No *Year established/built:* 1949 *Latitude:* 33.72306 *Longitude:* -118.18667

LOS ANGELES HARBOR LIGHTHOUSE

Address: Los Angeles Harbor Light *City:* San Pedro *State:* CA *Visitors welcome?* Yes *Hours:* Dawn to dusk *Admission:* FREE *Operated by:* U.S. Coast Guard (District 11) *NR?* No *NHL?* No *Year established/built:* 1913 *Latitude:* 33.70833 *Longitude:* -118.25139

MILE ROCK LIGHTHOUSE

Established and built in 1906, the Mile Rock Lighthouse was automated in 1966 and a helicopter pad added by the Coast Guard. *Address:* Mile Rock *City:* San Francisco *State:* CA *Visitors welcome?* No *Operated by:* U.S. Coast Guard (District 11) *NR?* No *NHL?* No *Year established/built:* 1906 *Latitude:* 37.7928 *Longitude:* -122.5100

NEW POINT LOMA LIGHTHOUSE

Built in 1889 to replace the Old Point Loma Lighthouse, the New Point Loma Lighthouse on Pigeon Point is used today as Coast Guard quarters. *Address:* Cabrillo National

Monument *City:* San Diego *State:* CA *Visitors welcome?* No *Operated by:* U.S. Coast Guard (District 11) *NR?* No *NHL?* No *Year established/built:* 1889 *Latitude:* 37.1819 *Longitude:* -122.3950

OAKLAND HARBOR LIGHTHOUSE

Established and built in 1890, the 1903 Oakland Harbor Lighthouse building was moved in the 1960s to its current location at Embarcadero Cove Marina. It is now a restaurant. *Address:* 1951 Embarcadero East *City:* Oakland *State:* CA *Zip:* 94606 *Phone:* 510-536-2050 *Web:* www.quinnslighthouse.com#www.quinnslighthou *Email:* quinnslighthouse@aol.com *Visitors welcome?* Yes *Hours:* Contact attraction directly *Admission:* FREE *Operated by:* Quinn's Lighthouse Restaurant & Pub *NR?* No *NHL?* No *Year established/built:* 1890 *Latitude:* 37.78175 *Longitude:* -122.2429

OLD POINT LOMA LIGHTHOUSE

One of the first set of eight lighthouses on the California coast, Old Point Loma stands near the place where the first European set foot on California in 1542. Completed in 1854, the station was the highest in the nation for many years, at 462 feet above sea level. *Address:* Point Loma Light *City:* San Diego *State:* CA *Zip:* 88505 *Phone:* 619-557-5450 *Visitors welcome?* Yes *Hours:* Daily, 9 a.m. to 5 p.m. *Admission:* FREE *Operated by:* Cabrillo National Monument *NR?* Yes *NHL?* No *Year established/built:* 1854 *Latitude:* 32.6717 *Longitude:* -117.2410

PIEDRAS BLANCAS LIGHTHOUSE

Named for a white rock outcrop near the point itself, Piedras Blancas Lighthouse was built in 1875. A two-story Victorian-style dwelling was added later that year, though it was later torn down. *Address:* Piedras Blancas Light Station *State:* CA *Visitors welcome?* Yes *Hours:* By appointment *Admission:* Donation requested for tours. *Operated by:* Piedras Blancas Light Station Association *NR?* Yes *NHL?* No *Year established/built:* 1875 *Latitude:* 35.6653 *Longitude:* -121.2840

PIGEON POINT LIGHTHOUSE

✛ Built in 1872, the Pigeon Point Lighthouse south of San Francisco is one of the tallest in the U.S. at 115 feet. It is still an active aid to navigation. *Address:* 210 Pigeon Point Road *City:* Pescadero *State:* CA *Zip:* 94060 *Phone:* 650-879-2120 *Web:* www.parks.ca.gov/default.asp?page_id=533#ww *Visitors welcome?* Yes *Hours:* 8 a.m. to sunset *Admission:* Contact attraction directly *Operated by:* California Dept. of Parks and Recreation *NR?* Yes *NHL?* No *Year established/built:* 1872 *Latitude:* 37.1821 *Longitude:* -122.3940 **Accommodations for overnight and/or long-term stays available.**

POINT ARENA LIGHTHOUSE

✛ Established in 1870, the current Point Arena Lighthouse was constructed in 1908, and it is still an active aid to navigation. The lighthouse was automated in 1977, and the keepers quarters are rented out to visitors. *Address:* Point Arena Light *City:* Point Arena *State:* CA *Zip:* 95468 *Phone:* 877-725-4448 *Web:* www.pointarenalighthouse.com *Email:* palight@mcn.org *Visitors welcome?* Yes *Hours:* Daily, 10 a.m. to 3:30 p.m. *Admission:* $5 adults; $1 children under 12 *Operated by:* Point Arena Lighthouse Keepers *NR?* No *NHL?* No *Year established/built:* 1870 *Latitude:* 38.95472 *Longitude:* -123.74056 **Accommodations for overnight and/or long-term stays available.**

POINT ARGUELLO LIGHTHOUSE

First lit in 1901, the Point Arguello Lighthouse looked over one of the most treacherous areas of California coastline, famed for taking dozens of ships and many lives, before and after it began operations. *Address:* Point Arguello Light *State:* CA *Visitors welcome?* No *Operated by:* U.S. Coast Guard (District 11) *NR?* No *NHL?* No *Year established/built:* 1901 *Latitude:* 34.57695 *Longitude:* -120.64722

POINT BLUNT LIGHTHOUSE

Point Blunt Lighthouse, really a large shed on a prominent point on Angel Island, helped marked the entrance to San Francisco Bay beginning in 1915. The lighthouse was torn down in the 1960s when the Coast Guard automated the station. *Address:* Point Blunt Light *City:* San Francisco *State:* CA *Visitors welcome?* No *Operated by:* U.S. Coast Guard (District 11) *NR?* No *NHL?* No *Year established/built:* 1915 *Latitude:* 37.85312 *Longitude:* -122.41907

POINT BONITA LIGHTHOUSE

Established in 1855, the current Point Bonita Lighthouse was constructed in 1877 and automated in 1980. It is still an active aid to navigation. *Address:* Point Bonita Lighthouse *City:* Sausalito *State:* CA *Visitors welcome?* No *Operated by:* Golden Gate National Parks *NR?* Yes *NHL?* No *Year established/built:* 1855 *Latitude:* 37.81592 *Longitude:* -122.52885

POINT CABRILLO LIGHTHOUSE

✛ Established and built in 1909, the Point Cabrillo Lighthouse was automated in 1973 and is still an active aid to navigation. *Address:* Point Cabrillo Light *City:* Mendocino *State:* CA *Visitors welcome?* Yes *Hours:* Daily, 9 a.m. to dusk *Admission:* FREE *Operated by:* Point Cabrillo Lightkeepers Association *NR?* Yes *NHL?* No *Year established/built:* 1909 *Latitude:* 39.3483 *Longitude:* -123.8260 **Accommodations for overnight and/or long-term stays available.**

POINT CONCEPTION LIGHTHOUSE

Established in 1854, the current Point Conception Lighthouse was constructed in 1882 and automated in 1973. It is still an active aid to navigation. *Address:* Point Conception Lighthouse *City:* Concepcion *State:* CA *Visitors welcome?* No *Operated by:* U.S. Coast Guard (District 11) *NR?* Yes *NHL?* No *Year established/built:* 1856 *Latitude:* 34.4485 *Longitude:* -120.4710

POINT DIABLO LIGHTHOUSE

Established and built in 1923, the Point Diablo Lighthouse is now an automated aid to navigation. *Address:* Point Diablo Light *City:* Sausalito *State:* CA *Visitors welcome?* No *Operated by:* Golden Gate National Parks *NR?* No *NHL?* No *Year established/built:* 1923 *Latitude:* 37.8200 *Longitude:* -122.49965

POINT FERMIN LIGHTHOUSE

Established and buit in 1874, the Point Fermin Lighthouse was deactivated in 1942, and it is now owned by the City of Los Angeles as a public facility. *Address:* 807 W. Paseo Del Mar *City:* San Pedro *State:* CA *Zip:* 90731 *Phone:* 310-241-0684 *Web:* www.point-ferminlighthouse.org *Visitors welcome?* Yes *Hours:* Tuesday through Sunday, 1 p.m. to 4 p.m. *Admission:* Donation requested *Operated by:* Point Fermin Lighthouse Historic Site and Museum *NR?* Yes *NHL?* No *Year established/built:* 1874 *Latitude:* 33.7122 *Longitude:* -118.3040

POINT HUENEME LIGHTHOUSE

Established in 1874, the current Point Hueneme Lighthouse was constructed in 1941, and it is still an active aid to navigation. *Address:* Point Hueneme Light *City:* Port Hueneme *State:* CA *Zip:* 93041 *Phone:* 310-541-0334 *Web:* huenemelight.org *Visitors welcome?* Yes *Hours:* Contact attraction directly *Admission:* Contact attraction directly *Operated by:* U.S. Coast Guard (District 11) *NR?* No *NHL?* No *Year established/built:* 1874 *Latitude:* 34.1450 *Longitude:* -119.2098

POINT KNOX LIGHTHOUSE

Established in 1885, the Point Knox Lighthouse is located on the southwest corner of Angel Island in San Francisco Bay. *Address:* Point Knox *State:* CA *Visitors welcome?* No *Operated by:* California Dept. of Parks and Recreation *NR?* No *NHL?* No *Year established/built:* 1885 *Latitude:* 37.85639 *Longitude:* -122.44209

POINT MONTARA LIGHTHOUSE

✦ Established in 1875, the current Point Montara Lighthouse was constructed in 1928. Automated in 1970, the lighthouse is still an active aid to navigation. *Address:* Point Montara Light *City:* Moss Beach *State:* CA *Visitors welcome?* Yes *Hours:* Grounds open, tower closed. *Admission:* FREE *Operated by:* California Dept. of Parks and Recreation *NR?* Yes *NHL?* No *Year established/built:* 1875 *Latitude:* 37.5363 *Longitude:* -122.5190 **Accommodations for overnight and/or long-term stays available.**

POINT PINOS LIGHTHOUSE

Established and built in 1855, the Point Pinos Lighthouse was automated in 1975. The lighthouse was decommissioned in 1993, but it is still operated as a private aid to navigation. *Address:* 165 Forest Avenue *City:* Pacific Grove *State:* CA *Zip:* 93950 *Phone:* 831-648-5716 *Web:* www.pgmuseum.org *Visitors welcome?* Yes *Hours:* 1 p.m. to 4 p.m., Thursday through Monday *Admission:* $1 youths; $2 adults *Operated by:* Pacific Grove Museum of Natural History *NR?* Yes *NHL?* No *Year established/built:* 1855 *Latitude:* 36.6219 *Longitude:* -121.91744

POINT REYES LIGHTHOUSE

Established and built in 1870, the Point Reyes Lighthouse was deactivated in 1975. It is part of the Point Reyes National Seashore. *Address:* Point Reyes National Seashore *City:* Point Reyes Station *State:* CA *Zip:* 94956 *Phone:* 415-464-5100 *Visitors welcome?* Yes *Hours:* 10 a.m. to 4:30 p.m., Thursday through Monday *Admission:* **FREE** *Operated by:* Point Reyes National Seashore *NR?* Yes *NHL?* No *Year established/built:* 1870 *Latitude:* 38.0670 *Longitude:* -122.87613

POINT SUR LIGHTHOUSE

Established and built in 1889, the sandstone Point Sur Lighthouse was automated in 1972 and is still an active aid to navigation. *Address:* Point Sur Lighthouse Reservation *City:* Carmel *State:* CA *Zip:* 93923 *Phone:* 831-625-4419 *Web:* www.pointsur.org *Email:* info@pointsur.org *Visitors welcome?* Yes *Hours:* Daily *Admission:* $8 adults; children six to 17, $4; under six FREE. *Operated by:* Point Sur State Historic Park and Lighthouse *NR?* Yes *NHL?* No *Year established/built:* 1889 *Latitude:* 36.30635 *Longitude:* -121.90163

POINT VICENTE LIGHTHOUSE

Established and built in 1926, the Point Vicente Lighthouse was automated in 1973 and is still an active aid to navigation. *Address:* Point Vicente Light *City:* Rancho Palos Verdes *State:* CA *Zip:* 90275 *Phone:* 310-541-0334 *Web:* www.vicentelight.org/ *Email:* auxsites@gmail.com *Visitors welcome?* Yes *Hours:* Some tours *Admission:* Contact attraction directly *Operated by:* U.S. Coast Guard (District 11) *NR?* Yes *NHL?* No *Year established/built:* 1926 *Latitude:* 33.7419 *Longitude:* -118.4106

PUNTA GORDA LIGHTHOUSE

Established in 1911 and built the following year, the Punta Gorda Lighthouse was deactivated in 1951. *Address:* Punta Gorda Light *State:* CA *Visitors welcome?* Yes *Hours:* Daily *Admission:* **FREE** *Operated by:* King Range National Conservation Area *NR?* Yes *NHL?* No *Year established/built:* 1911 *Latitude:* 40.2493 *Longitude:* -124.3503

SAN LUIS OBISPO LIGHTHOUSE

Established and built in 1890, the San Luis Obispo Lighthouse is also known as the Port Harford Lighthouse. Deactivated in 1975, the station was recently restored by a local not-for-profit organization. *Address:* San Luis Light *City:* San Luis Obispo *State:* CA *Visitors welcome?* Yes *Hours:* Contact attraction directly *Admission:* Contact attraction directly *Operated by:* Point San Luis Lighthouse Keepers *NR?* Yes *NHL?* No *Year established/built:* 1890 *Latitude:* 35.1601 *Longitude:* -120.7600

SANTA BARBARA LIGHTHOUSE

Established in 1856, the original lighthouse was lost in a 1925 earthquake and is now a skeletal metal tower. *Address:* Santa Barbara Light *City:* Santa Barbara *State:* CA *Visitors welcome?* No *Operated by:* U.S. Coast Guard (District 11) *NR?* No *NHL?* No *Year established/built:* 1856 *Latitude:* 34.3958 *Longitude:* -119.7232

SANTA CRUZ BREAKWATER LIGHTHOUSE

Constructed in 2001, the Santa Cruz breakwater has shown a beacon since the 1960s. The local community wanted a more traditional-looking lighthouse, and money was raised to build the current structure. *Address:* Santa Cruz Breakwater Light *City:* Santa Cruz *State:* CA *Visitors welcome?* Yes *Hours:* Grounds open, tower closed *Admission:* FREE *Operated by:* U.S. Coast Guard (District 11) *NR?* No *NHL?* No *Year established/built:* 2001 *Latitude:* 36.9604 *Longitude:* -122.0023

SANTA CRUZ LIGHTHOUSE

Established in 1869, the current Santa Cruz Lighthouse is a reconstruction of a lighthouse that was demolished in 1948. The structure is now home to the Santa Cruz Surfing Museum. *Address:* 701 West Cliff Drive *City:* Santa Cruz *State:* CA *Zip:* 95060 *Phone:* 831-420-6289 *Web:* www.santacruzsurfingmuseum.org *Visitors welcome?* Yes *Hours:* Winter: Thursday through Monday, noon to 4 p.m.; Summer: Summer hours (July 4th through Labor Day): Wednesday through Monday, 10 a.m. to 5 p.m. *Admission:* FREE *Operated by:* Santa Cruz Surfing Museum *NR?* No *NHL?* No *Year established/built:* 1869 *Latitude:* 36.9687 *Longitude:* -122.0160

SOUTHAMPTON SHOALS LIGHTHOUSE

Built in 1905, the Southampton Shoal lighthouse stood on navigational hazard along the eastern side of the shipping channel that runs between Angel Island and the Tiburon Peninsula near Berkeley. *Address:* Tinsley Island *City:* Stockton *State:* CA *Phone:* 209-607-3199 *Visitors welcome?* Yes *Hours:* Members only *Admission:* Members only *Operated by:* St. Francis Yacht Club *NR?* No *NHL?* No *Year established/built:* 1905 *Latitude:* 38.0377 *Longitude:* 121.4960

ST. GEORGE REEF LIGHTHOUSE

Established in 1867, the current St. George Reef Lighthouse was deactivated from 1975 to 2002, when it was returned to active service. It is often known as the most expensive lighthouse in America, taking ten years to construct. *Address:* St. George Reef Light *State:* CA *Visitors welcome?* No *Operated by:* St. George Reef Lighthouse Preservation Society *NR?* Yes *NHL?* No *Year established/built:* 1867 *Latitude:* 41.83633 *Longitude:* -124.37587

TABLE BLUFF LIGHTHOUSE

Established and built in 1892, the Table Bluff Lighthouse was moved to its current location in 1987. *Address:* Table Bluff Light *City:* Eureka *State:* CA *Zip:* 95502 *Visitors welcome?*

Yes *Hours:* Grounds only; tower is closed *Admission:* FREE *Operated by:* Humboldt Bay Harbor Recreation & Conservation District *NR?* No *NHL?* No *Year established/built:* 1890 *Latitude:* 40.69584 *Longitude:* -124.27393

TRINIDAD HEAD LIGHTHOUSE

Established in 1866, the current Trinidad Head Lighthouse was buit in 1871 and automated in 1974. It is still an active aid to navigation. *Address:* Trinidad Head Light *City:* Trinidad *State:* CA *Visitors welcome?* No *Operated by:* U.S. Coast Guard (District 11) *NR?* Yes *NHL?* No *Year established/built:* 1866 *Latitude:* 41.0518 *Longitude:* -124.1514

TRINIDAD MEMORIAL LIGHTHOUSE

The Trinidad Memorial Lighthouse was constructed in 1949 as a memorial to local residents lost at sea. The bell is rung daily at noon. The structure was improved with new windows and a new dome in 1998. The actual Trinidad Head Lighthouse is located nearby. *Address:* Edwards Street *City:* Trinidad *State:* CA *Zip:* 95570 *Visitors welcome?* Yes *Hours:* Grounds open, tower closed *Admission:* FREE *Operated by:* City of Trinidad *NR?* No *NHL?* No *Year established/built:* 1949 *Latitude:* 41.0585 *Longitude:* -124.1450

YERBA BUENA LIGHTHOUSE

Established and built in 1875, the Yerba Buena Lighthouse, also known as the Goat Island Lighthouse, was automated in 1958 and is still an active aid to navigation. The keepers quarters, built in 1873, is home to the local U.S. Coast Guard district commandant. *Address:* Yerba Buena Light *City:* San Francisco *State:* CA *Visitors welcome?* No *Operated by:* U.S. Coast Guard (District 11) *NR?* Yes *NHL?* No *Year established/built:* 1873 *Latitude:* 37.8073 *Longitude:* -122.3630

HAWAII

BARBERS POINT LIGHTHOUSE

Established in 1888, the current Barbers Point Lighthouse was constructed in 1933. Automated since 1964, the lighthouse is still an active aid to navigation. *Address:* Barbers Point Light *City:* Honolulu *State:* HI *Visitors welcome?* Yes *Hours:* Grounds only *Admission:* FREE *Operated by:* U.S. Coast Guard (District 14) *NR?* No *NHL?* No *Year established/built:* 1888 *Latitude:* 21.2964 *Longitude:* -158.1062

CAPE KUMUKAHI LIGHTHOUSE

Established in 1929, the current skeletal metal tower of the Cape Kumukahi Lighthouse was constructed in 1934. Automated in 1960, the lighthouse is still an active aid to navigation. *Address:* Cape Kumukahi Light *City:* Hilo *State:* HI *Visitors welcome?* Yes *Hours:*

Grounds only *Admission:* FREE *Operated by:* U.S. Coast Guard (District 14) *NR?* No *NHL?* No *Year established/built:* 1929 *Latitude:* 19.5160 *Longitude:* -154.8110

DIAMOND HEAD LIGHTHOUSE

Established in 1899, the current Diamond Head Lighthouse was constructed in 1918. Automated in 1924, the light is still an active aid to navigation. It is now housing for Coast Guard personnel. *Address:* Below Diamond Head State Monument *City:* Honolulu *State:* HI *Visitors welcome?* No *Operated by:* U.S. Coast Guard (District 14) *NR?* Yes *NHL?* No *Year established/built:* 1899 *Latitude:* 21.25934 *Longitude:* -157.81096

KAUHOLA POINT LIGHTHOUSE

Established in 1897, the current Kauhola Point Lighthouse was constructed in the 1930s. Automated in 1951, the lighthouse is still an active aid to navigation. *Address:* Kauhola Point Light *State:* HI *Visitors welcome?* Yes *Hours:* Grounds only *Admission:* FREE *Operated by:* U.S. Coast Guard (District 14) *NR?* No *NHL?* No *Year established/built:* 1897 *Latitude:* 20.2453 *Longitude:* -155.7716l

KILAUEA POINT LIGHTHOUSE

Established and built in 1913, the Kilauea Point Lighthouse was deactivated in 1976. The lighthouse is now within a national wildlife refuge. *Address:* Kilauea Point Light *City:* Kilauea *State:* HI *Zip:* 96754 *Phone:* 808-828-1413 *Visitors welcome?* Yes *Hours:* Grounds only *Admission:* FREE *Operated by:* Kilauea Point National Wildlife Refuge *NR?* Yes *NHL?* No *Year established/built:* 1913 *Latitude:* 22.2316 *Longitude:* -159.40199

LAHAINA LIGHTHOUSE

Ordered constructed by King Kamehameha in 1840, the first Lahaina Lighthouse was a wooden structure to guide ships into Lahaina Harbor. A second lighthouse was constructed, replacing the old wooden tower, sometime before 1860. *Address:* Lahiana Harbor *City:* Lahaina *State:* HI *Zip:* 96761 *Phone:* 808-661-3262 *Visitors welcome?* Yes *Hours:* Grounds only *Admission:* FREE *Operated by:* Lahaina Restoration Foundation *NR?* No *NHL?* No *Year established/built:* 1840 *Latitude:* 20.8739 *Longitude:* -156.6810

MAKAPUU LIGHTHOUSE

Established and built in 1909, the Makapu'u Lighthouse was automated in 1974 and is still an active aid to navigation. *Address:* Makapuu Light *City:* Waimanalo Beach *State:* HI *Visitors welcome?* Yes *Hours:* Grounds only *Admission:* FREE *Operated by:* U.S. Coast Guard (District 14) *NR?* Yes *NHL?* No *Year established/built:* 1909 *Latitude:* 21.3099 *Longitude:* -157.6498

Molokai Lighthouse, Kalaupapa National Historical Park

MOLOKAI LIGHTHOUSE

Established and constructed in 1909, the Molokai Lighthouse, also called the Kalaupapa Lighthouse, was automated in 1970 and is still an active aid to navigation. It is now part of the Kalaupapa National Historical Park. *Address:* Kalaupapa National Historical Park *City:* Kalaupapa *State:* HI *Zip:* 96742 *Phone:* 808-567-6802 *Visitors welcome?* No *Operated by:* Kalaupapa National Historic Park *NR?* Yes *NHL?* No *Year established/built:* 1909 *Latitude:* 21.1925 *Longitude:* -156.98612

NAWILIWILI LIGHTHOUSE

Established in 1906, the current Nawiliwili Lighthouse was constructed in 1933. Automated in 1953, the lighthouse is still an active aid to navigation. *Address:* Ninini Point *City:* Lihue *State:* HI *Visitors welcome?* Yes *Hours:* Grounds only *Admission:* FREE *Operated by:* U.S. Coast Guard (District 14) *NR?* No *NHL?* No *Year established/built:* 1906 *Latitude:* 21.95477 *Longitude:* -159.3358

OREGON

CAPE ARAGO LIGHTHOUSE

Established in 1866, the current Cape Arago Lighthouse, also called the Cape Gregory Lighthouse, was constructed in 1934 and automated in 1966. Now deactivated, the lighthouse is served by an 1889 iron bridge. *Address:* Cape Arago Light *City:* Coos Bay *State:* OR *Visitors welcome?* No *Operated by:* U.S. Coast Guard (District 13) *NR?* Yes *NHL?* No *Year established/built:* 1866 *Latitude:* 43.34361 *Longitude:* -124.37528

Caption Cape Blanco Lighthouse, Port Orford, Oregon

CAPE BLANCO LIGHTHOUSE

✦ Established and built in 1870, the Cape Blanco Lighthouse is the oldest and southernmost of Oregon's Lighthouses. It is now within a state park, although the lighthouse itself is managed by the federal Bureau of Land Management. *Address:* Cape Blanco Light *City:* Port Orford *State:* OR *Zip:* 97465 *Phone:* 541-332-0248 *Web:* www.oregonstateparks. org/park_62.php *Visitors welcome?* Yes *Hours:* Daily, April to October *Admission:* $2 adults, $1 children under 12, $5 family *Operated by:* Friends of Cape Blanco *NR?* Yes *NHL?* No *Year established/built:* 1870 *Latitude:* 42.8358 *Longitude:* -124.5610 **Accommodations for overnight and/or long-term stays available.**

CAPE MEARES LIGHTHOUSE

✛ Established and built in 1890, the Cape Meares Lighthouse marks the entrance to Tillamook Bay. The lighthouse, replaced by a nearby tower in 1963, is now a local attraction. *Address:* Cape Meares Light *City:* Tillamook *State:* OR *Phone:* 503-842-3182 *Web:* www.capemeareslighthouse.org *Email:* capemeareslighthouse@earthlink.net *Visitors welcome?* Yes *Hours:* Daily, April to October, 11 a.m. to 4 p.m. *Admission:* **FREE** *Operated by:* Friends of Cape Meares Lighthouse *NR?* Yes *NHL?* No *Year established/built:* 1890 *Latitude:* 45.4866 *Longitude:* -123.9780 **Accommodations for overnight and/or long-term stays available.**

CLEFT-OF-THE-ROCK LIGHTHOUSE

Built by maritime historian Jim Gibbs, the Clef-of-the-Rock Lighthouse, also called the Cape Perpetua Lighthouse, was added to the official list of navigation aids in 1979. *Address:* Cleft-of-the-Rock Light *City:* Yachats *State:* OR *Visitors welcome?* No *Operated by:* Private owner *NR?* No *NHL?* No *Year established/built:* 1976 *Latitude:* 44.29048 *Longitude:* -124.11077

COQUILLE RIVER LIGHTHOUSE

✛ Established and built in 1896, the Coquille River Lighthouse, also called the Bandon Lighthouse, was constructed to guide lumber ships into the Coquille River and its sawmills. The lighthouse is now within a state park. *Address:* Coquille River Light *City:* Bandon *State:* OR *Zip:* 97411 *Phone:* 541-347-3501 *Visitors welcome?* Yes *Hours:* Daily, May to October, 10 a.m. to 4 p.m.; Daily, June to September, Monday and Tuesday, 10 a.m. to 4 p.m., Wednesday to Sunday, 9 a.m. to 6 p.m. *Admission:* Contact attraction directly *Operated by:* Oregon Parks and Recreation Dept. *NR?* Yes *NHL?* No *Year established/built:* 1896 *Latitude:* 43.12391 *Longitude:* -124.42423 **Accommodations for overnight and/ or long-term stays available.**

HECETA HEAD LIGHTHOUSE

✛ Established and built in 1894, Heceta Head Lighthouse sits on a high bluff, making it one of the most photographed lighthouses in Oregon. Now part of a state park, the grounds include the keepers dwelling, which operates as a bed and breakfast. *Address:* Heceta Head Light *City:* Florence *State:* OR *Phone:* 541-547-3416 *Web:* www.oregonstateparks.org/park_124.php *Visitors welcome?* Yes *Hours:* May to September: Daily, 11 a.m. to 5 p.m.; March, April, October: daily, 11 a.m. to 3 p.m. *Admission:* **FREE** *Operated by:* Oregon Parks and Recreation Dept. *NR?* Yes *NHL?* No *Year established/built:* 1894 *Latitude:* 44.1374 *Longitude:* -124.1280 **Accommodations for overnight and/or long-term stays available.**

Heceta Head Lighthouse, Florence, Oregon

TILLAMOOK ROCK LIGHTHOUSE

Established and built in 1881, the Tillamook Rock Lighthouse, known affectionately at Terrible Tilly, was decommissioned by the U.S. Coast Guard in 1957. *Address:* Tillamook Rock Light *State:* OR *Visitors welcome?* No *Operated by:* Private owner *NR?* Yes *NHL?* No *Year established/built:* **1881** *Latitude:* 45.9375 *Longitude:* -124.0190

UMPQUA RIVER LIGHTHOUSE

✛ Established in 1856, the current Umpqua River Lighthouse was constructed in 1894 to aid ships entering the Umpqua River. The light was automated in 1966, and it's now within a state park. *Address:* Umpqua River Light *State:* OR *Phone:* 541-957-7007 *Visitors welcome?* Yes *Hours:* May to October, daily, 10 a.m. to 4 p.m. *Admission:* Contact attraction directly *Operated by:* Douglas County Museum *NR?* Yes *NHL?* No *Year established/built:* 1856 *Latitude:* 43.66179 *Longitude:* -124.1982 **Accommodations for overnight and/or long-term stays available.**

WARRIOR ROCK LIGHT

Established in 1889, the current concrete Warrior Rock Lighthouse was constructed in the 1930s. It is still an active aid to navigation. *Address:* Warrior Rock Light *City:* St.

Helens *State:* OR *Visitors welcome?* Yes *Hours:* Grounds only *Admission:* **FREE** *Operated by:* U.S. Coast Guard (District 13) *NR?* No *NHL?* No *Year established/built:* 1889 *Latitude:* 45.84858 *Longitude:* -122.78835

YAQUINA BAY LIGHTHOUSE

✦ Established and built in 1871 and decommissioned just three years later, the Yaquina Bay Lighthouse is now a private aid to navigation and a museum. *Address:* Yaquina Bay Light *City:* Newport *State:* OR *Zip:* 97365 *Phone:* 541-265-5679 *Web:* www. yaquinalights.org *Visitors welcome?* Yes *Hours:* Daily, Memorial Day to September, 11 a.m. to 5 p.m.; October to Memorial Day, noon to 4 p.m. *Admission:* **FREE** *Operated by:* Friends of Yaquina Lighthouses *NR?* Yes *NHL?* No *Year established/built:* 1871 *Latitude:* 44.62415 *Longitude:* -124.0629 **Accommodations for overnight and/or long-term stays available.**

YAQUINA HEAD LIGHTHOUSE

✦ Established and built in 1873, Yaquina Head Lighthouse on Cape Foulweather replaced the Yaquina Bay Lighthouse as an aid to navigation. Rehabilitated in 1992, the lighthouse is now a museum and local attraction. *Address:* Yaquina Head Light *City:* Agate Beach *State:* OR *Phone:* 541-574-3100 *Web:* www.yaquinalights.org *Visitors welcome?* Yes *Hours:* Summer, daily, 9 a.m to 5 p.m.; Winter, daily, 10 a.m. to 4 p.m. *Admission:* Contact attraction directly *Operated by:* Friends of Yaquina Lighthouses *NR?* Yes *NHL?* No *Year established/built:* 1873 *Latitude:* 44.67678 *Longitude:* -124.07941 **Accommodations for overnight and/or long-term stays available.**

WASHINGTON

ADMIRALTY HEAD LIGHTHOUSE

Established in 1860, the current Admiralty Head Lighthouse was constructed in 1903 and deactivated in 1922. It is now within a state park. *Address:* Admiralty Head Light *City:* Coupeville *State:* WA *Visitors welcome?* Yes *Hours:* June to August: Daily, 11 a.m. to 5 p.m; Other times, contact owner *Admission:* **FREE** *Operated by:* Keepers of Admiralty Head Lighthouse *NR?* Yes *NHL?* No *Year established/built:* 1860 *Latitude:* 48.16076 *Longitude:* -122.68117

ALKI POINT LIGHTHOUSE

Established in 1887, the current Alki Point Lighthouse was constructed in 1913. Automated in 1984, the light is still an active aid to navigation. *Address:* Alki Point Light *City:* Seattle *State:* WA *Visitors welcome?* Yes *Hours:* Contact attraction directly *Admission:* Contact attraction directly *Operated by:* U.S. Coast Guard (District 13) *NR?* No *NHL?* No *Year established/built:* 1913 *Latitude:* 47.5764 *Longitude:* -122.4210

Alki Point Lighthouse, Seattle, Washington

Browns Point Lighthouse, Tacoma, Washington

BROWNS POINT LIGHTHOUSE

✛ Established in 1887, the current Browns Point Lighthouse was constructed in 1933. Automated in 1963, the lighthouse is still an active aid to navigation. It is now a museum, with the keepers quarters available for overnight rental. *Address:* 201 Tulalip Street NE *City:* Tacoma *State:* WA *Web:* www.pointsnortheast.org *Email:* pointsnortheast@comcast.net *Visitors welcome?* Yes *Hours:* Daily *Admission:* **FREE** *Operated by:* Points Northeast Historical Society *NR?* Yes *NHL?* No *Year established/built:* 1887 *Latitude:* 47.3054 *Longitude:* -122.4410 **Accommodations for overnight and/or long-term stays available.**

BURROWS ISLAND LIGHTHOUSE

Established and built in 1906, the Burrows Island Lighthouse is still an active aid to navigation. *Address:* Burrows Island Light *City:* Anacortes *State:* WA *Visitors welcome?* Yes *Hours:* Contact attraction directly *Admission:* **FREE** *Operated by:* Washington State Parks *NR?* No *NHL?* No *Year established/built:* 1906 *Latitude:* 48.47805 *Longitude:* -122.71361

BUSH POINT LIGHTHOUSE

The Bush Point Lighthouse was built in 1933 to guide mariners through the middle reaches of Admiralty Inlet into Puget Sound. *Address:* Bush Point *City:* Freeland *State:* WA *Visitors welcome?* Yes *Hours:* Daily *Admission:* **FREE** *Operated by:* U.S. Coast Guard (District 13) *NR?* No *NHL?* No *Year established/built:* 1933 *Latitude:* 48.0309 *Longitude:* -122.6070

Cape Disappointment Lighthouse, Ilwaco, Washington

CAPE DISAPPOINTMENT LIGHTHOUSE

Established and built in 1856, the Cape Disappointment Lighthouse is located within a state park and it is still an active aid to navigation. *Address:* Cape Disappointment Light *City:* Ilwaco *State:* WA *Visitors welcome?* Yes *Hours:* Call 360-642-3078 *Admission:* Call 360-642-3078 *Operated by:* U.S. Coast Guard (District 13) *NR?* Yes *NHL?* No *Year established/built:* 1856 *Latitude:* 46.2756 *Longitude:* -124.0520

Cape Flattery Lighthouse, Washington State

CAPE FLATTERY LIGHTHOUSE

Established and built in 1857, the Cape Flattery Lighthouse was automated in 1977 and is still an active aid to navigation. *Address:* Cape Flattery Light *City:* Neah Bay *State:* WA *Visitors welcome?* Yes *Hours:* Contact attraction directly *Admission:* Contact attraction directly *Operated by:* U.S. Coast Guard (District 13) *NR?* Yes *NHL?* No *Year established/built:* 1857 *Latitude:* 48.3917 *Longitude:* -124.7366

CATTLE POINT LIGHTHOUSE

Built in 1935, the Cattle Point Lighthouse is near the San Juan Islands National Historical Park. *Address:* Cattle Point Light *City:* Friday Harbor *State:* WA *Visitors welcome?* Yes *Hours:* Contact attraction directly *Admission:* Contact attraction directly *Operated by:* San Juan National Historical Park *NR?* No *NHL?* No *Year established/built:* 1935 *Latitude:* 48.45598 *Longitude:* -122.9624

DESTRUCTION ISLAND LIGHTHOUSE

Established and built in 1891, the Destruction Island Lighthouse was automated in 1968 and is still an active aid to navigation. *Address:* Destruction Island Light *State:* WA *Visitors welcome?* Yes *Operated by:* U.S. Coast Guard (District 13) *NR?* No *NHL?* No *Year established/built:* 1891 *Latitude:* 47.6752 *Longitude:* -124.4870

DOFFLEMYER POINT LIGHTHOUSE

The Dofflemyer Point Lighthouse was built in 1934 to guard the entrance to Budd Inlet, the location of the Port of Olympia and the state capital. *Address:* Dofflemyer Point Light *City:* Olympia *State:* WA *Visitors welcome?* No *Operated by:* U.S. Coast Guard (District 13) *NR?* No *NHL?* No *Year established/built:* 1934 *Latitude:* 47.1404 *Longitude:* -122.9070

EDIZ HOOK LIGHTHOUSE

Established by Abraham Lincoln in 1862, the Ediz Hook Lighthouse was first lit in 1865. The keepers residence is now a private home in Port Angeles. *Address:* Marine Dr. and W. Hill St. *City:* Port Angeles *State:* WA *Visitors welcome?* No *Operated by:* U.S. Coast Guard (District 13) *NR?* No *NHL?* No *Year established/built:* 1862 *Latitude:* 48.12872 *Longitude:* -123.46281

GIG HARBOR LIGHTHOUSE

Built in 1988, the Gig Harbor Lighthouse marks the entrance to Gig Harbor, a small inlet northwest of Tacoma. *Address:* Goodman Dr. NW and 26th Ave. NW *City:* Gig Harbor *State:* WA *Visitors welcome?* Yes *Hours:* Contact attraction directly *Admission:* Contact attraction directly *Operated by:* Gig Harbor Lighthouse Association *NR?* No *NHL?* No *Year established/built:* 1988 *Latitude:* 47.3293 *Longitude:* -122.5730

GRAYS HARBOR LIGHTHOUSE

Established and built in 1898, the Grays Harbor Lighthouse, also called the Westport Lighthouse, is still an active aid to navigation cared for a local maritime museum. *Address:* 1020 West Ocean Avenue *City:* Westport *State:* WA *Phone:* 360-268-0078 *Fax:* 360-268-1288 *Web:* maritimemuseum-ghlighthouse.org/ *Email:* wmmvista@comcast.net *Visitors welcome?* Yes *Hours:* April to September: Daily, 10 a.m. to 4 p.m.; October to March: Friday to Monday, noon to 4 p.m. *Admission:* $5 *Operated by:* Westport South Beach Historical Society *NR?* Yes *NHL?* No *Year established/built:* 1898 *Latitude:* 46.8877 *Longitude:* -124.1170

LIME KILN LIGHTHOUSE

Established in 1914 and built in 1919, the Lime Kiln Lighthouse was automated in 1962 and is still an active aid to navigation. *Address:* Lime Kiln Point *City:* Friday Harbor *State:* WA *Visitors welcome?* Yes *Hours:* Daily, dawn to dusk *Admission:* FREE *Operated by:* Washington State Parks *NR?* Yes *NHL?* No *Year established/built:* 1914 *Latitude:* 48.5161 *Longitude:* -123.1520

MARROWSTONE POINT LIGHTHOUSE

Established in 1882, the current Marrowstone Point Lighthouse was built in 1912 and automated in 1962. It is still an active aid to navigation. *Address:* Marrowstone Light *City:* Port Townsend *State:* WA *Visitors welcome?* Yes *Hours:* Site open daily *Admission:* FREE *Operated by:* Washington State Parks *NR?* Yes *NHL?* No *Year established/built:* 1882 *Latitude:* 48.1018 *Longitude:* -122.6880

Mukilteo Lighthouse, Mukilteo, Washington

MUKILTEO LIGHTHOUSE

Established and built in 1906, the Mukilteo Lighthouse is still an active aid to navigation. It is now operated by a local not-for-profit organization. *Address:* Mukilteo Light *City:* Mukilteo *State:* WA *Visitors welcome?* Yes *Hours:* April to September, weekends and holidays, noon to 5 p.m. *Admission:* **FREE** *Operated by:* Mukilteo Historical Society *NR?* Yes *NHL?* No *Year established/built:* 1906 *Latitude:* 47.9487 *Longitude:* -122.3060

NEW DUNGENESS LIGHTHOUSE

✦ Established and built in 1857, the New Dungeness Lighthouse was automated in 1976 and is now operated by a local not-for-profit which allows guest lightkeepers. *Address:* Marine Dr. and Cays Rd. *City:* Sequim *State:* WA *Visitors welcome?* Yes *Hours:* Contact attraction directly *Admission:* Contact attraction directly *Operated by:* New Dungeness Light Station Association *NR?* Yes *NHL?* No *Year established/built:* 1857 *Latitude:* 48.14862 *Longitude:* -123.16676 **Accommodations for overnight and/or long-term stays available.**

NORTH HEAD LIGHTHOUSE

✦ Established and built in 1889, the North Head Lighthouse is still an active aid to navigation within a state park. *Address:* North Head Light *City:* Ilwaco *State:* WA *Visitors welcome?* Yes *Hours:* Call 360-642-3078 *Admission:* Call 360-642-3078 *Operated by:* Keepers of the North Head Lighthouse *NR?* Yes *NHL?* No *Year established/built:* 1898 *Latitude:* 46.2989 *Longitude:* -124.0780 **Accommodations for overnight and/or long-term stays available.**

PATOS ISLAND LIGHTHOUSE
Established in 1893, the current Patos Island Lighthouse was built in 1893, with the tower added in 1908. Automated in 1974, the lighthouse is now within a state park. *Address:* Patos Island Light *State:* WA *Phone:* 360-468-3518 *Web:* patoslightkeepers.org *Email:* patoslightkeers@hotmail.com *Visitors welcome?* Yes *Hours:* Daily, grounds only, occassional tours *Admission:* FREE *Operated by:* Keepers of the Patos Light *NR?* Yes *NHL?* No *Year established/built:* 1893 *Latitude:* 48.7890 *Longitude:* -122.9710

POINT NO POINT (WASHINGTON) LIGHTHOUSE
✛ Established and built in 1879, the Point No Point Lighthouse gain earlier prominence as the site of a critical treaty between the U.S. and local Indian tribes giving the Americans control of most of Puget Sound. *Address:* Point No Point Light *City:* Hansville *State:* WA *Visitors welcome?* Yes *Hours:* Dawn to dusk *Admission:* FREE *Operated by:* Friends of Point No Point Lighthouse *NR?* Yes *NHL?* No *Year established/built:* 1879 *Latitude:* 47.9119 *Longitude:* -122.5260 **Accommodations for overnight and/or long-term stays available.**

POINT ROBINSON LIGHTHOUSE
✛ Established in 1885, the current Point Robinson Lighthouse was constructed in 1915. Automated in 1978, the light is still an active aid to navigation and operated by a local not-for-profit. *Address:* Point Robinson Light *City:* Vashon Island *State:* WA *Phone:* 206 463-9602 *Visitors welcome?* Yes *Hours:* Dawn to dusk *Admission:* FREE *Operated by:* Keepers of Point Robinson *NR?* No *NHL?* No *Year established/built:* 1885 *Latitude:* 47.3881 *Longitude:* -122.3746 **Accommodations for overnight and/or long-term stays available.**

POINT WILSON LIGHTHOUSE
Established in 1879, the Point Wilson Lighthouse marks the entrance to Admiralty Inlet, the main route to Puget Sound in the 19th and early 20th centuries. *Address:* Point Wilson Light *City:* Port Townsend *State:* WA *Visitors welcome?* Yes *Hours:* Contact attraction directly *Admission:* Contact attraction directly *Operated by:* U.S. Coast Guard (District 13) *NR?* No *NHL?* No *Year established/built:* 1914 *Latitude:* 48.14417 *Longitude:* -122.7550

SKUNK BAY LIGHTHOUSE
Built in 1965, the Skunk Bay Lighthouse near the northern tip of Bainbridge Island is a fully operational lighthouse owned and operated by a private association. *Address:* Skunk Bay Light *City:* Hansville *State:* WA *Visitors welcome?* No *Operated by:* Skunk Bay Lighthouse Association *NR?* No *NHL?* No *Year established/built:* 1965 *Latitude:* 47.91871 *Longitude:* -122.55431

SLIP POINT LIGHTHOUSE

Located at Slip Point on the east end of Clallam Bay, overlooking the Strait of Juan de Fuca, the Slip Point Lighthouse faded into local memory after the lighthouse and the structures were demolished in the mid-20th century. However, the original two-story lighthouse keepers quarters survive. *Address:* Slip Point Light *State:* WA *Visitors welcome?* Yes *Hours:* Contact attraction directly *Admission:* Contact attraction directly *Operated by:* Clallam County *NR?* No *NHL?* No *Year established/built:* 1905 *Latitude:* 48.2645 *Longitude:* -124.2510

TURN POINT LIGHTHOUSE

Established in 1893, the current Turn Point Lighthouse was constructed in 1936. Automated in 1974, the lighthouse is still an active aid to navigation. A local not-for-profit operates the lighthouse as a museum. *Address:* Turn Point *City:* Friday Harbor *State:* WA *Visitors welcome?* Yes *Hours:* Tuesday, Wednesday, Friday, Saturday, Sunday; Noon to 4 p.m. *Admission:* Donation *Operated by:* Turn Point Lighthouse Preservation Society *NR?* No *NHL?* No *Year established/built:* 1893 *Latitude:* 48.68844 *Longitude:* -123.23714

WEST POINT LIGHTHOUSE

Established and built in 1881, the West Point Lighthouse was automated in 1984. Still an active aid to navigation, the lighthouse is within a city park. *Address:* West Point Light *City:* Seattle *State:* WA *Visitors welcome?* Yes *Hours:* Dawn to dusk *Admission:* FREE *Operated by:* Seattle Parks and Recreation *NR?* Yes *NHL?* No *Year established/built:* 1881 *Latitude:* 47.6619 *Longitude:* -122.4360

Want to be a volunteer lighthouse keeper? Look for notes in listings on accommodations.

CHAPTER 5

LIGHTSHIPS

Lightship Swiftsure (LV 83), Seattle, Washington

Unlike most ships, which usually have a home and a destination, the lightship was designed to stay in one place on the open ocean for months at a time. It only moved when heading out to its station and heading home for maintenance. They marked shoals or harbor entrances where a lighthouse wasn't practical. Bobbing on the ocean like a cork anchored to the bottom might seem safe, but lightships duty was actually among the most dangerous assignments for their U.S. Coast Guard crews. Lightships were expected to stay put, even in the worst storms, because they marked critical points that a merchant and military vessel heading for the safety of shore should avoid. Occasionally, a wayward ship would collide with a lightship. Although a large word such as "Swiftsure" might be painted on the ship's side, most lightships were actually known by their military designation, such as "LV-83," because several vessels might share a duty station. By the 1970s, active lightships were replaced with large floating platforms with automated lights and ranging gear. Today, most lightships afloat are maintained by museums and historical societies. Use your smart phone QR or bar code reader to visit this Fyddeye web page.

Use your smart phone QR or bar code reader to visit this Fyddeye web page

FYDDEYE RECOMMENDS:

Lightship Overfalls, Lewes, Delaware	Lightship Huron, Port Huron, Michigan

LIGHTSHIP UMATILLA (LV 196)

The Lightship Umatilla (LV 196) was the fourth vessel to mark Umatilla Reef off Washington State's coast. Retired in 1971, the Coast Guard decommissioned her, and it is now owned by a Ketchikan businessman. *Address:* Lewis Reef *City:* Ketchikan *State:* AK *Visitors welcome?* No *Operated by:* Southeast Stevedoring *NR?* No *NHL?* No *Latitude:* 55.3750 *Longitude:* -131.73805

LIGHTSHIP RELIEF (WLV-605)

Lightship Relief (WLV-605), one of six lightships constructed for the Coast Guard, was built by Rice Brothers Shipyard in Boothbay, Maine, in 1950. *Address:* Jack London Square *City:* Oakland *State:* CA *Zip:* 94607 *Phone:* 510-272-0544 *Visitors welcome?* Yes *Hours:* Friday, Saturday and Sunday, 11 a.m. to 4 p.m. *Admission:* Contact attraction directly *Operated by:* United States Lighthouse Society *NR?* Yes *NHL?* Yes *Year established/built:* 1950 *Latitude:* 37.79569 *Longitude:* -122.28059

LIGHTSHIP OVERFALLS (LV 118)

The Lightship Overfalls (LV 118) was the last lightship built by the U.S. government. Commissioned in 1938, LV 118 served off Connecticut and Massachusetts between 1938 and 1972. *Address:* 219 Pilottown Road *City:* Lewes *State:* DE *Zip:* 19958 *Phone:* 302-645-7377 *Web:* www.overfalls.org *Email:* bernheisel@juno.com *Visitors welcome?* Yes *Hours:* Memorial Day to Columbus Day: Monday, Thursday, Friday, Saturday, 10 a.m. to 4 p.m.; Sunday, noon to 4 p.m. *Admission:* Donation *Operated by:* Overfalls Maritime Museum Foundation *NR?* Yes *NHL?* Yes *Year established/built:* 1938 *Latitude:* 38.77725 *Longitude:* -75.1423

LIGHTSHIP NANTUCKET (LV-112)

Built in 1936, Lightship Nantucket (LV-112) was powered by a 600 IEP steam engine driven by two oil-fired Babcock-Wilcox boilers. In 1960, the ship was re-powered with a Cooper-Bessemer 900 HP diesel and the tall smoke stack was replaced with a smaller stack. It is now a museum ship in Boston and open by appointment. *City:* Boston *State:* MA *Web:* www.nantucketlightshiplv-112.org/ *Email:* rj0648@comcast.net *Visitors welcome?* No *Operated by:* United States Lightship Museum *NR?* Yes *NHL?* Yes *Year established/built:* 1936 *Latitude:* 42.35843 *Longitude:* -71.05978

LIGHTSHIP NANTUCKET (WLV-612)

Built in Curtis Bay, Maryland, Lightship Nantucket (WLV-612) was the last lightship built by the Coast Guard. It is now a private vessel available for charter. *Address:* Nantucket Harbor *City:* Nantucket *State:* MA *Zip:* 02554 *Phone:* 617-821-6771 *Web:* www.nantucketlightship.com *Email:* info@nantucketlightship.com *Visitors welcome?* Yes *Hours:*

Contact attraction directly *Admission:* Contact attraction directly *Operated by:* Nantucket Lightship WLV-612 *NR?* No *NHL?* No *Year established/built:* 1950 *Latitude:* 41.30429 *Longitude:* -70.0453

LIGHTSHIP NANTUCKET II (WLV-613)

The Lightship Nantucket II (WLV-613) was built in 1952 and originally stationed at Ambrose Channel in New York until 1967. In 1979, it was stationed off Nantucket Island. It alternated duty with WLV-612, also known as Lightship Nantucket I. *Address:* Agawam River *City:* Wareham *State:* MA *Visitors welcome?* No *Operated by:* Private owner *NR?* No *NHL?* No *Year established/built:* 1952 *Latitude:* 41.7626 *Longitude:* -70.6762

LIGHTSHIP CHESAPEAKE (LV-116)

U.S. Lightship 116 Chesapeake marked the mouth of the Chesapeake Bay for over 29 years. Lightship 116 was initially assigned to Fenwick Island, Delaware in 1930. In 1933, Lightship 116 was transferred to the approaches of the Chesapeake Bay where her bright red hull, masthead lamp, and loud foghorn guided mariners to safe harbor for 29 years. From 1965-1970, Lightship 116 finished her career marking the Delaware Bay approaches. *Address:* Pier 3, Baltimore Inner Harbor (301 E. Pratt St.) *City:* Baltimore *State:* MD *Zip:* 21202 *Phone:* 410-539-1797 *Web:* www.historicships. org/ *Email:* administration@historicships.org *Visitors welcome?* Yes *Hours:* Contact attraction directly *Admission:* Contact attraction directly *Operated by:* Historic Ships in Baltimore *NR?* Yes *NHL?* Yes *Year established/built:* 1930 *Latitude:* 39.2866 *Longitude:* -76.6087

Port Huron Lightship, Port Huron, Michigan

LIGHTSHIP HURON (LV 103)

Buit in 1920, Lightship Huron (LV 103) is now a museum ship in Port Huron, Mich. *Address:* Pine Grove Park *City:* Port Huron *State:* MI *Zip:* 48060 *Phone:* 810-982-0891 *Web:* www.ph-museum.org *Email:* lightship@phmuseum.org *Visitors welcome?* Yes *Hours:* Daily, Memorial Day to Labor Day, 11 a.m. to 5 p.m.; Sept. to Dec., Thursday to Monday; April to May, Thursday to Monday; Jan. to March, closed *Admission:* Contact attraction directly *Operated by:* Port Huron Museum *NR?* Yes *NHL?* Yes *Year established/built:* 1921 *Latitude:* 42.9882 *Longitude:* -82.4275

LIGHTSHIP BARNEGAT (LV 79/WAL 506)

Commissioned in 1904, the Lightship Barnegat (LV 79/WAL 506)'s station was off the Barnegat Lighthouse. The ship was decommissioned in 1967, and it has passed through the hands of several owners. It is now awaiting restoration. *Address:* Foot of North Seventh Street *City:* Camden *State:* NJ *Visitors welcome?* Yes *Hours:* Grounds only *Admission:* Contact attraction directly *Operated by:* Private owner *NR?* No *NHL?* No *Year established/built:* 1904 *Latitude:* 39.92595 *Longitude:* -75.11962

LIGHTSHIP LIBERTY (LV 107)

Built in 1923 at the Bath Iron Works in Bath, Maine, Lightship Libery (LV 107) first served at Cape Lookout Shoals, North Carolina, from 1924 to 1933. Its next station was Winter Quarter Shoals on Chesapeake Bay, where it marked the entrance until 1960. *Address:* 80 Audrey Zapp Drive *City:* Jersey City *State:* NJ *Zip:* 07304 *Phone:* 201-985-8000 *Email:* info@libertylandingmarina.com *Visitors welcome?* Yes *Hours:* Contact attraction directly *Admission:* Contact attraction directly *Operated by:* Liberty Landing Marina *NR?* No *NHL?* No *Year established/built:* 1923 *Latitude:* 40.7094 *Longitude:* -74.0478

LIGHTSHIP AMBROSE (WLV-613)

A lightship designated Ambrose has served as the main beacon marking Ambrose Channel, the main shipping channel for New York Harbor from 1823 to 1967. Several ships served as the lightship, and the last, WLV 613, was commissioned in 1952. The lightship is owned and operated by Seaport Museum New York, formerly the South Street Seaport Museum. *Address:* 12 Fulton St. *City:* New York *State:* NY *Zip:* 10038 *Phone:* 212-748-8600 *Web:* www.seany.org *Email:* minfo@seany.org *Visitors welcome?* Yes *Hours:* January to March: Thursday to Sunday:10 a.m. to 5 p.m., All galleries open, noon to 4 p.m., ships (weather permitting); April to December: Tuesday to Sunday, 10 a.m. to 6 p.m., All galleries and ships *Admission:* $15 adults, $12 students/seniors, $12 children 2-12, under 2 **FREE** *Operated by:* Seaport Museum New York *NR?* Yes *NHL?* Yes *Year established/built:* 1907 *Latitude:* 40.7066 *Longitude:* -74.0034

LIGHTSHIP FRYING PAN SHOALS (LV-115)

Built in 1929, Lightship Frying Pan Shoals (LV-115) guarded Frying Pan Shoals, 30 miles off of Cape Fear, North Carolina, from 1930 to 1965. She is 133 feet and 3 inches in length with a 30 foot beam and she is 632 gross tons. *Address:* Pier 63, Chelsea Waterside Park *City:* New York *State:* NY *Phone:* 212-989-6363 *Web:* www.fryingpan.com *Email:*

info@fryingpan.com *Visitors welcome?* Yes *Hours:* Contact attraction directly *Admission:* Contact attraction directly *Operated by:* Lightship Frying Pan *NR?* Yes *NHL?* No *Year established/built:* 1929 *Latitude:* 40.7143 *Longitude:* -74.0060

LILAC

Launched in 1933, the lighthouse tender Lilac is a floating exhibit on New York's waterfront. *Address:* Hudson River Park, Pier 25 *City:* New York *State:* NY *Phone:* 212-431-6100 *Web:* lilacpreservationproject.org *Email:* mary@lilacpreservationproject.org *Visitors welcome?* Yes *Hours:* Contact attraction directly *Admission:* Contact attraction directly *Operated by:* Lilac Preservation Project *NR?* Yes *NHL?* No *Year established/built:* 1933 *Latitude:* 40.7202 *Longitude:* -74.01463

LIGHTSHIP COLUMBIA (WLV-604)

Built in 1950 in Boothbay, Maine, Lightship Columbia (WLV-604) served as the lightship marking the entrance to the Columbia River and its treacherous bar. Decommissioned in 1979, the lighship now welcomes visitors at the Columbia River Maritime Museum. *Address:* 1792 Marine Drive *City:* Astoria *State:* OR *Zip:* 97103 *Phone:* 503-325-2323 *Web:* www.crmm.org *Email:* admin@crmm.org *Visitors welcome?* Yes *Hours:* Daily, 9:30 a.m. to 5:00 p.m. *Admission:* Children under 6, FREE; Children 6-17, $4; Seniors, $7; Adults, $8; Families, $24 *Operated by:* Columbia River Maritime Museum *NR?* Yes *NHL?* Yes *Year established/built:* 1950 *Latitude:* 46.1893 *Longitude:* -123.8230

LIGHTSHIP PORTSMOUTH (LV-101)

Built in 1915, the Plymouth Lightship, also known as the Cape Charles Lightship, served at several stations until she was retired in 1964. The ship is now a land-based museum. *Address:* 2 High Street *City:* Portsmouth *State:* VA *Zip:* 23704 *Phone:* 757-393-8591 *Web:* www.portsnavalmuseums.com *Email:* navalmuseums@portsmouthva.gov *Visitors welcome?* Yes *Hours:* Memorial Day to Labor Day: Monday to Saturday, 10 a.m. to 5 p.m., Sunday, 1 p.m. to 5 p.m.; September to November, March to May: Saturday, 10 a.m. to 5 p.m., Sunday 1 p.m. to 5 p.m. *Admission:* Memorial Day to Labor Day: $3; September to May: $1.50 adults, $.50 students two to 18, under two FREE *Operated by:* Portsmouth Naval Shipyard Museum *NR?* Yes *NHL?* Yes *Year established/built:* 1915 *Latitude:* 36.8355 *Longitude:* -76.2969

LIGHTSHIP SWIFTSURE (LV-83)

Launched in 1904, the lightship Swiftsure (LV-83) is a floating exhibit in Seattle. *Address:* 860 Terry Ave. N. *City:* Seattle *State:* WA *Zip:* 00000 *Phone:* 206-447-9800 *Web:* www.nwseaport.org *Email:* seaport@oz.net *Visitors welcome?* Yes *Hours:* Contact attraction directly *Admission:* Donation *Operated by:* Northwest Seaport Maritime Heritage Ctr *NR?* No *NHL?* Yes *Year established/built:* 1904 *Latitude:* 47.6276 *Longitude:* -122.3370

Is your favorite lighthouse missing from the *Guide*? Email info to contact@fyddeye.com.

CHAPTER 6

LIFE-SAVING STATIONS

Lifeboat from Grays Harbor Lifeboat Station, Westport, Washington

The modern facilities operated by the U.S. Coast Guard trace their roots to the life-saving station, where highly trained men waited for a call of distress from the sea. Many life-saving stations were associated with lighthouses as part of a safety and rescue service. The first stations were established in New England and the mid-Atlantic states in the mid-19th century and manned by volunteers who braved the surf and rocky coasts in open boats. As shipping grew and accidents increased, the loosely organized stations were brought under a newly created U.S. Life-Saving Service in 1878, later merged into the modern Coast Guard, which oversees lighthouses as well. This chapter lists life-saving stations preserved as museums dedicated to the volunteers and professionals who risked their lives to bring seamen in peril safely home. Use your smart phone QR or bar code reader to visit this Fyddeye web page.

Use your smart phone QR or bar code
reader to visit this Fyddeye web page.

FYDDEYE RECOMMENDS:	
Indian River Life-Saving Station, Rehoboth Beach, Delaware	Point Allerton Life-Saving Station, Hull, Massachusetts

CALIFORNIA

ARENA COVE LIFESAVING STATION

✦ Established and built in 1901, the Arena Cove Lifesaving Station (#314) is now a bed and breakfast. *Address:* 695 Arena Cove *City:* Point Arena *State:* CA *Zip:* 95468 *Phone:* 707-882-2442 *Web:* www.coastguardhouse.com *Email:* coast@mcn.org *Visitors welcome?* Yes *Hours:* Contact attraction directly *Admission:* Contact attraction directly *Operated by:* Coast Guard House Historic Inn *NR?* Yes *NHL?* No *Year established/built:* 1901 *Latitude:* 38.9141 *Longitude:* -123.7090 **Accommodations for overnight and/or long-term stays available.**

HUMBOLDT BAY (SAMOA) LIFEBOAT STATION

The Humboldt Bay Lifeboat Station is still an active service operated by the U.S. Coast Guard. *Address:* Samoa Peninsula *City:* Samoa *State:* CA *Phone:* 707-443-2213 *Visitors welcome?* Yes *Hours:* Contact attraction directly *Admission:* Contact attraction directly *Operated by:* U.S. Coast Guard (District 11) *NR?* No *NHL?* No *Latitude:* 40.8226 *Longitude:* -124.1850

POINT REYES LIFEBOAT STATION

Established in 1890, the Point Reyes Lifeboat Station, now known as the Historic Lifeboat Station at Point Reyes National Seashore, is used an educational facility. *Address:* Point Reyes Lifeboat Station *City:* Point Reyes *State:* CA *Phone:* 415-663-8522 *Visitors welcome?* Yes *Hours:* Contact attraction directly *Admission:* Contact attraction directly *Operated by:* Point Reyes National Seashore *NR?* No *NHL?* No *Year established/built:* 1890 *Latitude:* 37.9939 *Longitude:* -122.9740

CONNECTICUT

NEW SHOREHAM LIFESAVING STATION

The New Shoreham Lifesaving Station once stood at Block Island, and it is now part of the Mystic Seaport collection. *Address:* 75 Greenmanville Avenue *City:* Mystic *State:* CT *Zip:* 05365 *Phone:* 860-572-5315 *Web:* www.mysticseaport.org *Visitors welcome?* Yes *Hours:*

Daily, April to October, 9 a.m. to 5 p.m.; November to March, 10 a.m. to 4 p.m. *Admission:* Adults, $18.50; Seniors, $16.50; Children 6-17, $13; Under six, FREE *Operated by:* Mystic Seaport: The Museum of America and the Sea *NR?* No *NHL?* No *Latitude:* 41.36174 *Longitude:* -71.96339

Indian River Life-Saving Station, Rehoboth Beach, Delaware

DELAWARE

INDIAN RIVER LIFE-SAVING STATION

Established in 1876, the current Indian River Life-Saving Station was built in 1905 and recently restored. It is now a state park. *Address:* 25039 Coastal Highway *City:* Rehoboth Beach *State:* DE *Zip:* 19971 *Phone:* 302-227-6991 *Web:* www.destateparks.com/attractions/life-saving-station/ *Email:* Dorothy.Sheehan@state.de.us *Visitors welcome?* Yes *Hours:* Contact attraction directly *Admission:* Contact attraction directly *Operated by:* Indian River Life-Saving Station: Delaware Seashore State Park *NR?* Yes *NHL?* No *Year established/built:* 1876 *Latitude:* 38.699413 *Longitude:* -75.078064

FLORIDA

HOUSE OF REFUGE MUSEUM AT GILBERT'S BAR

The House of Refuge Museum at Gilbert Bar is the oldest structure on the Treasure Coast. *Address:* 301 SE MacArthur Boulevard *City:* Stuart *State:* FL *Zip:* 34996 *Phone:* 772-225-1875 *Web:* elliottmuseumfl.org/pages/house_refuge.php *Email:* info@elliottmuseumfl.org *Visitors welcome?* Yes *Hours:* Monday to Saturday, 10 a.m. to 4 p.m.; Sunday, 1 p.m. to 5 p.m. *Admission:* $5 adults, $2 children six to 12, under six FREE *Operated by:* Historical Society of Martin County *NR?* Yes *NHL?* No *Year established/built:* 1876 *Latitude:* 27.1992 *Longitude:* -80.1654

SANTA ROSA LIFE-SAVING STATION

Established in 1885, the Santa Rosa Life-Saving Station was deactivated in 1986. The current structure, which serves as a ranger station and office for a campground about one mile away, was built circa 1908. It is now a campground within the Gulf Islands *Address:* Santa Rosa Island, Gulf Islands National Seashore *City:* Gulf Breeze *State:* FL *Phone:* 850-934-2600 *Web:* www.nps.gov/guis/ *Visitors welcome?* Yes *Hours:* Daily, 8 a.m. to 5 p.m. *Admission:* Contact attraction directly *Operated by:* Gulf Islands National Seashore *NR?* No *NHL?* No *Year established/built:* 1908 *Latitude:* 30.3478 *Longitude:* -87.0449

ILLINOIS

CALUMET HARBOR LIFEBOAT STATION

The Calumet Life-Saving Station, also called the South Chicago Life-Saving Station, is part of U.S. Coast Guard Station Calumet Harbor. *Address:* 4001 E. 98th Street *City:* South Chicago *State:* IL *Zip:* 60617 *Phone:* 773-768-4093 *Visitors welcome?* Yes *Hours:* By appointment *Admission:* FREE *Operated by:* U.S. Coast Guard (District 9) *NR?* No *NHL?* No *Latitude:* 41.71761 *Longitude:* -87.52678

KENTUCKY

MAYOR ANDREW BROADDUS

Launched in 1929, the floating lifesaving station Mayor Andrew Broaddus is now floating offices for the Belle of Louisiana Operating Board. *Address:* 401 W. River Road *City:* Louisville *State:* KY *Zip:* 40202 *Phone:* 502-574-2992 *Web:* belleoflouisville.org *Visitors welcome?* Yes *Hours:* Contact attraction directly *Admission:* Contact attraction directly *Operated by:* Belle of Louisville & Spirit of Jefferson Cruises *NR?* Yes *NHL?* Yes *Year established/built:* 1929 *Latitude:* 38.25888 *Longitude:* -85.75234

MAINE

CRANBERRY ISLAND LIFE-SAVING STATION

The former Cranberry Island Life-Saving Station is now a private residence and summer rental. *Address:* Little Cranberry Island *State:* ME *Web:* islesford.com/idcrent.html *Email:* uslsstation@gmail.com *Visitors welcome?* Yes *Hours:* Contact attraction directly *Admission:* Contact attraction directly *Operated by:* Private owner *NR?* No *NHL?* No *Year established/ built:* 1878 *Latitude:* 44.25814 *Longitude:* -68.22946

CROSS ISLAND LIFE-SAVING STATION

The Cross Island Life-Saving Station is now owned by an Outward Bound facility. *Address:* Cross Island Life-Saving Station *City:* Machiasport *State:* ME *Phone:* 207-594-5548 *Email:* info@hurricaneisland.org *Visitors welcome?* Yes *Hours:* Contact attraction directly *Admission:* Contact attraction directly *Operated by:* Hurricane Island Outward Bound School *NR?* No *NHL?* No *Latitude:* 44.6987 *Longitude:* -67.3947

FLETCHERS NECK LIFE-SAVING STATION

The former Fletchers Neck Life-Saving Station is now a private residence. *City:* Biddeford Pool *State:* ME *Visitors welcome?* No *Operated by:* Private owner *NR?* Yes *Year established/ built:* 1873 *Latitude:* 43.44264 *Longitude:* -70.34237

POPHAM BEACH LIFE-SAVING STATION

✦ Established and built in 1883, the Popham Beach Life-Saving Station, also known as the Hunniwells Beach Life-Saving Station, was decommissioned in 1971 and is now a bed and breakfast. *Address:* 4 Riverview Avenue *City:* Phippsburg *State:* ME *Zip:* 04562 *Phone:* 207-389-2409 *Web:* www.pophambeachbandb.com *Email:* stay@pophambeachbandb.com *Visitors welcome?* Yes *Hours:* Contact attraction directly *Admission:* Contact attraction directly *Operated by:* Popham Beach Bed & Breakfast *NR?* No *NHL?* No *Year established/ built:* 1883 *Latitude:* 43.7499 *Longitude:* -69.7823 **Accommodations for overnight and/ or long-term stays available.**

PORTSMOUTH HARBOR LIFE-SAVING STATION

Portsmouth Harbor Life-Saving Station, also called Wood Island Life-Saving Station, is accessed through Fort Foster State Park. *Address:* Fort Foster State Park *City:* Kittery Point *State:* ME *Visitors welcome?* Yes *Hours:* Contact attraction directly *Admission:* Contact attraction directly *Operated by:* Wood Island Preservation Group *NR?* No *NHL?* No *Latitude:* 43.06908 *Longitude:* -70.68636

QUODDY HEAD LIFE-SAVING STATION

✦ Quoddy Head Station is located on West Quoddy Head in Downeast Maine in the historic seafaring town of Lubec. It's adjacent to Quoddy State Park with a five-minute walk to West Quoddy Lighthouse. *Address:* PO Box 98 *City:* Lubec *State:* ME *Zip:* 04652 *Phone:* 860-535-4714 *Toll-free:* 877-535-4714 *Web:* www.quoddyvacation.com *Email:* info@quoddyvacation.com *Visitors welcome?* Yes *Hours:* Contact attraction directly *Admission:* Contact attraction directly *Operated by:* Quoddy Head Station *NR?* No *NHL?* No *Year established/built:* 1874 *Latitude:* 44.81692 *Longitude:* -66.96751 **Accommodations for overnight and/or long-term stays available.**

WHITEHEAD LIFE-SAVING STATION

Address: Spruce Head *City:* St. George *State:* ME *Visitors welcome?* No *Operated by:* Private owner *NR?* No *NHL?* No *Latitude:* 44.0115 *Longitude:* -69.1328

MARYLAND

ASSATEAGUE LIFEBOAT STATION

Established in 1875, the current Assateague Lifeboat Station was constructed in 1922 and is now part of the Assateague Island National Seashore. *Address:* 726 National Seashore Lane *City:* Berlin *State:* MD *Zip:* 21811 *Phone:* 410-641-1441 *Visitors welcome?* Yes *Hours:* Daylight hours *Admission:* FREE *Operated by:* Assateague Island National Seashore *NR?* No *NHL?* No *Year established/built:* 1875 *Latitude:* 38.24993 *Longitude:* -75.15585

OCEAN CITY LIFE-SAVING STATION MUSEUM

Established about 1874, the current Ocean City Life-Saving Station was constructed in 1901. In 1977, the building was moved to its present location, where it is used as a museum and local attraction. *Address:* 813 S Boardwalk *City:* Ocean City *State:* MD *Zip:* 21843 *Phone:* 410-289-4991 *Web:* www.ocmuseum.org *Email:* curator@ocmuseum.org *Visitors welcome?* Yes *Hours:* June to Sept., daily, 10 a.m. to 10 p.m.; May and October, daily, 10 a.m. to 4 p.m. *Admission:* $3 adults, $1 children six to 12, under six FREE *Operated by:* Ocean City Museum Society *NR?* No *NHL?* No *Year established/built:* 1874 *Latitude:* 38.3387 *Longitude:* -75.08098

MASSACHUSETTS

CAHOONS HOLLOW LIFE-SAVING STATION

Established in 1897, the Cahoons Hollow Life-Saving Station was decommissioned and sold to a local businessman in 1853. It is now the Beachcomber Restaurant. *Address:* 1120 Cahoon Hollow Rd. *City:* Wellfleet *State:* MA *Zip:* 02667 *Phone:* 508-349-6055 *Web:* www.thebeachcomber.com *Email:* dan@thebeachcomber.com *Visitors welcome?* Yes *Hours:*

Contact attraction directly *Admission:* Contact attraction directly *Operated by:* Private owner *NR?* No *NHL?* No *Year established/built:* 1897 *Latitude:* 41.9437 *Longitude:* -69.9856

GURNET POINT LIFE-SAVING STATION

The former Gurnet Point Life-Saving Station is now a private residence. *Address:* Gurnet Point Life-Saving Station *City:* Duxbury *State:* MA *Visitors welcome?* No *Operated by:* Private owner *NR?* No *NHL?* No *Latitude:* 42.04177 *Longitude:* -70.67226

HORSENECK POINT LIFE-SAVING STATION

Established in 1888, the Horseneck Point Life-Saving Station is now being restored. *Address:* Horseneck Point *City:* Westport *State:* MA *Web:* westportriver.org/life-saving-station.html *Email:* wfa@westportriver.org *Visitors welcome?* Yes *Hours:* Contact attraction directly *Admission:* Contact attraction directly *Operated by:* Westport Fisherman's Association *NR?* No *NHL?* No *Year established/built:* 1888 *Latitude:* 41.5112 *Longitude:* -71.0884

NANTUCKET SHIPWRECK & LIFESAVING MUSEUM

Located next to important shipping lanes running along the East Coast when maritime travel was in its heyday, Nantucket Island saw hundreds of vessels passing by each day. *Address:* 158 Polpis Road *City:* Nantucket *State:* MA *Zip:* 02554 *Phone:* 508-228-1885 *Web:* www.nantucketlifesavingmuseum.com *Visitors welcome?* Yes *Hours:* July 1 to October 13, daily, 10 a.m. to 4 p.m. *Admission:* Contact attraction directly *Operated by:* Nantucket Shipwreck & Lifesaving Museum *NR?* No *NHL?* No *Year established/built:* 1968 *Latitude:* 41.2912 *Longitude:* -70.0449

OLD HARBOR LIFE-SAVING STATION

Established and built in 1897, the Old Harbor Life-Saving Station was deactivated in 1944. In 1977, the building was moved from Nauset Beach to Race Point Beach when the structure was threatened by erosion. It is now within the Cape Cod National Seashore. *Address:* Race Point Beach *City:* Provincetown *State:* MA *Phone:* 508-771 - 2144 *Web:* www.nps.gov/caco/historyculture/old-harbor-life-saving-station.htm *Visitors welcome?* Yes *Hours:* Daily *Admission:* FREE *Operated by:* Cape Cod National Seashore *NR?* Yes *NHL?* No *Year established/built:* 1897 *Latitude:* 42.0812 *Longitude:* -70.2161

PAMET RIVER LIFEBOAT STATION

✦ The Pamet River Lifeboat Station is now a youth hostel. *Address:* North Pamet Road *City:* Truro *State:* MA *Zip:* 02666 *Phone:* 508-349-3889 *Web:* www.usahostels.org/cape/hitr/index.shtml *Visitors welcome?* Yes *Hours:* Contact attraction directly *Admission:* Contact attraction directly *Operated by:* Hostelling International-New England *NR?* No *NHL?* No *Latitude:* 42.0010 *Longitude:* -70.0373 **Accommodations for overnight and/or long-term stays available.**

POINT ALLERTON LIFE-SAVING STATION

The Hull Lifesaving Museum, the museum of Boston Harbor heritage, preserves the region's lifesaving tradition and maritime culture through collections, exhibits, experiential and interpretive education, research and service to others. *Address:* 1117 Nantasket Ave. *City:* Hull *State:* MA *Zip:* 02045 *Phone:* 781-925-5433 *Web:* www.lifesavingmuseum.org *Email:* lifesavingmuseum@comcast.net *Visitors welcome?* Yes *Hours:* Daily *Admission:* $5 adults, $3 seniors, children under 18 FREE *Operated by:* Hull Lifesaving Museum *NR?* No *NHL?* No *Latitude:* 42.3055 *Longitude:* -70.8974

SURFSIDE LIFE-SAVING STATION

✦ Established in 1873, the Surfside Life-Saving Station is now a youth hostel. *Address:* 31 Western Ave. *City:* Nantucket *State:* MA *Zip:* 02554 *Phone:* 508-228-0433 *Web:* www.usa-hostels.org/cape/hint/index.shtml *Visitors welcome?* Yes *Hours:* Contact attraction directly *Admission:* Contact attraction directly *Operated by:* Hostelling International-New England *NR?* Yes *NHL?* No *Year established/built:* 1873 *Latitude:* 41.2443 *Longitude:* -70.0980 **Accommodations for overnight and/or long-term stays available.**

MICHIGAN

GRAND MARAIS HARBOR OF REFUGE

The Harbor of Refuge house was built in 1908 by the U.S. Life Saving Service as the Light-keeper's dwelling. It was constructed at a cost of $5,000, and is a duplicate to the station at the Munising Range Lights. U.S. Coast Guard families lived in the home. *Address:* Coast Guard Point Road *City:* Grand Marais *State:* MI *Phone:* 906-387-2607 *Web:* www.nps.gov/piro/ *Visitors welcome?* Yes *Hours:* Contact attraction directly *Admission:* **FREE** *Operated by:* Pictured Rocks National Lakeshore *NR?* No *NHL?* No *Year established/built:* 1908 *Latitude:* 46.6708 *Longitude:* -85.9852

GRAND MARAIS LIFEBOAT STATION

Established in 1899, the current Grand Marais Life-Saving Station was constructed in 1938 and deactivated in 1981. The station is now within the Pictured Rocks National Lakeshore. *Address:* Coast Guard Point Road *City:* Grand Marais *State:* MI *Phone:* 906-387-2607 *Web:* www.nps.gov/piro/ *Visitors welcome?* Yes *Hours:* Contact attraction directly *Admission:* FREE *Operated by:* Pictured Rocks National Lakeshore *NR?* No *NHL?* No *Year established/built:* 1899 *Latitude:* 46.67081 *Longitude:* -85.98517

MUNISING LIFEBOAT STATION

Established in 1932, the Munising Life-Saving Station, also known as the Sand Point Life-Saving Station, was operated by the U.S. Coast Guard until 1960. It is now the headquarters for the Pictured Rocks National Lakeshore. *Address:* Sand Point Road *City:* Munising

State: MI *Phone:* 906-387-2607 *Web:* www.nps.gov/piro/ *Visitors welcome?* Yes *Hours:* Contact attraction directly *Admission:* FREE *Operated by:* Pictured Rocks National Lakeshore *NR?* No *NHL?* No *Year established/built:* 1932 *Latitude:* 46.4369 *Longitude:* -86.6128

NORTH MANITOU ISLAND LIFE-SAVING STATION

Established and built in 1854, the North Manitou Island Life-Saving Station was deactivated in 1939. It is now within the Sleeping Bear Dunes National Lakeshore. *Address:* Manitou Passage, Lake Michigan *City:* Leland *State:* MI *Phone:* 231-326-5134 *Visitors welcome?* Yes *Hours:* Grounds only *Admission:* FREE *Operated by:* Sleeping Bear Dunes National Lakeshore *NR?* Yes *NHL?* Yes *Year established/built:* 1854 *Latitude:* 45.0231 *Longitude:* -85.7598

POINTE AUX BARQUES LIFE-SAVING STATION

Established in 1876, the Pointe aux Barques Life-Saving Station is now deactivated. The building was moved to Huron City Museum in 1964. *Address:* 7995 Pioneer Drive *City:* Port Austin *State:* MI *Phone:* 989-428-4123 *Email:* info@huroncitymuseums.com *Visitors welcome?* Yes *Hours:* Daily, Memorial Day through Sept. 30, Monday through Saturday, 10 a.m. to 6 p.m., Sunday, 11 a.m. to 6 p.m. *Admission:* Contact attraction directly *Operated by:* Point aux Barques Lighthouse Society *NR?* No *NHL?* No *Year established/built:* 1876 *Latitude:* 44.02944 *Longitude:* -82.83622

SLEEPING BEAR POINT LIFE-SAVING STATION

Established in 1902, the Sleeping Bear Point Life-Saving Station was deactivated in 1942 and is now part of the Sleeping Bear Dunes National Lakeshore. *Address:* Michigan State Route 209 *City:* Glen Arbor *State:* MI *Phone:* 616-326-5134 *Visitors welcome?* Yes *Hours:* Daily *Admission:* FREE *Operated by:* Sleeping Bear Dunes National Lakeshore *NR?* Yes *NHL?* No *Year established/built:* 1902 *Latitude:* 44.8960 *Longitude:* -85.9873

SOUTH MANITOU ISLAND LIFE-SAVING STATION

Established in 1901, the South Manitou Island Life-Saving Station was deactivated in 1958. It is now part of the Sleeping Bear Dunes National Lakeshore. *Address:* South Manitou Island, Lake Michigan *City:* Leland *State:* MI *Phone:* 231-326-5134 *Visitors welcome?* Yes *Hours:* Grounds only *Admission:* FREE *Operated by:* Sleeping Bear Dunes National Lakeshore *NR?* Yes *NHL?* No *Year established/built:* 1901 *Latitude:* 45.0231 *Longitude:* -85.7598

ST. JOSEPH LIFE-SAVING STATION

Established in 1874, the St. Joseph Life-Saving Station is now Station St. Joseph of the U.S. Coast Guard. *Address:* 127 North Pier Street *City:* St. Joseph *State:* MI *Zip:* 49085 *Phone:* 269-983-6114 *Visitors welcome?* Yes *Hours:* Contact attraction directly *Admission:* FREE *Operated by:* U.S. Coast Guard (District 9) *NR?* No *NHL?* No *Year established/built:* 1874 *Latitude:* 42.11402 *Longitude:* -86.48561

WHITEFISH POINT LIFE-SAVING STATION

⚓ Established in 1923 on the grounds of the Whitefish Point Lighthouse, the Whitefish Point Lifeboat Station is now owned by a local museum. The building is available for overnight stays. *Address:* Whitefish Point Light *City:* Paradise *State:* MI *Zip:* 49768 *Phone:* 888-492-3747 *Web:* www.shipwreckmuseum.com *Visitors welcome?* Yes *Hours:* Contact attraction directly *Admission:* Contact attraction directly *Operated by:* Great Lakes Shipwreck Historical Society *NR?* Yes *NHL?* No *Year established/built:* 1923 *Latitude:* 46.7706 *Longitude:* -84.9567 **Accommodations for overnight and/or long-term stays available.**

NEW JERSEY

MONMOUTH BEACH LIFE-SAVING STATION

Established in 1849, the current Monmouth Beach Life-Saving Station was constructed in 1895. Deactivated by the Coast Guard in the late 1950s, the building is now home to a local cultural center. *Address:* 128 Ocean Avenue *City:* Monmouth Beach *State:* NJ *Zip:* 07750 *Phone:* 732-229-4527 *Web:* www.surfmen.com *Email:* mbculturalcenter@comcast.net *Visitors welcome?* Yes *Hours:* Wednesday to Saturday, 10 a.m. to 2 p.m. *Admission:* Contact attraction directly *Operated by:* Monmouth Beach Cultural Center *NR?* No *NHL?* No *Year established/built:* 1849 *Latitude:* 40.34235 *Longitude:* -73.97401

SPERMACETI COVE LIFE-SAVING STATION

Established in 1849, the Spermaceti Cove Life-Saving Station was deactivated in 1946. It is now a visitors center for the Sandy Hook unit of the Gateway National Recreation Area. *Address:* Rt. 36 at Hartshorne Dr. *City:* Fort Hancock *State:* NJ *Zip:* 07732 *Phone:* 732-872-5970 *Visitors welcome?* Yes *Hours:* Daily, 10 a.m. to 5 p.m. *Admission:* FREE *Operated by:* Gateway National Recreation Area *NR?* Yes *NHL?* Yes *Year established/built:* 1849 *Latitude:* 40.42616 *Longitude:* -73.98564

NEW YORK

FORGE RIVER LIFEBOAT STATION

The Forge River Lifeboat Station is now a restaurant in Ocean Bay Park. *Address:* 1 Cayuga St. *City:* Ocean Bay Park *State:* NY *Zip:* 11770 *Phone:* 631-583-5000 *Visitors welcome?* Yes *Hours:* Contact attraction directly *Admission:* Contact attraction directly *Operated by:* Private owner *NR?* No *NHL?* No *Latitude:* 40.65134 *Longitude:* -73.1369

OAK ISLAND BEACH LIFE-SAVING STATION
Established and built in 1861, the Oak Island Beach Life-Saving Station is now a community center. *City:* Babylon *State:* NY *Zip:* 11757 *Phone:* 631-957-3000 *Visitors welcome?* Yes *Hours:* Contact attraction directly *Admission:* Contact attraction directly *Operated by:* Town of Babylon *NR?* No *NHL?* No *Year established/built:* 1861 *Latitude:* 40.69202 *Longitude:* -73.37676

NORTH CAROLINA

CAFFEY'S INLET LIFE-SAVING STATION
✦ Established and built in 1874, the Caffeys Inlet Life-Saving Station is now a resort. *Address:* 1461 Duck Road *City:* Kitty Hawk *State:* NC *Zip:* 27949 *Phone:* 252-261-8419 *Web:* www.thesanderling.com *Visitors welcome?* Yes *Hours:* Contact attraction directly *Admission:* Contact attraction directly *Operated by:* Sanderling Inn Resort *NR?* No *NHL?* No *Year established/built:* 1874 *Latitude:* 36.22343 *Longitude:* -75.77089 **Accommodations for overnight and/or long-term stays available.**

CHICAMACOMICO LIFE-SAVING STATION
Established and built in 1874 as one of North Carolina's original group of life-saving stations, the Chicamacomico Life-Saving Station was decommissioned in 1954 and is now a museum. *Address:* 23645 N.C. Highway 12 *City:* Rodanthe *State:* NC *Zip:* 27968 *Phone:* 252-987-1552 *Web:* www.chicamacomico.net *Email:* clss@embarqmail.com *Visitors welcome?* Yes *Hours:* Mid-April to November, Monday to Friday, noon to 5 p.m. *Admission:* $6 adults, $4 seniors and students *Operated by:* Chicamacomico Historical Association *NR?* Yes *NHL?* No *Year established/built:* 1874 *Latitude:* 35.6898 *Longitude:* -75.48982

KITTY HAWK LIFE-SAVING STATION
Established and built in 1874 as one of North Carolina's orginal group of life-saving stations, the Kitty Hawk Life-Saving Station is now a restaurant. *Address:* MP 4 Oceanfront *City:* Kitty Hawk *State:* NC *Zip:* 27949 *Phone:* 252-261-3171 *Web:* www.blackpelican.com *Email:* events@blackpelican.com *Visitors welcome?* Yes *Hours:* Contact attraction directly *Admission:* Contact attraction directly *Operated by:* Black Pelican Restaurant *NR?* Yes *NHL?* No *Year established/built:* 1874 *Latitude:* 36.06461 *Longitude:* -75.70573

OCRACOKE LIFEBOAT STATION
The Ocracoke Lifeboat Station is a sub-unit of U.S. Coast Guard Station Hatteras Inlet. *Address:* Ocracoke Island *City:* Ocracoke *State:* NC *Visitors welcome?* Yes *Hours:* Contact attraction directly *Admission:* Contact attraction directly *Operated by:* U.S. Coast Guard (District 5) *NR?* No *NHL?* No *Year established/built:* 1883 *Latitude:* 35.10487 *Longitude:* -75.96155

OREGON

COOS BAY LIFEBOAT STATION

In 1878, the first life-saving station, later to become a Coast Guard station, was located at Cape Arago below the lighthouse on a small sandy beach. *Address:* Coos Bay Lifeboat Station *City:* Charleston *State:* OR *Zip:* 96791 *Phone:* 541-888-3267 *Visitors welcome?* Yes *Hours:* Contact attraction directly *Admission:* Contact attraction directly *Operated by:* U.S. Coast Guard (District 13) *NR?* No *NHL?* No *Year established/built:* 1874 *Latitude:* 43.35318 *Longitude:* -124.07823

COQUILLE RIVER LIFEBOAT STATION

Located on the south bank of the Coquille River, the Coquille River Lifeboat Station is now a multipurpose structure. *Address:* 390 SW First St. *City:* Bandon *State:* OR *Zip:* 97411 *Visitors welcome?* Yes *Hours:* Contact attraction directly *Admission:* Contact attraction directly *Operated by:* Port of Bandon *NR?* No *NHL?* No *Latitude:* 43.12054 *Longitude:* -124.41795

PORT ORFORD LIFEBOAT STATION

Established and built in 1934, the Port Orford Lifeboat Station is now a museum. *Address:* Port Orford Head State Park *City:* Port Orford *State:* OR *Zip:* 97465 *Phone:* 541-332-0521 *Web:* www.portorfordlifeboatstation.org *Email:* info@portorfordlifeboatstation.org *Visitors welcome?* Yes *Hours:* April to October, Monday to Thursday, 10 a.m. to 3:30 p.m. *Admission:* FREE *Operated by:* Port Orford Heritage Society *NR?* Yes *NHL?* No *Year established/built:* 1934 *Latitude:* 42.74566 *Longitude:* -124.49733

YAQUINA BAY LIFEBOAT STATION

The Yaquina Bay Lifeboat Station is an active U.S. Coast Guard facility. *Address:* 925 SW Naterlin Dr. *City:* Newport *State:* OR *Zip:* 97365 *Phone:* 541-265-5381 *Visitors welcome?* Yes *Hours:* By appointment *Admission:* FREE *Operated by:* U.S. Coast Guard (District 13) *NR?* No *NHL?* No *Latitude:* 44.62649 *Longitude:* -124.05732

RHODE ISLAND

NARRAGANSETT PIER LIFE-SAVING STATION

Constructed in 1888, the Narrangansett Pier Life-Saving Station is now a restaurant. *Address:* 40 Ocean Road *City:* Narragansett *State:* RI *Zip:* 02882 *Phone:* 401-789-0700 *Web:* www.thecoastguardhouse.com *Email:* office@thecoastguardhouse.com *Visitors welcome?* Yes *Hours:* Contact attraction directly *Admission:* FREE *Operated by:* Coast Guard House *NR?* Yes *NHL?* No *Year established/built:* 1885 *Latitude:* 41.43022 *Longitude:* -71.45536

POINT JUDITH LIFE-SAVING STATION

The Point Judith Life-Saving Station is adjacent to the Point Judith Lighthouse. *Address:* Point Judith Coast Guard Station *City:* Point Judith *State:* RI *Visitors welcome?* Yes *Hours:* Grounds only *Admission:* FREE *Operated by:* U.S. Coast Guard (District 1) *NR?* Yes *NHL?* No *Year established/built:* 1810 *Latitude:* 41.36538 *Longitude:* -71.48673

VIRGINIA

VIRGINIA BEACH LIFE-SAVING STATION

Established and built in 1903, the Virginia Beach Life-Saving Station, also called the Seatack Life-Saving Station, is now operated as the Old Coast Guard Museum. *Address:* 2400 Atlantic Ave. *City:* Virginia Beach *State:* VA *Zip:* 23451 *Phone:* 757-422-1587 *Web:* www.oldcoastguardstation.com *Email:* director@oldcoastguardstation.com *Visitors welcome?* Yes *Hours:* Monday through Saturday, 10 a.m. to 5 p.m.; Sunday, noon to 5 p.m. *Admission:* $4 adults, $3 seniors/military, $2 children six to 18, under six FREE *Operated by:* Old Coast Guard Station *NR?* No *NHL?* No *Year established/built:* 1903 *Latitude:* 36.8525 *Longitude:* -75.9766

WASHINGTON

GRAYS HARBOR LIFEBOAT STATION

Established in 1939, the Grays Harbor Lifeboat Station is now operated as the Westport Maritime Museum. An historic lifeboat once used at Grays Harbor is located at the U.S. Coast Guard station 1/2 mile south of the museum. *Address:* 2201 Westhaven Dr. *City:* Westport *State:* WA *Zip:* 98595 *Phone:* 360-268-0078 *Web:* www.westportwa. com/museum/ *Email:* westport.maritime@comcast.net *Visitors welcome?* Yes *Hours:* Daily, April to Sept., 10 a.m. to 4 p.m.; Oct. to March, Friday to Monday, 12 p.m. to 4 p.m. *Admission:* Contact attraction directly *Operated by:* Westport South Beach Historical Society *NR?* No *NHL?* No *Year established/built:* 1939 *Latitude:* 46.9077 *Longitude:* -124.1120

WISCONSIN

RACINE HARBOR LIGHTHOUSE & LIFE-SAVING STATION

Established and built in 1866, the Racine Harbor Lighthouse & Life-Saving Station, located at the mouth of the Root River, was deactivated in 1903. The light is atop a skeletal steel tower, and the site is now on private property. *Address:* Entrance to Racine Harbor at Pugh Marina *City:* Racine *State:* WI *Zip:* 53402 *Phone:* 262-632-8515 *Visitors welcome?* Yes *Hours:* Grounds only *Admission:* Contact attraction directly *Operated by:* Private owner *NR?* No *NHL?* No *Year established/built:* 1866 *Latitude:* 42.7261 *Longitude:* -87.7829

TWO RIVERS LIFEBOAT STATION

Believed established in the Civil War era, the current Two Rivers Lifeboat Station was constructed in 1909. It is still an active Coast Guard unit, known as Station Two Rivers. *Address:* 13 East Street *City:* Two Rivers *State:* WI *Zip:* 54241 *Phone:* 920-793-1304 *Visitors welcome?* Yes *Hours:* Contact attraction directly *Admission:* Contact attraction directly *Operated by:* U.S. Coast Guard (District 9) *NR?* No *NHL?* No *Year established/built:* 1865 *Latitude:* 44.14872 *Longitude:* -87.56302

TWO RIVERS LIFE-SAVING STATION

The Two Rivers Life-Saving Station is part of the Rogers Street Fishing Village museum. *Address:* 2010 Rogers St. *City:* Two Rivers *State:* WI *Zip:* 54241 *Phone:* 920-793-5905 *Web:* www.rogersstreet.com *Email:* szipperer@rogersstreet.com *Visitors welcome?* Yes *Hours:* May to October: Daily, 10 a.m. to 4 p.m. *Admission:* $4 adults, $2 children under 16 *Operated by:* Rogers Street Fishing Village & Great Lakes Coast Guard Museum *NR?* No *NHL?* No *Year established/built:* 1877 *Latitude:* 44.1518 *Longitude:* -87.56256

Check for the latest lighthouse news on our *Fyddeye Guide* Facebook page!

APPENDIX

U.S. Lighthouse and Maritime Festivals

Most community festivals focus on a central theme: music, the arts, food, local history. The community maritime festival often brings all these themes together under an umbrella of life in, on, and around the water. The biggest lighthouse festival in the country is the Great Lakes Lighthouse Festival in Alpena, Mich., which showcases several lighthouse sites in Lake Michigan. Other maritime festivals celebrate the hard work of maritime industry, such as the Seattle Maritime Festival in early May, which features tugboat races that draw working and historic tugs from as far away as Canada. Other festivals revolve around folk traditions, particularly music, such as September's Portsmouth Maritime Folk Festival in Portsmouth, N.H. Seafood is a major element of most maritime festivals, and sometime the main element, as in the Florida Seafood Festival in Apalachicola, Fla., in November. And though most festivals happen in the warmer months of the year, especially spring and early summer, you can find a maritime festival somewhere in the U.S. almost any month of the year. Here's a list of the most popular maritime-themed festival from around the nation.

FEBRUARY

CHICAGO MARITIME FESTIVAL
Chicago, IL
Chicago Maritime Festival
http://www.chicagomaritimefestival.org/
chriskastle@yahoo.com

FISHER POETS GATHERING
Astoria, OR
Clatsop Community College
503-325-4972
http://www.clatsopcollege.com/fisherpoets/
fsage@clatsopcc.edu

GREAT LAKES SHIPWRECK FESTIVAL
Ann Arbor, MI
Dossin Great Lakes Museum
http://www.shipwreckfestival.org/

MARCH

GHOST SHIPS FESTIVAL
Milwaukee, WI
Great Lakes Shipwreck Research Foundation
http://www.ghost-ships.org/
info@ghost-ships.org

GULF MARITIME FESTIVAL
Tarpon Springs, FL
City of Tarpon Springs
http://floridamaritimeheritage.org/

ST. AUGUSTINE LIGHTHOUSE FESTIVAL
St. Augustine, FL
St. Augustine Lighthouse & Museum
904-829-0745
http://www.staugustinelighthouse.com/
info@staugustinelighthouse.com

APRIL

ASTORIA WARRENTON CRAB, SEAFOOD & FESTIVAL
Astoria, OR

Astoria & Warrenton Area Chamber of Commerce
800-875-6807
http://www.oldoregon.com/events/entry/astoria-warrenton-crab-seafood-wine-festival/
info@oldoregon.com

BLESSING OF THE FLEET

Darien, GA
Darien-McIntosh County Chamber of Commerce
http://www.blessingofthefleet.com/

CRYSTAL RIVER BOAT BASH

Crystal River, FL
Crystal River Reserve State Park
850-245-2157
http://www.floridastateparks.org/crystalriverpreserve/

MAY

CAPE COD MARITIME DAYS

Hyannis, MA
Cape Cod Chamber of Commerce
508-362-3225
http://www.ecapechamber.com/MaritimeDays/
info@capecodchamber.org

HUDSON RIVER SHAD FESTIVAL

Kingston, NY
Hudson River Maritime Museum
845-338-0071
http://www.hrmm.org/
hrmm@hvc.rr.com

JUNEAU MARITIME FESTIVAL

Juneau, AK
Juneau Maritime Festival
907-523-2330
http://juneaumaritimefestival.org/
jrintala@jedc.org

MACKINAW MARITIME FESTIVAL

Mackinaw City, MI
Great Lakes Lighthouse Keepers Association
231-436-5580
http://www.mackinawmaritimefestival.com/
info@gllka.com

MARYLAND MARITIME HERITAGE FESTIVAL

Annapolis, MD
Maryland Maritime Heritage Festival
410-693-8394
davehanson1011@gmail.com

PASSAIC RIVER MARITIME FESTIVAL

Newark, NJ
Passaic River Maritime Festival
http://www.passaicrivermaritimefestival.com/
info@passaicrivermaritimefestival.com

PENN COVE WATER FESTIVAL

Coupeville, WA
Penn Cove Water Festival
http://www.penncovewaterfestival.com/
RoseAnn@IslandCountyTourism.com

SEA FESTIVAL

Santa Barbara, CA
Santa Barbara Maritime Museum
805-962-8404
http://www.sbmm.org/Featured-Events/seafestival.html

SEATTLE MARITIME FESTIVAL

Seattle, WA
Seattle Propeller Club
206-282-6858
http://www.seattlepropellerclub.org/maritimefestival.html
Ken@HamiltonSaunderson.com

SOLOMONS MARITIME FESTIVAL

Solomons, MD
Calvert Marine Museum

410-326-2042
http://www.calvertmarinemuseum.com/

JUNE

ANTIQUE & CLASSIC BOAT FESTIVAL
St. Michaels, MD
Chesapeake Bay Maritime Museum
410-745-2916
http://www.cbmm.org/
mthomas@cbmm.org

CAPE COD MARITIME FESTIVAL
Hyannis, MA
Cape Cod Maritime Museum
508-775-1723
http://www.capecodmaritimemuseum.org/
info@capecodmaritimemuseum.org

CHANNEL ISLANDS TALL SHIPS FESTIVAL
Oxnard, CA
Channel Islands Harbor
805-382-3001
http://www.tallshipschannelislands.com/
CHHarborVisitors@ventura.org

DELAWARE BAY DAY
Port Norris, NJ
Bayshore Discovery Project
856-785-2060
http://www.bayshorediscovery.org
jtraas@bayshorediscovery.org

DETROIT RIVER DAYS
Detroit, MI
Detroit Riverfront Conservancy
313-566-8200
http://www.riverdays.com/

JAMES RIVER BATTEAU FESTIVAL
Lynchburg, VA
Virginia Canals & Navigations Society
http://www.batteau.org/

LONG ISLAND PIRATE FESTIVAL
West Sayville, NY
Long Island Maritime Museum
631-494-9888
http://limaritime.org/
limm@limaritime.org

NORTHPORT LIGHTHOUSE AND MARITIME FESTIVAL
Northport, MI
Grand Traverse Lighthouse Museum
231-386-7195
http://www.grandtraverselighthouse.com/
gtlthse@triton.net

RUSTY SCUPPER PIRATE DAZE
Westport, WA
Rusty Scupper Pirates
360-268-9817
http://rustyscupperpirates.com/
oldcoasty69@msn.com

SAILING SEAWAY CLAYTON
Clayton, NY
Sailing Seaway Clayton
http://www.sailingseawayclayton.com/
theshipwatcher@yahoo.com

WINDJAMMER DAYS FESTIVAL
Boothbay Harbor, ME
Maine Windjammer Association
207-374-2993
http://www.sailmainecoast.com/about_mwa/fleetevents.htm

WOODEN BOAT SHOW
Mystic, CT
Wooden Boat Magazine
800-273-7447

http://www.thewoodenboatshow.com/
michele@woodenboat.com

WOODENBOAT SHOW
Mystic, CT
WoodenBoat Magazine
800-273-7447
http://www.thewoodenboatshow.com/
woodenboatshow@woodenboat.com

JULY

BALLARD SEAFOODFEST
Seattle, WA
Ballard Chamber of Commerce
206-784-9705
http://www.seafoodfest.org/
seafoodfest@ballardchamber.com

BEAUFORT WATER FESTIVAL
Beaufort, SC
Beaufort Water Festival
843-524-0600
http://www.bftwaterfestival.com/
info@bftwaterfestival.com

CITY OF WATER DAY FESTIVAL
Jersey City, NJ
Metropolitan Waterfront Alliance
212-935-9831
http://www.cityofwaterday.org/
lkleinman@waterfrontalliance.org

DULUTH MUSIC & MARITIME FESTIVAL
Duluth, MN
Visit Duluth
877-435-9849
http://visitduluth.com/maritimefestival/
cvb@visitduluth.com

HEREFORD INLET MARITIME FESTIVAL
North Wildwood, NJ
Hereford Inlet Lighthouse
609-348-5826
http://www.herefordlighthousefestival.org/
herefordfestival@aol.com

LAKE UNION WOODEN BOAT FESTIVAL
Seattle, WA
Center for Wooden Boats
206-382-2628
http://www.cwb.org/
cwb@cwb.org

MANDEVILLE SEAFOOD FESTIVAL
Mandeville, LA
Greater Mandeville Seafood Association
985-624-9762
http://www.seafoodfest.com/

MARITIME HERITAGE DAYS
New Bedford, MA
New Bedford Whaling National Historical Park
508-996-4095
http://www.nps.gov/nebe/

MERRIMACK RIVER MARITIME FESTIVAL
Salisbury Beach, MA
Salisbury Beach State Reservation
978-462-7874
http://www.beachfests.org/

NORTH RIVER HISTORIC SHIP FESTIVAL
New York, NY
North River Historic Ship Society
212-533-6552
http://nrhss.org/
nycentral13@gmail.com

OSWEGO HARBORFEST
Oswego, NY
Oswego Harbor Festivals

315-343-6858
http://www.oswegoharborfest.com/

REHOBOTH BEACH MARITIME HERITAGE FESTIVAL
Rehoboth Beach, NJ
Indian River Life-Saving Station
302-739-9175
http://www.destateparks.com
Necia.Beck@state.de.us

RIVERDALE RIVERFEST
Riverdale, NY
Hudson River Greenway
http://www.riverdaleriverfest.org/
info@riverdaleriverfest.org

SAN DIEGO SEA CHANTEY FESTIVAL
San Diego, CA
San Diego Maritime Museum
619-234-9153
http://www.sdmaritime.org/sea-chantey-festival/
info@sdmaritime.org

THUNDER BAY MARITIME FESTIVAL
Alpena, MI
Thunder Bay National Marine Sanctuary
989-356-8805
http://thunderbay.noaa.gov/

AUGUST

COMMENCEMENT BAY MARITIME FESTIVAL
Tacoma, WA
Commencement Bay Maritime Fest
253-318-2210
http://www.maritimefest.org/
maritime_fest@yahoo.com

FAMILY MARITIME FESTIVAL
Essex, CT

Connecticut River Museum
860-767-8269
http://www.ctrivermuseum.org

LAKE CHAMPLAIN MARITIME FESTIVAL
Burlington, VT
Lake Champlain Maritime Festival
802-482-3313
http://www.lcmfestival.com/
bigredpenproductions@hotmail.com

MAINE LOBSTER FESTIVAL
Rockland, ME
Maine Lobster Festival
207-596-0376
http://www.mainelobsterfestival.com/
info@mainelobsterfestival.com

NATIONAL LIGHTHOUSE DAY
American Lighthouse Foundation
207-594-4174
http://www.lighthousefoundation.org/museum/natllighthouseday_info.htm
info@lighthousefoundation.org

NEW JERSEY MARITIME HERITAGE FESTIVAL
Tuckerton, NJ
Tuckerton Seaport
609-296-8868
http://www.tuckertonseaport.org/

PORT WASHINGTON MARITIME HERITAGE FESTIVAL
Port Washington, WI
Port Washington Maritime Heritage Festival
262-268-1132
http://www.portmaritimefestival.com/
maritimeheritagefestival@yahoo.com

ROGERS CITY NAUTICAL FESTIVAL
Rogers City, WI
Nautical City Festival
http://www.nauticalfestival.org/
nautical@charterinternet.com

SALEM MARITIME FESTIVAL
Salem, MA
Salem Maritime National Historic Site
978-740-1650
http://www.nps.gov/sama/

TASTE OF TALL SHIPS CHICAGO
Chicago, IL
Navy Pier
312-595-5300
http://www.navypier.com/tasteoftallships/
navypierinfo@mpea.com

SEPTEMBER

CAMDEN WINDJAMMER FESTIVAL
Camden, ME
Rockport Lincolnville Chamber of Commerce
http://www.camdenwindjammerfestival.com/

DANA POINT TALL SHIPS FESTIVAL
Dana Point, CA
Ocean Institute
949-496-2274
http://www.ocean-institute.org/

GLOUCESTER SCHOONER FESTIVAL
Gloucester, MA
Cape Ann Chamber of Commerce
978-283-1601
http://www.capeannvacations.com/schooner/
info@CapeAnnChamber.com

GREAT NORTH RIVER TUGBOAT RACE
New York, NY
Working Harbor Committee
212-757-1600
http://workingharbor.com/
John@Workingharbor.Org

GREENPORT MARITIME FESTIVAL
Greenport, NY
East End Seaport Museum and Marine Foundation
631-477-2100
eseaport@verizon.net

HAMPTON BEACH SEAFOOD FESTIVAL
Hampton, NH
Hampton Area Chamber of Commerce
603-926-8718
http://www.hamptonbeachseafoodfestival.com/
info@hamptonchamber.com

MICHIGAN SCHOONER FESTIVAL
Traverse City, MI
Maritime Heritage Alliance
231-946-2647
http://www.michiganschoonerfestival.org/
Mark@MaritimeHeritageAlliance.org

OCEANSIDE HARBOR DAYS
Oceanside, CA
Oceanside Chamber of Commerce
760-722-1534
http://www.oceansidechamber.com/harbordays/
info@oceansidechamber.com

OHIO RIVER STERNWHEEL FESTIVAL
Marietta, OH
Washington County Convention and Visitors Bureau
800-288-2577
http://www.ohioriversternwheelfestival.org/

OLYMPIA HARBOR DAYS
Olympia, WA
Olympia Harbor Days
http://www.harbordays.com/
harbordays@comcast.net

PITTSBURG SEAFOOD FESTIVAL
Pittsburg, CA
Pittsburg Chamber of Commerce

925-432-7301
http://www.pittsburgchamber.org/

PORT TOWNSEND WOODEN BOAT FESTIVAL
Port Townsend, WA
Wooden Boat Foundation
360-385-3628
http://www.woodenboat.org/festival/
ask@woodenboat.org

PORTSMOUTH MARITIME FOLK FESTIVAL
Portsmouth, NH
New England Folk Network
http://www.newenglandfolknetwork.org/pmff/
pmff@comcast.net

REDONDO BEACH LOBSTER FESTIVAL
Redondo Beach, CA
Redondo Beach Chamber of Commerce & Visitors Bureau
310-376-6911
http://www.lobsterfestival.com/
info@redondochamber.org

SAN DIEGO FESTIVAL OF SAIL
San Diego, CA
San Diego Maritime Museum
619-234-9153
http://www.sdmaritime.org/
info@sdmaritime.org

TOSHIBA TALL SHIPS FESTIVAL
Dana Point, CA
Ocean Institute
949-496-2274
http://www.tallshipsfestival.com/

OCTOBER

BOAST THE COAST MARITIME FESTIVAL
Lewes, DE

Lews Chamber of Commerce
877-465-3937
http://www.leweschamber.com

CAMBRIDGE SCHOONER RENDEZVOUS
Cambridge, MD
Cambridge Schooner Rendezvous
410-221-1871
http://www.cambridgeschoonerrendezvous.com/
info@richardsonmuseum.org/

CLASSIC & WOODEN BOAT FESTIVAL
Sturgeon Bay, WI
Door County Maritime Museum
920-743-5958
http://www.dcmm.org/
info@dcmm.org

DOWNRIGGING WEEKEND
Chestertown, MD
Sultana Projects
410-778-5954
http://www.sultanaprojects.org/downrigging/
dmcmullen@sultanaprojects.org

GREAT LAKES LIGHTHOUSE FESTIVAL
Alpena, MI
Great Lakes Lighthouse Festival
586-566-1603
http://www.lighthousefestival.org/

LAKE PONTCHARTRAIN WOODEN BOAT FESTIVAL
Madisonville, LA
Lake Pontchartrain Basin Maritime Museum
985-845-9200
http://lpbmm.org/
info@lpbmm.org

LAKESIDE-MARBLEHEAD LIGHTHOUSE FESTIVAL
Marblehead, OH
Marblehead Chamber of Commerce
866-952-5374

http://www.lakesideohio.com/
guestinfo@lakesideohio.com

NORTH CAROLINA SEAFOOD FESTIVAL

Morehead City, NC
North Carolina Seafood Festival
252-726-NCSF
http://www.ncseafoodfestival.org/
fun@ncseafoodfestival.org

NORTH COAST SEAFOOD FESTIVAL

Tillamook, OR
North Coast Seafood Festival
503-398-5223
http://www.northcoastseafoodfestival.com/
seafoodfestival@oregoncoast.com

NOVEMBER

FLORIDA SEAFOOD FESTIVAL

Apalachicola, FL
Florida Seafood Festival
888-653-8011
http://www.floridaseafoodfestival.com/
information@floridaseafoodfestival.com

PIRATES IN PARADISE FESTIVAL

Key West, FL
Pirates in Paradise Festival
305-296-9694
http://piratesinparadise.com/
info@piratesinparadise.com

INDEX

The following index contains all cities in the *Fyddeye Guide to America's Lighthouses*. Some cities appear more than once on a directory page. However, their pages are listed only once in the index.

PHOTO CREDITS

MAP INSERTS
California Lighthouses Itinerary: Photos of Point Cabrillo and Port Hartford lighthouses courtesy Wikimedia Commons; Michigan Lighthouses Itinerary: Photo of Au Sable Point Lighthouse courtesy National Park Service; New England Lighthouses Itinerary: Photo of Portsmouth Harbor Lighthouse by Jeremy D'Entremont; Photo of Cape May Lighthouse by Craig Terry.

OTHER PHOTOS
Big Bay Lighthouse (Big Bay Point Lighthouse); Delaware Parks Department (Indian River Life-Saving Station); Donna Connor (Absecon Lighthouse); Jeremy D'Entremont (Portland Head Lighthouse, Portsmouth Harbor Lighthouse); Joe Follansbee (Alki Point Lighthouse, Browns Point Lighthouse, Cape Disappointment Lighthouse, Grays Harbor Lighthouse, Grays Harbor Lifeboat Station, Lightship Swiftsure, Mukilteo Lighthouse); Linda Nenn (Port Washington Lighthouse); National Oceanographic and Atmospheric Administration (Cape Decision Lighthouse, Cape Flattery Lighthouse, Sanibel Island Lighthouse, St. Simons Island Lighthouse, Tortugas Harbor); Michigan Travel Bureau (Manistique East Breakwater Lighthouse); Monhegan Museum (Monhegan Island Lighthouse); National Park Service (Cape Hatteras Lighthouse, Michigan Island [New] Lighthouse, Au Sable Point Lighthouse, Devils Island Lighthouse, Raspberry Island Lighthouse, Sand Island Lighthouse); Ohio State Parks (Marblehead Lighthouse); Old Baldy Foundation (Bald Head Island Lighthouse); Oregon Parks and Recreation Department (Cape Blanco Lighthouse, Heceta Head Lighthouse); Paul St. Germain (Cape Ann Lighthouse); Pensacola Lighthouse and Museum (Pensacola Lighthouse);

Brian Pope (Montauk Point Lighthouse); Public domain (Ida Lewis); Tim Robinson (Seguin Island Lighthouse); Darlene Rome (Lightship Huron); State of New Jersey

(Barnegat Lighthouse); U.S. Coast Guard (Ship Shoal Lighthouse drawing, Sombrero Key Lighthouse, Molokai Lighthouse); Chris Winters (Whitefish Point Lighthouse).

Heceta Head Lighthouse); Paul St. Germain (Cape Ann Lighthouse); Pensacola Lighthouse and Museum (Pensacola Lighthouse); Brian Pope (Montauk Point Lighthouse); Public domain (Ida Lewis); Tim Robinson (Seguin Island Lighthouse); Darlene Rome (Lightship Huron); State of New Jersey (Barnegat Lighthouse); U.S. Coast Guard (Ship Shoal Lighthouse drawing, Sombrero Key Lighthouse, Molokai Lighthouse); Chris Winters (Whitefish Point Lighthouse).

ACKNOWLEDGEMENTS

The Fyddeye Guide to America's Lighthouses builds on the work on thousands of people, ranging from Guide contributors to the individuals and not-for-profit organizations in small and large communities fighting to preserve our maritime heritage. Without the hard work of volunteers and staff at heritage organizations across the country, a directory series such as the Fyddeye Guides would not have been possible, because so much of our heritage would otherwise have been lost.

Joe Follansbee, Winter 2012

MORE TITLES FROM FYDDEYE MEDIA

The Fyddeye Guide to America's Maritime History -- *The Fyddeye Guide to America's Maritime History* is a one-of-a-kind directory for tall ships, lighthouses, historic warships, maritime museums, and other attractions you can visit today that preserve, protect, and interpret our nation's maritime history. Use the *Guide* to plan a family trip, map out a heritage travel experience, research your local history, or find a heritage organization to help you discover the sea captain in your family tree. The *Guide* covers maritime history attractions in the lower 48 states, Alaska, Hawaii, Puerto Rico, and the Virgin Islands.

- More than 200 authentic tall ships, many offering family and couple excursions.

- More than 300 ferries, tugs, steamboats, submarines, battleships, aircraft carriers, destroyers, and small craft covering two centuries of history.

- More than 750 photogenic lighthouses and lightships.

- More than 260 family-friendly maritime museums.

Available now through Amazon, Barnes & Noble, Indiebound, and independent bookstores. Also available as an e-book for Kindle, Nook, and other mobile devices running the Kindle and Nook e-reader apps.

Bet: Stowaway Daughter -- Lisbet "Bet" Lindstrom is the 13-year-old daughter of a sea captain convicted of theft and sent to prison. Bet is convinced her father is innocent, but she has no way to prove it. Desperate to free her father, she visits his old fishing boat, and spots a horribly scarred sailor who might know the truth about the crime. Ignoring the warnings of her friends, risking her life, she secretly jumps aboard the ship and sails to Alaska. She braves huge storms, performs daring rescues, and faces the man who threatens everything she loves.

Available now as an e-book for Kindle and Nook e-readers, as well as other mobile devices with the Kindle and Nook e-reader apps.

More information about these books and upcoming titles is available at www.fyddeye.com.